Protestation

In all that I shall say in this book I submit to what is taught by Our mother, the Holy Roman Church; if there is anything in it contrary to this, it will be without my knowledge. Therefore, for the love of Our Lord, I beg the learned men who are to read it to look at it very carefully and to make known to me any faults of this nature which there may be in it and the many others which it will have of other kinds. If there is anything good in it, let this be to the glory and honor of God in the service of His most sacred Mother, our Patroness and Lady.

Matthew Plese

In past ages, the lives of Catholics were studded with joyful celebrations of saints and somber calls to penance. The ebb and flow of feasting and fasting gave the Christian religion a distinctive 'thickness' and 'texture': it wasn't a bunch of ideas floating in the clouds but a daily planner filled with concrete actions. In the heady rationalism and hearty optimism that gripped modern reformers, nearly all of this holistic ecosystem was overthrown, and the loss of it meant far more than the loss of parties or Lenten recipes; it meant, for too many, the loss of any relevance of faith to everyday life. What is a Catholic to do in this desert of deprivation? Simple: follow a knowledgeable guide out of it. In this informative book, Matthew Plese, who has devoted himself to studying and living the traditional calendar, takes us step by step through some of the most important 'lost customs of Christendom.' Restoring them, here and there, one by one, we restore ourselves and our families to all that Catholic life can be.

–Dr. Peter A. Kwasniewski, scholar, lecturer, composer
author, *The Once and Future Roman Rite*
www.peterkwasniewski.com

As a patriarch of a veritable battalion of nine offspring, navigating the tumultuous seas of modernity while striving to anchor them in the resolute harbor of the rich tradition of Catholicism, I recently encountered a literary beacon: *Restoring Lost Customs of Christendom* by Matthew R. Plese. This tome, akin to a cartographer's detailed map, guides the wayward traveler back to the almost-forgotten lands of Catholic tradition and custom.

The author, acting as a sagacious chronicler, delves into the labyrinthine depths of the liturgical calendar, illuminating each corner with historical acumen and practical sagacity. From the expectant quietude of Advent to the jubilant alleluias of Easter, the book resurrects these sacred temporal landmarks, imbuing them with a vividness that resonates profoundly within the familial sanctum.

In the grand tapestry of Catholic tradition, Plese weaves a narrative that is both grandiloquent and approachable, making the monumental task of integrating these customs into the bustling life of a large family seem not only possible but imperative. The book transcends mere observation of rites; it is an exhortation to breathe life into them, to ensconce them in the everyday, thus fortifying the bulwarks of faith against the relentless siege of secularism.

The tome's exploration of penance, prayer, and liturgical understanding is nothing short of an intellectual banquet, offering a sumptuous feast of theological and spiritual insight. As a father, tasked with the arduous challenge of instilling unshakeable faith in my progeny, I found in these pages a clarion call to elevate our daily practices from the mundane to the celestial.

In conclusion, *Restoring Lost Customs of Christendom* is not merely a book; it is a clarion call to arms for those of us who dare to combat the insidious creep of modernity with the sword and shield of tradition. It is a lantern in the dark, guiding families like mine to not only remember but to relive and reinvigorate the glorious traditions of our faith. For those intrepid souls seeking to traverse the narrow path of tradition in a world enamored with the broad highways of modernism, this tome is an indispensable companion.

–Keith Jones
Director & Producer
Foudations Restored: A Catholic Perspective on Origins

Catholics who want to integrate the Catholic customs of ages past will deeply appreciate *Restoring Lost Customs of Christendom*. Beginning with Advent and continuing through the feasts and seasons of the liturgical year, this complete compendium of Catholic traditions by Matthew Plese will help integrate the ancient traditions of our faith in our families and homes. This treasured volume presents the fasts and feasts, the indulgences and blessings which are the patrimony of our Catholic people.

–Fr. Scott A. Haynes
www.mysticaltheologyofthemass.com

RESTORING LOST CUSTOMS OF CHRISTENDOM

Matthew R. Plese

2nd Edition

Restoring Lost Customs of Christendom

Matthew R. Plese

© Our Lady of Victory Press, MMXXIV

ISBN 979-8-9877607-5-8

Our Lady of Victory Press is an imprint of The Meaning of Catholic, a lay apostolate dedicated to uniting Catholics against the enemies of Holy Church.

MeaningofCatholic.com

All chapters originally published at OnePeterFive.com

Design and layout by W. Flanders.

Our Lady of Victory, pray for us!

First edition published by Our Lady of Victory Press on Our Lady of Guadalupe, MMXXIII. The second edition includes three new chapters and additions to the penultimate chapter on saint days.

Table of Contents

Temporal Cycle

Preface 11

1. Advent 15
2. Christmas 24
3. Epiphanytide 31
4. Septuagesima 40
5. Lent 48
6. Easter 57
7. Rogation Days 69
8. Ascensiontide 77
9. Pentecost 87
10. Corpus Christi 97
11. Sacred Heart 106
12. Precious Blood 113
13. Ember Days 121

Sanctoral Cycle

14. Octave of Christian Unity 130
15. St. Valentine 136
16. St. Patrick 142
17. St. Joseph 148
18. May – Month of Mary 161
19. St. John the Baptist 170

20. Saints Peter and Paul 182
21. St. Anne 194
22. St. Lawrence 202
23. Assumptiontide 210
24. Marymas 215
25. Roodmas 219
26. Michaelmas 227
27. Allhallowtide 240
28. All Saints Days for Religious Orders & Nations 254
29. Martinmas and St. Martin's Lent 269
30. Immaculate Conception 278
31. Other Saints Days 287
Catholic Culture: Our Birthright 306

Preface

Under the Old Testament laws, God's people observed annual ceremonies commemorating important events in salvation history which prefigured the completion of the Old Law through Christ. Similarly, Holy Church commemorates important mysteries, events, and persons, using an annual cycle of prayers, Scriptures, hymns, and various spiritual disciplines. In the same way, each of the twelve months has a unique focus, and each day of the week has a unique focus as well. Even in the day, the hours of the day are divided up into canonical hours. In so doing, all time is, in a manner of speaking, consecrated to God since He alone created all time and redeemed all of time.

Unlike the pagan religions which often view time as an endless cycle of death and rebirth, the Christian view of time is linear. While God alone has always existed and has no beginning, time had a beginning. There was a first day on earth. And there will be a last day. There will be a day ultimately when the sun will rise for the last time and when it will set for the last time. Time will end. And God Himself will end it as time belongs to Him. It is our duty to honor God in time. And we can do so by sanctifying the days, weeks, months, and seasons of the year.

The Church's Liturgical Year is a harmonious interplay of feasts and fasts interwoven in both the temporal and sanctoral cycles that define the rhythm and rhyme of Catholic life. While there are many customs associated with the seasons of the liturgical year and high ranking feast days, the entire year is replete with opportunities to live out our Catholic heritage through the customs our forefathers instituted.

The Church's annual liturgical calendar is comprised of two different, concurrent annual cycles. First, the Proper of the Seasons, or Temporal Cycle, traces the earthly life of Our Lord Jesus Christ. In the Roman Catholic Church, it consists mainly of Sundays related to the various liturgical seasons – that is, the seven liturgical seasons contained in two cycles of its own: the Christmas Cycle and the Easter Cycle. It starts with Advent then goes through Christmas, Epiphany, Septuagesima, Lent, Easter, and Time after Pentecost. The determination of the date of Easter dictates nearly all the other dates in this cycle. But there is a second cycle: the Proper of the Saints, called the Sanctoral Cycle, which is the annual cycle of feast days not necessarily connected with the seasons.

It's also important to realize that each rite in the Catholic Church (e.g., Roman, Maronite, Chaldean, etc.) has its own liturgical calendar, and some have multiple uses or forms of the calendar. Even within the same use or form, there are variations according to local customs. For instance, the patron saint of a church or of the cathedral would be ranked higher in the liturgical calendar of that local jurisdiction. Even in the Roman Rite itself, different dioceses, countries, and religious orders would keep some different feast days. These were listed in the Mass in Some Places (*pro aliquibus locis*) supplement to the Missal. Beyond the Roman Rite, the Ambrosian, Mozarabic, Lyon, and Bragan Rites are also all part of the Western liturgical tradition. So too are the various Rites for religious orders (e.g., the Carmelite Rite, the Carthusian Rite, the Dominican Rite). These are also part of the Roman Catholic Church. No one has ever doubted the legitimacy of this liturgical diversity.

Those who try to discredit the Traditional Latin Mass may try to falsely claim that all Catholics must observe the same calendar of saints. But this is not the case as seen in the liturgical calendar diversity in the different Rites of the Church and in the Roman Rite itself. Even *Summorum Pontificium* affirmed that the continued use of the older Roman calendar in the traditional Mass and Breviary is permissible.

Beyond assisting at Mass and praying the Divine Office, we can and should observe the forgotten customs that further underscored authentic Catholic culture. Catholic culture is more than just going to Mass – much more. Catholic culture is built on fasting periods, assisting at Processions, having various items blessed at different parts of the year (e.g. herbs on August 15th, grapes on September 8th, wine on December 27th). It features days of festivity like Martinmas and promotes family time and charitable works like visits to grandparents on Easter Monday. It is replete with food customs to celebrate the end of fasting periods and filled with special devotions during periods of penance. It is our heritage. These traditions are our birthright. They are ours as much as they were our ancestors. We must reclaim them. We must spread them. We must love them and observe them. And this book will show today's Catholic how.

I

Advent

Brethren, knowing that it is now the hour for us to rise from sleep. For now our salvation is nearer than when we believed. The night is passed, and the day is at hand. Let us therefore cast off the works of darkness and put on the armor of light. Let us walk honestly, as in the day: not in rioting and drunkenness, not in chambering and impurities, not in contention and envy: but put ye on the Lord Jesus Christ (Romans 13:11-14 as taken from the Epistle on the First Sunday of Advent).

A Season of Penance to Start the Liturgical Year

Advent as a season is quite ancient. The season itself went through slow development, taking form in the 4th century and reaching a definite form in Rome by 6th century. Advent starts on the Sunday nearest Nov 30th, which is the Feast of Saint Andrew, and it formed the beginning of the liturgical year by the 10th century. It started earlier at one time (as early as Nov 11) because it was fashioned after Lent, so it had forty days originally in some areas, and even earlier in other areas with a beginning in September, which forms the basis of the monastic fast.[1] By the 6th – 7th centuries the number was set as a span

---

[1] See Matthew Plese, "The Monastic Fast," *The Fatima Center* (Feb 8, 2021) <https://fatima.org/news-views/the-monastic-fast>, accessed December 11th, 2023.

of four Sundays. The 1962 Missal texts preserve most of the ancient Masses of this season.

Dom Prosper Guéranger in *The Liturgical Year* writes in part on the history of Advent, noting how we should apply this time to our own spiritual development:

> The name Advent [from the Latin word Adventus, which signifies a coming] is applied, in the Latin Church, to that period of the year, during which the Church requires the faithful to prepare for the celebration of the feast of Christmas, the anniversary of the birth of Jesus Christ. The mystery of that great day had every right to the honor of being prepared for by prayer and works of penance…We must look upon Advent in two different lights: first, as a time of preparation, properly so called, for the birth of our Savior, by works of penance; and secondly, as a series of ecclesiastical Offices drawn up for the same purpose.

Customs in Advent

Advent is a liturgical season rich in customs that allow us to more spiritually enter into the mystery of these "two different lights." Especially in a society that rushes Christmas and obscures all penance and preparation, keeping these customs will help us keep true Catholic practices, allowing us to do fitting penance now before celebrating from December 25th through February 2nd.

Rorate Mass: The Rorate Mass takes its name from the opening words of the Introit, which comes to us from Isaiah 45:8: "Drop down dew, ye heavens, from above, and let the clouds rain the just: let the earth be opened and bud forth a Savior." The Rorate Mass is traditionally illuminated only by candlelight. Because it is a votive Mass in Mary's honor, white vestments are worn instead of Advent violet. There is a custom in which every day of Advent outside of certain major days the sung low Rorate Mass takes place. While it is difficult to have in most places, very few know the rubric which allows this as *Matters Liturgical* documents.[2]

In the dimly lit setting, priests and faithful prepare to honor the Light of the world, who is soon to be born, and offer praise to God for the gift of Our Lady. As the Mass proceeds and sunrise approaches, the church becomes progressively brighter, illumined by the sun as our Faith is illumined by Christ. The readings and prayers of the Mass foretell the prophecy of the Virgin who would bear a Son called Emmanuel and call on all to raise the gates of their hearts and their societies to let Christ the King enter.

Advent Wreath: The Advent wreath, which has German origins, is probably the most recognized Advent custom. It is a wreath made of evergreens that is often, but not necessarily, bound to a circle of wire. It symbolizes the many years from Adam to Christ in which the world awaited its Redeemer; it also represents the years that we have awaited His Final Coming in glory. The wreath holds four equally spaced candles, the three purple ones lit on the "penitential" Sundays and a pink one for Gaudete, the joyful third Sunday in Advent. The traditional blessing of an Advent wreath and the weekly prayers for the Advent wreath lighting, can be found online.[3]

Jesse Tree & Advent Calendar: The Jesse tree depicts Christ's ancestry through symbols and relates Scripture to salvation history, progressing from creation to the birth of Christ. See *Fish Eaters* for more information on making one as a

---

[2] *Matters Liturgical* (1959 ed.), 490.
[3] "Advent: Wreath & Candles," *Fish Eaters* (undated) <https://www.fisheaters.com/customsadvent2.html>, accessed December 9, 2023.

family.[4] These often coincide with Advent calendars which also can help us count down the days to Christmas.[5]

Shoes Filled with Candy on St. Nicholas' Day: The feast of St. Nicholas is on Dec. 6th and it is a highlight of the Advent season. St. Nicholas was from the 4th Century and was Bishop of Myra. The many churches built to honor him and the stories about him are all testimonials to his holiness. St. Nicholas is best remembered for his compassion towards the poor. Born at Patara in Lycia, a province of Asia Minor, he became bishop of Myra and became known for his zeal and piety. He was present at the Council of Nicaea and condemned the heresy of Arianism. In one story, St. Nicholas saved three unjustly incarcerated officers one time, and at another time, he saved three boys from death. St. Nicholas helped one man, who couldn't pay the dowries for his three daughters by throwing gold through the window of the home. He did it several times and each was done secretly until the last time when he threw the gold in the home. The man inside saw him and was overjoyed in thanking him. Have your children leave their shoes by the door the evening of December 5th and fill them with candy so when they awake they will see the fruits of St. Nicholas' charity!

Fasting on the Vigil of the Immaculate Conception: For those not already fasting throughout Advent, December 7th is an ideal day to fast (on years when it does not fall on a Sunday). On July 25, 1957, Pope Pius XII transferred the fast in the Universal Church from the Vigil of the Assumption (i.e., August 14th) to the Vigil of the Immaculate Conception (i.e., December 7), even though he had previously abrogated the Mass for the Vigil of the Immaculate Conception. Thus, this

---

[4] Advent Customs at *Fish Eaters*:
<https://www.fisheaters.com/customsadvent9.html>, accessed December 9, 2023.
[5] Ibid., "Advent Calendars,"
<https://www.fisheaters.com/customsadvent12.html>, accessed December 9, 2023.

day starting in 1957 was a day of mandatory fasting and abstinence. This is preserved in the laws in force in 1962 for instance. Fasting helps prepare us to celebrate the one Holy Day of Obligation during Advent: The Immaculate Conception. Originally referred to as the "Conception of the Blessed Virgin Mary," December 8th became a Holy Day of Obligation in 1708 under Pope Clement XI, nearly 150 years before Pope Pius IX dogmatically and infallibly defined the dogma of the Immaculate Conception.

Ember Days: Although the observation of Ember Days is no longer mentioned in mainstream Catholicism following the changes in the 1960s to fasting, they can – and should – still be observed by the faithful. Ember Days are set aside to pray and offer thanksgiving for a good harvest and God's blessings. If you are in good health, fast on the Wednesday, Friday, and Saturday immediately following the Feast of St. Lucy on December 13th.

St. Lucy: Beyond her patronage for those suffering from ailments of the eyes, those of Swedish and Italian descent have a particular reason to celebrate her feast day on December 13th. *Fish Eaters* writes,

> Her name, 'Lucia,' means 'Light,' and light plays a role in the customs of her Feast Day. In Italy, torchlight processions and bonfires mark her day, and bowls of a cooked wheat porridge known as cuccia is eaten because, during a famine, the people of Syracuse invoked St. Lucy, who interceded by sending a ship laden with grain (much as St. Joseph also did for the people of Sicily)…
>
> Some of the loveliest St. Lucy's Day customs are Swedish: in Sweden, the oldest daughter of a family will wake up before dawn on St. Lucy's Day and dress in a white gown for purity, often with a red sash as a sign of

martyrdom. On her head she will wear a wreath of greenery and lit candles, and she is often accompanied by 'starboys,' her small brothers who are dressed in white gowns and cone-shaped hats that are decorated with gold stars, and carrying star-tipped wands. 'St. Lucy' will go around her house and wake up her family to serve them special St. Lucy Day foods, such as saffron buns and Lussekatter (St. Lucy's Cats), shaped into X's, figure-8s, S-shapes, or crowns.

These connections to the liturgical year help families live out the faith and teach the importance of imitating the virtues of the saints like the purity of St. Lucy which is surely needed in our modern society.

O Antiphons: The O Antiphons are a series of antiphons to the Magnificat, which are prayed as part of Vespers (evening prayer) from December 17th – 23rd inclusive. Each of the titles of the O Antiphons addresses Jesus with a special title given to the Messiah and refers to a prophecy from the Prophet Isaiah. It is unknown when the O Antiphons started, however, there is mention of them as far back as the 400s AD. They are often called the Great Antiphons too. Even if you do not usually pray Vespers each day, take time to listen to the ancient O Antiphons chanted.[6]

Novenas: While any time of year is appropriate to pray a Novena, Advent has a rich connection to several important ones that are worth praying every year as a family. Novenas are prayed for nine days in a row, usually before the beginning a feast. During Advent, we pray the Christmas Novena from December 16 – December 24th and the Novena in preparation for the Immaculate Conception from November 29 through

---

[6] Matthew Plese, "The O Antiphons," *A Catholic Life* (Dec 17, 2006) <https://acatholiclife.blogspot.com/2006/12/o-antiphons.html>, accessed December 11, 2023.

December 7th.[7] Yet even more popular than both of these is the St. Andrew's Christmas Novena which is prayed 15 times a day from November 30th until Christmas.[8] Incorporate this one in your family prayers after the nightly Rosary.

The Nativity Scene: Putting out the Nativity scene is an excellent way to teach children the story of Christmas. In Advent, the three wisemen should be stationed far away from the central figures of Mary and Joseph. And the Baby Jesus too should not be displayed yet. As Advent unfolds, day by day have someone – ideally a small child – in your family move the wisemen closer to the Holy Family. On Christmas Eve, put the Baby Jesus in the manger and say the traditional family prayer to bless the Nativity scene.[9] Keep advancing the wisemen until January 6th, the Feast of the Epiphany, when they finally arrive to adore the newborn King. Children should know the difference between Christmas and the Epiphany and understand the 12 Days of Christmas are those between the two feasts – not the 12 days leading up to Christmas.

Christmas Baking: A few days before Christmas, baking usually begins for Christmas. While we are then still in a period of penance, the day will soon dawn when the Lord will be born to us, and we will celebrate with a feast. In an age where family time is often distracted or completely lacking, spending time these days together in the kitchen can help forge lasting memories. Many people have fond memories baking with their parents or grandparents, and these memories can last a lifetime.

Christmas Eve: Christmas Eve is the final day in the Advent season, and it is one of fasting (for those aged 21 to 60) and abstinence (for those over age 7), following the traditional

---

[7] Ibid., <https://acatholiclife.blogspot.com/2005/12/christmas-novena.html>; <https://acatholiclife.blogspot.com/2006/12/novena-to-our lady of immaculate.html>.

[8] Ibid., <https://acatholiclife.blogspot.com/2014/11/st-andrew-christmas-novena-begins-today.html>.

[9] Aloisius J. Muench, *The Christmas Missal* (Bruce Publishing, 1951), 64.

requirements. Christmas Eve has been a vigil of fasting and abstinence for centuries. In fact, even when various groups or nations were exempted from various fast days, the Vigil of our Lord's Nativity virtually always remained. Sadly, this Vigil ceased being a day of fasting in the modern Catholic Church following the changes in 1966. Yet, Traditional Catholics continue to keep this day as a day of fasting and abstinence, as our forefathers in the Faith did for centuries. However, in one unique exception, the Church has for centuries permitted a double collation on this one particular fasting day on account of this day being a "joyful fast."[10] This underscores the sentiments of joy that should permeate the Catholic home on this final day of Advent.

Feast of the Seven Fishes: One particularly notable custom for observing Christmas Eve abstinence is the Italian custom of the Feast of Seven Fishes, on account of the abstinence on Christmas Eve. Many Italian families will customarily have a dinner of seven fishes in honor of the seven Sacraments and the seven days of Creation. For families who are accustomed to spending the evening together in a family meal before attending midnight Mass, look up appropriate recipes in keeping with this tradition.[11] For larger families, twelve kinds of fish may be eaten, in honor of the twelve apostles. And for smaller families, either three kinds of fish (in honor of the Trinity) or five kinds (in honor of the Five Wounds of Christ) may be used instead. In all of these variations, the meal remains meatless and ends the day's fast.

Blessing of the Christmas Tree: More and more frequently families are blessing their Christmas trees. It is good to remind

---

[10] Matthew Plese, "Christmas Eve: Fasting & Abstinence," *A Catholic Life* (Dec 23, 2013) <https://acatholiclife.blogspot.com/2013/12/christmas-eve-fasting-abstinence.html>, accessed December 11, 2023.

[11] Jacqueline Weiss, "50 Recipes for the Feast of the Seven Fishes," *Taste of Home* (May 19, 2023) <https://www.tasteofhome.com/collection/recipes-feast-seven-fishes/>, accessed December 11, 2023.

children that "the tree" relates to many aspects of our faith. For example, we are reminded that our first parents were not allowed to eat from one tree and that Christ paid the great price for our redemption by hanging on a tree (cf. Acts 5:29-32). The Traditional Blessing for a Christmas Tree is quite beautifully said on Christmas Eve as we finally transition from the penance and preparation of Advent to the joy of Christmastide.[12]

---

[12] Matthew Plesc, "Traditional Blessing of a Christmas Tree Pre-Vatican II," *A Catholic Life* (Dec 24, 2018) <https://acatholiclife.blogspot.com/2018/12/traditional-blessing-of-christmas-tree.html>, accessed December 9, 2023.

II

Christmas

> Let the heavens rejoice, and let the earth be glad before the face of the Lord: because He cometh (Psalm 95:13,11 Taken from the Offertory Verse of the First Mass of Christmas)

At the first stroke of midnight on December 25th, the Church in her Sacred liturgy bursts forth in joyous celebration for the birth of the God-Man, Jesus Christ, who is born of the Virgin Mary. The virgin birth occurs nine months after His conception in Her womb when God united His divinity with our humanity. At Christmas we celebrate the birth in the flesh of the Second Person of the Most Blessed Trinity who will ultimately redeem us on Calvary and who will one day come again in glory at the End of Time to judge the living and the dead and the world by fire.

Aware of this monumentally important celebration, various traditions, customs, and observances have been observed throughout the forty days of the Christmas season which begins on December 25th and concludes on February 2nd with Candlemas. During these forty days, the Church celebrates the Octave of our Lord's Nativity, Epiphany and its Octave, and continues with Time After Epiphany.

This chapter focuses on the traditions and customs specific to Christmastide leading up to the Vigil of the Epiphany. The next chapter will discuss specific customs for Epiphanytide. Some of the many practices to be aware of during this time, which are often forgotten in our era, are mentioned below.

The Divine Office on Christmas Day

All Catholics are aware of our obligation to attend Holy Mass and rest from servile works on Christmas Day. Christmas gift exchanges, caroling, joy-filled family time, and a meat-rich dinner are staples of Catholic life on December 25th.[13]

One forgotten tradition of Christmas Day is the praying of the Divine Office. Lest we forget the spiritual treasures of the Church and the importance Holy Mother Church places on this Sacred day of our Lord's Nativity, here is a reminder of what is contained in the *Raccolta* which, regardless of the current status of this indulgence, underscores the importance the Church places on praying the Divine Office on Christmas Day:

> In order to increase the devotion of all faithful Christians towards the feast of the birthday of our Divine Savior Jesus Christ, and that they may celebrate it with spiritual profit to their souls, Pope Sixtus V, by his brief, *Ut fidelium*

---

[13] The 1917 Code also introduced the notion that a Holy Day of Obligation would *eo ipso* overrule the requirement of Friday abstinence for any Holy Days of Obligation outside of Lent. Previously the only day that would automatically abrogate the requirement of Friday abstinence was Christmas Day. Thus Christmas Day, which always falls on December 25th and which may thus fall on a Friday, is the one traditional exception to year-round Friday abstinence. On this singular exception, Dom Guéranger writes in *The Liturgical Year* published in 1886: "To encourage her children in their Christmas joy, the Church has dispensed with the law of abstinence, if this Feast fall on a Friday. This dispensation was granted by Pope Honorius III, who ascended the Papal Throne in 1216. It is true that we find it mentioned by Pope St Nicholas I, in the ninth century; but the dispensation was not universal; for the Pontiff is replying to the consultations of the Bulgarians, to whom he concedes this indulgence, in order to encourage them to celebrate these Feasts with solemnity and joy: Christmas Day, St Stephen, St John the Evangelist, the Epiphany, the Assumption of our Lady, St John the Baptist, and SS Peter and Paul. When the dispensation for Christmas Day was extended to the whole Church, these other Feasts were not mentioned."

devotio, dated Oct. 22, 1586, granted the following Indulgences:

1. The indulgence of 100 years to all those who, being truly penitent, having Confessed and Communicated, shall recite the Divine Office on that day, or assist in person in any church where Matins and Lauds are said;

2. One hundred years indulgence for the Mass, and the same for first and second Vespers;

3. The indulgence of forty years for each of the hours of Prime, Tierce, Sext, None, and Compline.

More Holy Days of Obligation

The Octave of Christmas, beginning on Christmas Day and continuing until its Octave Day on January 1, is unique since the Feasts of St. Stephen, St. John the Apostle, and the Holy Innocents – which are celebrated on the 2nd, 3rd, and 4th days, respectively, of the Christmas Octave – used to be Holy Days of Obligation. Few people are aware that these former holy days were days of obligation for centuries.[14] In fact, up until 1955, they had Octaves of their own too!

The three are sometimes known as the "Comites Christi" (Companions of Christ). Their connection is not an accident, and Catholics should be taught to honor these feast days in a truly special manner, even if they are no longer Holy Days of Obligation. A vestige of the prominence of the Comites was

---

[14] In times past, Holy Days would often be referred to as days of single or double precept, with those of double precept requiring both hearing Mass and abstaining from servile works, whereas days of single precept would permit servile work. Taking Ireland as an example, St. Stephen was a day of double precept (like Christmas Day) whereas St. John and the Holy Innocents were only single precept as of 1755. See Matthew Plese, "Feasts of Single vs. Double Precept," *A Catholic Life* (July 15, 2020) <https://acatholiclife.blogspot.com/2020/07/feasts-of-single-vs-double-precept.html>, accessed December 9, 2023.

retained up until the liturgical changes immediately preceding Vatican II. In fact, even though St. Stephen, St. John, and the Holy Innocents had ceased being holy days, their feasts would take precedence over the Sunday within the Octave of the Nativity until the 1960 reform of the Missal.

December 31st was also in centuries past another holy day of obligation in honor of St. Sylvester:

> Numerous legends dramatize his life and work, e.g., how he freed Constantine from leprosy by baptism; how he killed a ferocious dragon that was contaminating the air with his poisonous breath. Such legends were meant to portray the effects of baptism and Christianity's triumph over idolatry. For a long time the feast of St. Sylvester was a holy day of obligation. The Divine Office notes: 'He called the weekdays feria, because for the Christian every day is a "free day." The term is still in use; thus Monday is feria secunda.' *(Compiled from Heavenly Friends, Rosalie Marie Levy and The Church's Year of Grace, Pius Parsch).*

One interesting point to note is that using the same list of Holy Days as set forth by Pope Urban VIII, which kept the Comites as days of precept, England would have also observed as a Holy Day of Obligation the Feast of St. Thomas Beckett. As a result, Catholics in England would have observed five consecutive Holy Days of Obligation before only a one-day break (unless that day was a Sunday) before the Feast of the Circumcision on January 1st which is another day of precept.

Blessing of Wine on the Feast of St. John (December 27)

Many countries around the world have the tradition of blessing wine in the name of Saint John on his December feast day. Often a sweetened, spiced red wine is prepared and served hot (alcohol is evaporated after boiling for five minutes). At dinner on Saint John's Day, the father blesses a large cup of wine. Each member of the family takes a drink and passes the cup, saying "I drink to you in the love of Saint John."

Ask your priest to publicly bless wine for anyone who wishes to bring their bottles of wine to Mass on January 27th. A copy of the English translation of the prayers is available online (the original in Latin is the *Rituale Romanum*).[15]

The Blessing of Children on Childermas Day (December 28)

The following is taken from *Christmas to Candlemas in a Catholic Home* by Helen McLoughlin, regarding December 28:

> Holy Innocents or 'Childermas Day' is celebrated on December 28. The Gospel tells the story simply. ;Herod sent and slew all the boys in Bethlehem who were two years old or under.' He had intended to include the Son of God among the murdered babies. To recall the grief of their mothers the Church wears purple today.[16] In Mass she hushes her joyous Gloria in Excelsis and the Alleluias. And yet there is joy in her services. Children sing with the choirs in the great cathedrals; and in ancient times other functions were given to them — hence the name 'Childermas' or Children's Mass.

The feast of the Holy Innocents is an excellent time for parents to inaugurate the custom of blessing their children. From the

---

[15] Matthew Plese, "Blessing of the Wine for the Feast of St. John," *A Catholic Life* (Dec 27, 2010) <https://acatholiclife.blogspot.com/2010/12/blessing-of-wine-for-feast-of-st-john.html>, accessed December 9, 2023.

[16] The main differences between the pre-1955 liturgy for the Holy Innocents and the one used in the 1962 Missal is that before 1955 the vestments are purple and the gradual and alleluia are omitted today. This excerpt refers to the older tradition pre-1955.

Ritual comes the form which we use on solemn occasions, such as First Communion. But all parents need to do is to sign a cross on the child's forehead with the right thumb dipped in holy water and say: May God bless you, and may He be the Guardian of your heart and mind — the Father, + Son, and Holy Spirit. Amen.

Indulgence for New Years

On December 31st (i.e., the Feast of St. Sylvester), a plenary indulgence is granted when the *Te Deum* is recited publicly on the last day of the year. Otherwise, a partial indulgence is granted to those who recite the *Te Deum* in thanksgiving. On January 1st (i.e. the Feast of the Circumcision), a plenary indulgence is granted when the *Veni, Creator Spiritus* is recited.

What does "public recitation" mean? The common interpretation of this is labiation (i.e., the moving of one's lips) in a public place. The prayer does not need to be loud enough to be heard by others but it must still be said as in the lips move to form the words (i.e., it is not a mental prayer). Thus, it does not necessarily have to be said in a group to be "public recitation." Do not let these opportunities for grace pass by!

This of course requires us to fulfill the normal conditions of a plenary indulgence:

1. One is free from all attachment from sin[17]

2. One receives the Sacraments of Penance and the Eucharist (within 7 days of the prescribed work)

---

[17] Matthew Plese, "Free from All Attachment to Sin: Requirement for Plenary Indulgences," *A Catholic Life* (May 26, 2013) <https://acatholiclife.blogspot.com/2013/05/free-from-all-attachment-to-sin-gaining.html>, accessed November 26, 2024.

3. One prays for the intentions of the Pope (an Our Father and Hail Mary will suffice)[18]

Conclusion

Father Weiser in *Christian Feasts and Customs* devotes pages to Christmas carols, pageants, the Christmas tree, flowers associated with Christmas time, Christmas foods, and various customs from country to country during the Octave of Christmas. As the number of customs associated with Christmas is sufficient in itself to be a book in its own right, I encourage anyone interested in learning more to read through a copy of Father Weiser's classic text.

What our ancestors observed is not lost. We can recover these customs little by little with the help of God. And in so doing, they can help us better live out a liturgical life.

---

[18] Matthew Plese, "Praying for the Pope's Intentions: The 6 Intentions of the Holy Father," *Fatima Center* (Mar 20, 2019) <https://fatima.org/news-views/catholic-apologetics-9/>, accessed December 11, 2023.

III

Epiphanytide

> O God, of Whose mercies there is no number, and of Whose goodness the treasure is infinite: we render thanks to Thy most gracious Majesty for the gifts Thou hast bestowed upon us, always beseeching Thy clemency; that as Thou grantest the petitions of them that ask Thee, Thou wilt never forsake them, but wilt prepare them for the greater rewards that still await them. Through Christ Our Lord, amen. (The Final Prayer from the Solemn Blessing of Epiphany Water on January 5th).

For those Catholics committed to the Sacred Traditions of the past, Epiphanytide is a special period of time in the liturgical year. Instead of having Christmastide turn into some oddly name "Ordinary Time," traditional Catholics will celebrate Christmastide, Epiphanytide, Septuagesima, and then finally begin the penance of Lent. Epiphanytide commences on January 6th and traditionally had a vigil – one of the four principal vigils of the entire liturgical year.

The Blessing of Epiphany Water on January 5

The Vigil of the Epiphany is the traditional day for priests to bless Epiphany water. This tradition, which is older in the Eastern Rites than in the Roman Rite, involves a beautiful and long ceremonial. The history and prayers can be found online.[19] Ask your priest to offer this blessing this year.

Blessing of Homes & Chalk on January 6

The Feast of the Epiphany on January 6th is a culmination for the Christmas season and one of the major Christian feast days in the entire Church year. It was a Holy Day of Obligation in the United States until 1885.[20]

Epiphany Day is the day in many countries – primarily Hispanic ones – when Christmas gifts are exchanged in honor of the day's commemoration of the arrival of the Wisemen. The Epiphany simultaneously recalls the arrival of the Wisemen to worship the Child Christ, our Lord's Baptism at age 30, and His first public miracle in Cana.

Chalk is customarily blessed on January 6 by a priest using the *Rituale Romanum*, though nowadays typically only done by more traditional parishes. The chalk is a sacramental, intended for the blessings of homes. It may only be blessed by a priest.

Along with the blessing of chalk is the blessing of one's home on the Feast of the Epiphany or in the days immediately afterward. If a priest is unable to visit your home at this season, a simple blessing may be given by the father of the family using the blessed chalk. The full blessing of homes to be said as part of this custom can be found online.[21]

Whether said by a priest or the father of the family, he should mark the year and the initials of the three Magi (Caspar,

---

[19] Matthew Plese, "The Vigil of Epiphany & The Solemn Blessing of Epiphany Water," *A Catholic Life* (Jan 5, 2016) <https://acatholiclife.blogspot.com/2016/01/blessing-of-epiphany-water-for-vigil-of.html>, accessed December 11, 2023.

[20] Ibid., <https://acatholiclife.blogspot.com/2020/06/a-history-of-holy-days-of-obligation.html>.

[21] "Traditional Epiphany Home Blessing: "Chalking the Door," *Virgo Sacrata* (no date) <https://www.virgosacrata.com/epiphany-home-blessing.html>, accessed December 11, 2023.

Melchoir and Balthasar) on the lintel of the main door using the blessed chalk. The initials C, M, and B also stand for *Christus mansionem benedicat* (May Christ bless the house). This is the example for the year 2022): 20 + C + M + B + 22

The Twice a Year Venetian Tradition

Fisheaters shares some of the great regional customs for this Feast Day:

> Something else wonderful happens in Italy on the Feast of the Ascension and the days following: in Venice, there is a clock tower in the Piazza San Marco. This marvelous clock, made in A.D. 1499 (and recently restored) indicates not only the minutes and hours, but the days, months, Zodiacal signs, and phases of the Moon as well. At the top of the tower are two large figures known as the Moors ("Mori"), who signal the hour by striking a large bell. Underneath them is a large, golden lion – the symbol of St. Mark, patron of Venice. Underneath this is a niche which holds a figure of Our Lady and her Son. Twice a year – on the Feast of the Epiphany and during the festivities surrounding the Ascension (known as "*la Festa della Sensa*" in Venice) – doors on either side of Our Lady open up, and out come the three Magi, led by an angel. The angel and Kings make their way around Our Lady and Jesus, the angel regaling them with his trumpet, and the Kings bowing and removing their crowns.

Rosca de Reyes (King Cake)

As with most customs of our Faith, there is a tradition based on food for Epiphany Day and that is King Cake. Father Weiser in "Christian Feasts and Customs" shares:

An old tradition in most countries of Europe was the festival of the "Kings' Cake" (Dreikonigskuchen), which was baked on Epiphany in honor of the Magi and eaten at a special party in the home on the afternoon of the feast. Often a coin was put in the dough before baking, and the person who found it was the "king."

In Austria, Germany, France, and England, and also in Canada, this cake contained a bean and a pea, making the respective finders 'Tang' and 'queen' of the merry party. This custom has been explained as a relic of the ancient games of chance at the Roman Saturnalia. However, there is no proof of this connection; the first reports about the 'Kings' Cake' date from the end of the fourteenth century. Also, the wild and excessive reveling of the Saturnalia or Calendae was never a feature of this festival.

It was an old custom in France to put a big piece of the cake aside 'for our Lord' and to give it to some poor person after the feast. Another tradition in France demanded that rich people help collect a goodly sum of money by giving a substantial donation in return for their piece of the cake. This money was deposited on a tray and was called 'the gold of the Magi.' It was afterward used to pay the cost of higher education for some talented poor youngster.

The Octave of the Epiphany

The practice of celebrating an Octave, while not only traced to the time spent by the Apostles and the Blessed Virgin Mary awaiting the Paraclete, also has its origins in the Old Testament eight-day celebration of the Feast of Tabernacles (Leviticus 23:36) and the Dedication of the Temple (2

Chronicles 7:9). Very truly, Christ did not come to abolish the Old Law but to fulfill it.

By the 8th century, Rome had developed liturgical octaves not only for Easter, Pentecost, and Christmas but also for the Epiphany and the feast of the dedication of a church. After 1568, when Pope Pius V reduced the number of octaves (since by then they had grown considerably), the number of Octaves was still plentiful. Octaves were classified into several types. Easter and Pentecost had "specially privileged" octaves, during which no other feast whatsoever could be celebrated. Christmas, Epiphany, and Corpus Christi had "privileged" octaves, during which certain highly ranked feasts might be celebrated. The octaves of other feasts allowed even more feasts to be celebrated.

To reduce the repetition of the same liturgy for several days, Pope Leo XIII and Pope St. Pius X made further distinctions, classifying octaves into three primary types: privileged octaves, common octaves, and simple octaves. The changes under St. Pius X did not really change the practice of any of the Octaves, except for Simple Octaves – it just changed the category labels. The Octave of the Epiphany remained until its suppression by Pope Pius XII in 1955 but those priests who still keep the pre-1955 Missal will celebrate it. However, even for those priests offering the 1962 Missal, the feria days during the former Octave permit the priest to offer a Votive Mass of the Epiphany. This is an ideal way for us to keep this venerable tradition even while using the 1962 Liturgical Books.

Feast of the Holy Family

The Sunday within the Octave of the Epiphany (or January 12th if January 13th falls on a Sunday) was the feast of the Holy Family up until the reforms of 1955. The following Sundays, until Septuagesima, were named as the "Sundays after Epiphany." Before the changes in 1911, the Second Sunday of Epiphany was kept as the Feast of the Holy Name, since January 2nd, 3rd, and 4th were the Octave Days of the Comites and January 5th was the Vigil of the Epiphany.

The Feast of the Holy Family is an ideal day to consecrate our families to the Holy Family.[22] While this feast day was only recently inserted in the Universal Calendar in 1921 by Pope Benedict XV – it offers to modern mankind an example to aspire towards. We will never be as perfect as the Holy Family but the ideal shines forth as a north star to which we can aspire to get closer to. And with the Holy Family as our guide, we as a family must reject errors (e.g., artificial contraception, licentiousness, immodesty, etc.).

Blessing of Lambs on St. Agnes on January 21

While not specifically related to Epiphanytide, this season bears witness to the Feast of St. Agnes who is regarded as one of the most popular virgin martyrs. *Catholic Culture* remind us of a unique custom for this day:

> Because of the similarity of her name to the Latin for 'lamb' (Agnus), the lamb has been St. Agnes' symbol since the 6th century. On the feast day of St. Agnes on January 21st, the Trappist fathers of the Monastery of Tre Fontane (near Saint Paul's Basilica) provide two lambs from their sheepfold to the Benedictine nuns of Saint Cecilia. They arrive at Saint Agnes' Basilica wearing crowns, lying in 'baskets decorated with red and white flowers and red and white ribbons—red for martyrdom, white for purity.'
>
> For the festal Mass, the church, titular cardinal, the deacon, and subdeacon are decorated with red, white and gold. At the conclusion of the Holy Mass, there is a procession of little girls

---

[22] Matthew Plese, *loc. cit.*
<https://acatholiclife.blogspot.com/2005/12/feast-of-holy-family.html>.

veiled and dressed in white lace with pale blue ribbons, followed by four resplendent carabinieri carrying the baby lambs. The lambs are blessed and incensed before being taken to the Vatican for the Holy Father's blessing. Then they are delivered to the Convent of Saint Cecilia to become the pets of the sisters until Holy Thursday (when they are shorn) before being sacrificed on Good Friday.

The wool from these lambs is woven into 12 archbishops' palliums. The pallium is an older symbol of the papacy than that of the famed triregnum. The elect becomes 'Shepherd of Christ's Flock' when the pallium touches his shoulder and symbolizes that the new bishop is being 'yoked' with the bishop of Rome, who is the visible head of the Church. About 204 AD, Saint Felician of Foligno is the first recorded recipient of a pallium from Pope Saint Victor I.

Candlemas (The End of the 40 Days of Christmas)

Candlemas (i.e., the Feast of the Purification of our Lady) is another day which the modern world greatly overlooks in importance. The Feast of Candlemas, exactly 40 days after Christmas, commemorates the Blessed Virgin Mary's obedience to the Mosaic law by submitting herself to the Temple for ritual purification, as commanded in Leviticus.

The Feast of the Purification is called Candlemas for the traditional blessing and distribution of candles on that day. It is customary to bring candles from home to be blessed – at least 51% beeswax candles that one uses for devotional purposes (candles for the family altar, Advent candles, etc.) so they can be lit after dusk on All Saints' Day, during the Sacrament of Extreme Unction, and during storms and times of trouble. Nowadays, though, for those few parishes continuing this ancient observance, the parish will often provide the candles.

Mass on Candlemas is typically preceded by a procession with lighted candles. The lighted candles are held during the reading of the Gospel and from the beginning of the Canon of the Mass to Communion. And it is no coincidence that on this day which is devoted to light and shadows that the secular world celebrates groundhog day.

Blessing of Throats on St. Blaise

The day after Candlemas is the Feast of St. Blaise, who is invoked as a patron saint against diseases and ailments of the throat. In his honor, there is a special blessing of Candles proper to February 3rd followed by the blessing of throats.[23] The priest takes two unlit candles and crosses them. He places one on one side of the parishioner's neck and one on the other. And the priest says this prayer:

> By the intercession of St. Blaise, bishop and martyr, may God deliver you from every malady of the throat, and from every possible mishap; in the name of the Father, and of the Son, and of the Holy Ghost.
>
> R. Amen.

Conclusion

Let's remember not to neglect this season and give it our due observance. Those of us praying the Older Breviary will find much beauty in the hymns and antiphons during these days.

Share this information widely and ask your priests to offer these various blessings from the *Rituale Romanum*, offer Votive Masses for the Epiphany during the former Octave of the Epiphany, and teach these customs to the faithful so we

---

[23] Matthew Plese, *loc. cit.*
<https://acatholiclife.blogspot.com/2006/02/devotions-for-presentation-of-lord.html>.

might recover in our own homes brick by brick the foundation of Christian traditions once again.

IV

Septuagesima

> Brethren: Know you not that they that run in the race, all run indeed, but one receiveth the prize. So run that you may obtain. And every one that striveth for the mastery refraineth himself from all things. And they indeed that they may receive a corruptible crown: but we an incorruptible one. I therefore so run, not as at an uncertainty: I so fight, not as one beating the air. But I chastise my body and bring it into subjection: lest perhaps, when I have preached to others, I myself should become a castaway (1 Cor. 9:24-27 as taken from the Epistle on Septuagesima Sunday).

Septuagesima is the ancient period of time observed for two and a half weeks before the start of Lent. Celebrated on the Third Sunday before the First Sunday in Lent, Septuagesima is both the name of this third Sunday before Lent's beginning as well as the season itself that runs from this day up until Ash Wednesday. The season of Septuagesima comprises the Sundays of Septuagesima, Sexagesima, and Quinquagesima. The Fourth Council of Orleans in 541 AD documents the existence of this season.

This time, informally called "Pre-Lent," is a time for us to focus on the need for a Savior. It is a time to prepare a Lenten prayer schedule so that we can determine which extra devotions and Masses we will go to in Lent. It is a time to begin weaning ourselves from food so that we may more easily observe the strictest fast during Lent.

A Season of Penance Before Lent Shown in the Church's Liturgy

Starting with First Vespers of Septuagesima, which is prayed on the Saturday evening before Septuagesima Sunday, the Alleluia ceases to be said until we proclaim our Lord's resurrection. There is no exception. At first Vespers of Septuagesima Sunday, two alleluias are added to the closing verse of *Benedicamus Domino* and its response, *Deo gratias*, as during the Easter Octave. Starting with Compline, the word Alleluia is no longer said until the Easter Vigil and the proclamation of the Lord's Resurrection. As a result, many monasteries and some parishes began the custom of physically burying a banner with the word *alleluia* and only unearthing it on Easter. Some places also adopted rather elaborate farewell to alleluia ceremonies. Fr. Scott Haynes from the Archdiocese of Chicago writes on this custom:

> Pope Alexander II decreed that the dismissal of the Alleluia be solemnly marked on the eve of Septuagesima Sunday (i.e., three Sundays before Ash Wednesday) in the chanting of the Divine Office by inserting Alleluias in the sacred text. This custom also inspired the creation of new hymns sung at Vespers honouring the Alleluia... This burial of the Alleluia was nicknamed the deposition (i.e., "the giving on deposit"). Curiously enough, gravestones in Catholic cemeteries traditionally had the inscription Depositus, or simply "D," to indicate a Christian's burial. When this term indicates the burial of the Alleluia or of the faithful departed, the Christian belief in resurrection is clear. As we bury those who have been "marked with the sign of faith," (Roman Canon), and as we enter

> into the fasting of Lent, we do not silence our tongues because of despair or permanent loss. Rather, we do so with confidence that what has been deposited into the earth—our dead, our Alleluia—will rise again.

There are other noticeable changes in the Church's liturgy with the beginning of Septuagesima. Violet vestments are worn, except on feasts, from Septuagesima Sunday until Holy Thursday. As during Advent and Lent, the *Gloria* and *Te Deum* are no longer said on Sundays. The readings at Matins for the first week of Septuagesima are the first few chapters of Genesis, telling of the creation of the world, of Adam and Eve, the fall of man and resulting expulsion from the Garden of Eden, and the story of Cain and Abel. In the following weeks before and during Lent, the readings continue to Noah, Abraham, Isaac, Jacob, and Moses. The Gospel reading for Septuagesima Sunday is the parable of the Workers in the Vineyard (Matthew 20:1-16).

On the connection of this ancient season with Lent, Guéranger observed:

> The season upon which we are now entering is expressive of several profound mysteries. But these mysteries belong not only to the three weeks which are preparatory to Lent: they continue throughout the whole period of time which separates us from the great feast of Easter.

Pre-Lenten Fasting

Septuagesima is also an appropriate time for us to begin preparing our bodies for the upcoming Lenten fast by incorporating some fasting into our routine. In some places a custom of observing a fast of devotion, in anticipation of and in preparation for the Great Lenten fast, was observed as Father Weiser mentions in his *Handbook of Christian Feasts and Customs*:

> This preparatory time of pre-Lent in the Latin Church was suggested by the practice of the Byzantine Church, which started its great fast earlier, because their 'forty days' did not include Saturdays. Saint Maximum (465 AD), Bishop of Turin, mentioned the practice in one of his sermons. It is a pious custom, he said, to keep a fast of devotion (not of obligation) before the start of Lent.

We should in a special way recall the importance of observing some penance even in the days before Lent. To this end, *Sensus Fidelium* has a 13-minute video on the importance of penance in Septuagesima that would be worthwhile to reflect upon.[24]

Paczkis, Pancakes, & Carnival on Shrove Tuesday

For those who plan to keep the true Lenten fast (i.e., fasting for all forty weekdays of Lent and abstaining from all meat and all animal products all forty days of Lent and on all Sundays), Fat Tuesday represents one last day of merriment. Unfortunately, this day has grown into a debaucherous celebration by many who hardly fast at all during Lent. For this reason, while we can observe Fat Tuesday by enjoying food – including Polish paczkis which are customarily eaten on this day – we should ensure that our merriment never turns to gluttony.[25] Some cultures – like the English – adopted the custom of eating pancakes on Fat Tuesday – earning it the nickname of "Pancake Tuesday." This custom, like the Polish one, was observed because for centuries the use of any lacticinia (i.e., animal byproducts like cheese, butter, milk or

---

[24] "Lent Well Spent: Prepare for Forty Days with Forty Hours," *Sensus Fidelium* (Feb 27, 2020) <https://www.youtube.com/watch?v=v4boWXphUY>, accessed December 11, 2023.

[25] Matthew Plese, *loc. cit.*
<https://acatholiclife.blogspot.com/2007/02/fat-tuesday-prayer.html>.

eggs) was forbidden for the entirety of Lent.[26] We should consider adopting a similar observance this year with our Lenten fast.

The practice of observing Carnival celebrations was based on the approaching Lenten fast. The word "carnival" comes from the Latin words "carnis" (meaning meat or flesh) and "vale" (the Latin word for farewell). Carnival then became the last farewell to meat since meat was never permitted at all during Lent until the liberalizing changes of Pope Benedict XIV in 1741.[27] Lent was always a season of complete abstinence for centuries.

The name "Shrove Tuesday" also expresses the ancient practice of the faithful to go to Confession on the day before Ash Wednesday. Ælfric of Eynsham's "Ecclesiastical Institutes" from c. 1000 AD states: "In the week immediately before Lent everyone shall go to his confessor and confess his deeds and the confessor shall so shrive him as he then may hear by his deeds what he is to do [in the way of penance]." Father Weiser similarly remarks, "In preparation for Lent the faithful in medieval times used to go to confession on Tuesday before Ash Wednesday. From this practice, that day became known as 'Shrove Tuesday' (the day on which people are shriven from sins)."

(To be precise, in Poland itself, Catholics would eat "pączki" on Fat Thursday, not Fat Tuesday (when they traditionally eat herrings). It is today still a universal custom throughout Poland, although most people have no idea of this Pre-Lent period. The reason was that from Quinquagesima Sunday, Poles could not eat lacticina (e.g. dairy products) and on Friday and Saturday you fasted. Thus, the Thursday between

---

[26] Ibid., <https://acatholiclife.blogspot.com/2021/02/abstinence-from-meat-animal-products-on.html>.

[27] Matthew Plese, "Fasting Part 6: Fasting in the Early Modern Era," *Fatima Center* (Aug 18, 2020) <https://fatima.org/news-views/fasting-part-6-fasting-in-the-early-modern-era/>, accessed December 9, 2023.

Sexagesima and Quinquagesima was the last day to eat "pączki" in Poland.)

Make it a resolution to go to Confession on Shrove Tuesday or the weekend before. Since none of our penance done in the state of mortal sin earns merit for us, starting our Lenten penance in the state of sanctifying grace is of the utmost importance.

40 Hours Devotion & Reparation to the Holy Face

Unfortunately, Carnival season over time grew to that of excess. Dom Guéranger wrote of the excesses and sinfulness of Mardi Gras in his own time. And how much worse it is in our own times than his, who lived from 1805 to 1875:

> How far from being true children of Abraham are those so-called Christians who spend Quinquagesima and the two following days in intemperance and dissipation, because Lent is soon to be upon us! We can easily understand how the simple manners of our Catholic forefathers could keep a leave-taking of the ordinary way of living, which Lent was to interrupt, and reconcile their innocent carnival with Christian gravity; just as we can understand how their rigorous observance of the laws of the Church for Lent would inspire certain festive customs at Easter.
>
> Even in our times, a joyous carnival is not to be altogether reprobated, provided the Christian sentiment of the approaching holy season of Lent be strong enough to check the evil tendency of corrupt nature; otherwise the original intention of an innocent custom would be perverted, and the forethought of penance could in no sense be considered as the prompter of our joyous farewell to ease and comforts.

> While admitting all this, we would ask, what right or title have they to share in these carnival rejoicings, whose Lent will pass and find them out of the Church? And they, too, who claim dispensations from fasting during Lent and, for one reason or another, evade every penitential exercise during the solemn forty days of penance, and will find themselves at Easter as weighed down by the guilt and debt of their sins as they were on Ash Wednesday – what meaning, we would ask, can there possibly be in their feasting at 'Mardi Gras.'

As a result of the excesses of Fat Tuesday and the carnival season, the Church instituted the practice of observing the 40 Hours Devotion. Father Weiser remarks:

> In order to encourage the faithful to atone in prayer and penance for the many excesses and scandals committed at carnival time, Pope Benedict XIV, in 1748, instituted a special devotion for the three days preceding Lent, called 'Forty Hours of Carnival,' which is held in many churches of Europe and America, in places where carnival frolics are of general and long-standing tradition. The Blessed Sacrament is exposed all day Monday and Tuesday, and devotions are held in the evening, followed by the Eucharistic benediction.

The Church also instituted the Votive Feast of the Holy Face of Our Lord Jesus Christ Deformed in the Passion for the Tuesday after Quinquagesima (i.e., Fat Tuesday) as a means of making reparation for the sins of Mardi Gras. In fact, our Blessed Lord Himself asked for such reparation to His Holy Face in apparition to Mother Pierina in 1938:

> See how I suffer. Nevertheless, I am understood by so few. What gratitude on the

part of those who say they love me. I have given My Heart as a sensible object of My great love for man and I give My Face as a sensible object of My Sorrow for the sins of man. I desire that it be honored by a special feast on Tuesday in Quinquagesima (Shrove Tuesday – the Tuesday before Ash Wednesday). The feast will be preceded by novena in which the faithful make reparation with Me uniting themselves with my sorrow.[28]

To this end, the praying of the Golden Arrow prayer during Septuagesima has become an annual custom for some families.

Prepare a Lenten Resolution Plan During Septuagesima

Lent, with its three-fold foundation of prayer, fasting, and almsgiving, provides Catholics a grace-filled opportunity to atone for sin. To this end, Lent has been called the "tithe of the year." Preparing for Lent requires a plan for Lenten penance with all three pillars. To start your preparation see a list of 20 Pious Practices for Lent and consider adopting some of them.[29] Commit to your resolutions by writing them down on a Lenten preparation guide, ensuring you cover prayer, fasting, and almsgiving to a greater degree than required by Church law.[30]

---

[28] Matthew Plese, "Reparation to the Holy Face for the Offenses of Mardi Gras," *A Catholic Life* (Feb 19, 2018) <https://acatholiclife.blogspot.com/2018/02/reparation-to-holy-face-for-offenses-of.html>, accessed December 9, 2023.
[29] Ibid., <https://acatholiclife.blogspot.com/2012/02/20-pious-practices-for-lent-what-should.html>.
[30] Ibid., <https://acatholiclife.blogspot.com/2020/02/lent-preparation-guide.html>.

V

Lent

> The observance of Lent is the very badge of Christian warfare. By it we prove ourselves not to be enemies of Christ. By it we avert the scourges of divine justice. By it we gain strength against the princes of darkness, for it shields us with heavenly help. Should men grow remiss in their observance of Lent, it would be a detriment to God's glory, a disgrace to the Catholic religion, and a danger to Christian souls. Neither can it be doubted that such negligence would become the source of misery to the world, of public calamity, and of private woe.
> –Pope Benedict XIV (1740 – 1758).

The sacred season of Lent, called the Great Fast by our eastern Catholic brethren, was instituted by the Apostles themselves as Dom Guéranger writes:

> The forty days' fast, which we call Lent, is the Church's preparation for Easter, and was instituted at the very commencement of Christianity. Our blessed Lord Himself sanctioned it by fasting forty days and forty nights in the desert; and though He would not impose it on the world by an express commandment (which, in that case, could not have been open to the power of dispensation), yet He showed plainly enough, by His own example, that fasting, which God had so

> frequently ordered in the old Law, was to be also practiced by the children of the new…The apostles, therefore, legislated for our weakness, by instituting, at the very commencement of the Christian Church, that the solemnity of Easter should be preceded by a universal fast; and it was only natural that they should have made this period of penance to consist of forty days, seeing that our divine Master had consecrated that number by His own fast.

Lent, founded upon the three pillars of prayer, fasting, and almsgiving is the primary season of penance in the year and must be observed with the greatest strictness for the love of God who instituted this season for our healing.[31] Due to the primordial importance of Lent, over time, the history and customs of observed prayers, fasting and abstinence, and almsgiving have formed a definitive part of annual Catholic life. This Lent, adopt some of these – especially the fasting principles – which our forefathers in the Faith gladly observed.

Lenten Fasting

Lenten fasting is a cornerstone of Lent and rediscovering true Catholic fasting for Lent is necessary to resurrect Christendom. The Lenten fast began under the Apostles themselves and was practiced in various forms. St. Augustine in the fourth century remarked, "Our fast at any other time is voluntary; but during Lent, we sin if we do not fast." At the time of St. Gregory the Great at the beginning of the 7th century, the fast was universally established to begin on what we know as Ash Wednesday. While the name "Ash Wednesday" was not given to the day until Pope Urban II in 1099, the day was known as the "Beginning of the Fast."

---

[31] T. S. Flanders, "Fasting is a Virtue," *OnePeterFive* (Feb 21, 2022) <https://onepeterfive.com/fasting-is-a-virtue/>, accessed December 11, 2023; Ibid., <https://onepeterfive.com/almsgiving-catechism/>.

Regarding Holy Saturday's fast in particular, Canon 89 of the Council in Trullo in 692 AD provides an account of the piety and devotion of the faithful of that time: "The faithful, spending the days of the Salutatory Passion in fasting, praying and compunction of heart, ought to fast until the midnight of the Great Sabbath: since the divine Evangelists, Matthew and Luke, have shown us how late at night it was [that the resurrection took place]." That tradition of fasting on Holy Saturday until midnight would last for centuries.

Historical records further indicate that Lent was not a merely regional practice observed only in Rome. It was part of the universality of the Church. Lenten fasting began in England, for instance, sometime during the reign of Earconberht, the king of Kent, who was converted by the missionary work of St. Augustine of Canterbury in England. During the Middle Ages, fasting in England, and many other then-Catholic nations, was required both by Church law and the civil law. Catholic missionaries brought fasting, which is an integral part of the Faith, to every land they visited.

The rules on fasting remained largely the same for hundreds of years. Food was to be taken once a day after sunset. After the meal, the fast resumed and was terminated only after the sun had once again set on the horizon. But relaxations were to soon begin.

By the eighth century, the time for the daily meal was moved to the time that the monks would pray the Office of None in the Divine Office. This office takes place around 3 o'clock in the afternoon. As a consequence of moving the meal up in the day, the practice of a collation was introduced. The well-researched Father Francis Xavier Weiser summarizes this major change with fasting:

> It was not until the ninth century, however, that less rigid laws of fasting were introduced. It came about in 817 when the monks of the Benedictine order, who did much labor in the

> fields and on the farms, were allowed to take a little drink with a morsel of bread in the evening... Eventually the Church extended the new laws to the laity as well, and by the end of the medieval times they had become universal practice; everybody ate a little evening meal in addition to the main meal at noon.

In 604, in a letter to St. Augustine of Canterbury, Pope St. Gregory the Great announced the form that abstinence would take on fast days. This form would last for almost a thousand years: "We abstain from flesh meat and from all things that come from flesh: milk, cheese, and eggs." When fasting was observed, abstinence was likewise always observed.

Through the writings of St. Thomas Aquinas, we can learn how Lent was practiced in his own time and attempt to willingly observe such practices in our own lives. The Lenten fast as mentioned by St. Thomas Aquinas constituted of the following:

- o Monday through Saturday were days of fasting. The meal was taken at mid-day and a collation was allowed at night, except on days of the black fast
- o All meat or animal products were prohibited throughout Lent.
- o Abstinence from these foods remained even on Sundays of Lent, though fasting was not practiced on Sundays.[32]
- o No food was to be eaten at all on either Ash Wednesday or Good Friday
- o Holy Week was a more intense fast that consisted only of bread, salt, water, and herbs.

---

[32] Laetare Sunday would eventually become the one day of a reprieve during the Lenten observance when abstinence was relaxed.

The Lenten fast included fasting from all *lacticinia* (Latin for milk products) which included butter, cheese, eggs, and animal products.[33] From this tradition, Easter Eggs were introduced, and therefore the Tuesday before Ash Wednesday is when pancakes are traditionally eaten to use leftover *lacticinia*. And similarly, Fat Tuesday is known as Carnival, coming from the Latin words *carne levare* – literally the farewell to meat.

By the fourteenth century, the meal had begun to move up steadily until it began to take place even at 12 o'clock. The change became so common it became part of the Church's discipline. In one interesting but often unknown fact, because the monks would pray the liturgical hour of None before they would eat their meal, the custom of calling midday by the name "noon" entered into our vocabulary as a result of the fast. With the meal moved up, the evening collation remained.

Some of the most significant changes to fasting would occur under the reign of Pope Benedict XIV who reigned from 1740 – 1758. On May 31, 1741, Pope Benedict XIV issued *Non Ambiginius* which granted permission to eat meat on fasting days while explicitly forbidding the consumption of both fish and flesh meat at the same meal on all fasting days during the year in addition to the Sundays during Lent. Beforehand, the forty days of Lent were held as days of complete abstinence from meat. The concept of partial abstinence was born even though the term would not appear until the 1917 Code of Canon Law. Sadly, Lent would only continue to wane in the centuries to come.

---

[33] Regarding this point there are important exceptions to note as the Church has always exercised common sense. "Abstinence from lacticinia which included milk, butter, cheese, and eggs, was never strictly enforced in Britain, Ireland, and Scandinavia because of the lack of oil and other substitute foods in those countries. The Church using common sense granted many dispensations in this matter in all countries of Europe. People who did eat the milk foods would often, when they could afford it, give alms for the building of churches or other pious endeavors." Weiser, *Handbook of Christian Feasts & Customs*, 171-172.

Father Anthony Ruff relates in his article "Fasting and Abstinence: The Story" of the changes made by Pope Leo XIII in the document entitled *Indultum quadragesimale* as a further modification to the changes introduced by Pope Benedict XIV.

> In 1886 Leo XIII allowed meat, eggs, and milk products on Sundays of Lent and at the main meal on every weekday [of Lent] except Wednesday and Friday in the [United States]. Holy Saturday was not included in the dispensation. A small piece of bread was permitted in the morning with coffee, tea, chocolate, or a similar beverage.[34]

While the evening collation had been widespread since the 14th century, the practice of an additional morning collation was introduced only in the 19th century as part of the gradual relaxation of discipline.

Consequently, *The Baltimore Manual* published by the Third Plenary Council of Baltimore in 1884 states:

> Only one full meal is allowed, to be taken about noon or later. Besides this full meal, a collation of eight ounces is allowed. If the full meal is taken about the middle of the day, the collation will naturally be taken in the evening; if the full meal is taken late in the day, the collation may be taken at noon. Besides the full meal and collation, the general custom has made it lawful to take up to two ounces of bread (without butter) and a cup of some warm liquid – as coffee or tea – in the morning. This is important to observe, for by means of this many persons

---

[34] Anthony Ruff, "Fasting and Abstinence: The Story," *Pray Tell* (no date) <https://praytellblog.com/index.php/2018/02/21/fasting-and-abstinence-the-story/>, accessed December 9, 2023.

are enabled – and therefore obliged – the keep the fast who could not otherwise do so.

The Catechism of Father Patrick Powers published in Ireland in 1905 mentions that abstinence includes flesh meat and "anything produced from animals, as milk, butter, cheese, eggs." However, Father Patrick notes, "In some countries, however, milk is allowed at collation." The United States was one of those nations whereas Ireland and others were not granted such dispensations. The use of eggs and milk during Lent was to drastically change with the 1917 Code of Canon Law.

For more information on how the Lenten fast quickly deteriorated even more in the 1900s, see the article Fasting in the 1900s Pre-Vatican II.[35] With this history in mind we can better understand the importance of the Lenten fast to our ancestors and rediscover in our own lives this Lent the keeping of Lent as forty days of fasting and forty-six days of abstinence, even from dairy products, in order to continue these immemorial practices.[36] It is not too late to commit to some form of bodily penance for the remainder of Lent.

Lenten Prayers

Lent also has a focus on prayer and this thankfully is still seen by the many Catholics who gladly continue to pray the Stations of the Cross each Friday of Lent, which has indulgences attached to them for those who meet the conditions.[37] In addition to this practice, praying the indulged

---

[35] Matthew Plese, "Fasting Part 7: Fasting in the 1900s Pre-Vatican II," *The Fatima Center* (Aug 25, 2020) <https://fatima.org/news-views/pasting-part-7-fasting-in-the-1900s-pre-vatican-ii/>, accessed December 9, 2023.

[36] Ibid., "Abstinence from Meat & Animal Products on Sundays in Lent," *A Catholic Life* (Feb 27, 2021) <https://acatholiclife.blogspot.com/2021/02/abstinence-from-meat-animal-products-on.html>, accessed December 9, 2023.

[37] Ibid., <https://acatholiclife.blogspot.com/2005/06/the-stations-of-cross.html>.

prayer to the Cross each Friday in Lent should be something more Catholics rediscover.[38]

Additionally, each day of Lent has a special stational church in Rome. These churches often have a connection to the Traditional Mass readings and prayers of that day – especially for catechumens – and reading about the daily stational churches is a worthwhile practice this Lent.[39]

Similarly, we would be remiss if we did not try to attend Holy Mass more often during this sacred season and, even for those days we cannot attend, read the prayers of the Missal since everyday of Lent has a proper Mass as Dom Guéranger points out:

> Each feria of Lent has a proper Mass; whereas, in Advent, the Mass of the preceding Sunday is repeated during the week. This richness of the Lenten liturgy is a powerful means for our entering into the Church's spirit, since she hereby brings before us, under so many forms, the sentiments suited to this holy time… All this will provide us with most solid instruction; and as the selections from the Bible, which are each day brought before us, are not only some of the finest of the sacred volume, but are, moreover, singularly appropriate to Lent, their attentive perusal will be productive of a twofold advantage.

Lenten Almsgiving

In addition to prayer and fasting, almsgiving is one of the primary means of penance we perform during Lent. There is a custom in some churches in Europe of having alms boxes

---

[38] Ibid., <https://acatholiclife.blogspot.com/2014/03/indulged-prayer-to-cross-for-fridays-in.html>.
[39] Ibid., <https://acatholiclife.blogspot.com/2006/03/stational-churches.html>.

specifically for the poor souls.[40] This is a custom that is not commonly known nowadays but one that we might encourage parishes in our own area to adopt.

Almsgiving refers to giving to the poor. By giving to the poor, we make reparation for sins as we see in the poor the person of Christ Himself. Though, while not strictly almsgiving, the giving of our time to visit the sick, the elderly, or those in prison also makes reparation for sin. Our Lord at the End of Times will judge everyone, and He will judge us against the works of mercy. Everyone will be judged against them.

May the restoration in our own lives this Lent of increased prayer, fasting, and almsgiving be for the glory of God and the glory of Christendom.

---

[40] Ibid., <https://acatholiclife.blogspot.com/2019/06/alms-for-poor-souls.html>.

VI

Easter

Easter itself is an 8-day celebration, and even after the Octave concludes on Low Sunday, the Easter Season lasts for a total of fifty days until the completion of Ascensiontide and the celebration of Pentecost Sunday. This period of time, especially for the Octave of Easter, is enriched with many rich customs all expressing the heartfelt joy of the faithful that the Lord, brutally murdered on the Cross, is alive. Alleluia!

Father Weiser echoes these sentiments and shows the importance of Easter customs since times immemorial:

> The joy and exultation over this greatest of all Christian feasts is evident in the writings of the saints and Fathers from earliest times. Easter is referred to as the 'peak (akropolis) of all feasts' and the 'Queen of all solemnities.' Saint Gregory of Nazianzen (390) wrote, 'This highest Feast and greatest celebration so much surpasses not only civic holidays but also the other feast days of the Lord, that it is like the sun among stars.'

It is fitting that this most holy of celebrations be enhanced with customs by the faithful. And many of these customs are thankfully still found in our world. May they increase along with the number of faithful Catholics year by year!

The Paschal Greeting

The most conspicuous custom of Eastertide still in practice today, at least among Eastern Catholics, is the greeting "Christ is risen!"

Outside Paschaltide, it is traditional for Catholics to greet one another with the greeting, "*Laudetur Iesus Christus!*" [May Jesus Christ be praised!] to which the other responds with some variation of "*In Saecula!*" [Unto the Ages / Forever!].

Now, throughout the weeks of Eastertide, Christians greet one another with "Christ is risen!" to which the other responds with "He is risen indeed!" Some versions have the answer as "And He has appeared unto Simon."

Try teaching your children to greet another throughout the Easter season like this. So instead of "Good morning" and "Good night" and "Hello," instead say "Christ is risen! / He is risen indeed!"

This begins already in the liturgy of the Eastern Vigil and goes through the Octave. The greeting is maintained in the versicle for the *Regina Caeli* throughout Paschaltide.

Easter Monday and Tuesday as Holy Days of Obligation

When writing about the rank of days in the Catholic Liturgical calendar, there are various ways to label them. In the modern Church, they will use the terms solemnity, feast, memorial, or optional memorial. In the 1962 Missal, we have First, Second, Third, or Fourth Class feast days. But before the 1962 Missal up until the changes made by Pope Pius XII in 1955, there were from least to most important: Simples, Semidoubles, Lesser Doubles (also known as Doubles), Greater Doubles, Doubles of the second class, and Doubles of the first class.

Using the traditional pre-1955 calendar, we notice something very interesting about Easter Monday and Easter Tuesday. Easter Monday and Tuesday are doubles of the first class whereas the rest of the Easter Octave is a semi-double. Even with the variation in rank, the Easter Octave is privileged and no other feast day may occur in the Octave.

What's unique about Easter Monday and Easter Tuesday is that no other saints are commemorated those days in the Mass or the Divine Office. Why the special treatment for Easter Monday and Easter Tuesday? It is because they were universal holy days of obligation for a very long time. Easter Tuesday was not dropped from the list until 1771 by Pope Clement XIV; Easter Monday was dropped from the universal list at the beginning of the 20th century but is still a Holy Day of Obligation in many places to this very day. In Catholic European countries, it is still common to have Easter Monday off as a paid holiday, which gives rise to many customs practiced on that day. The other days of Easter Week (i.e., Easter Wednesday through Easter Saturday) ceased being holy days much earlier in the Middle Ages, yet nevertheless, some customs for these days do also remain.

The unequaled Dom Guéranger writes:

> So fervently did the faithful of those times appreciate and love the Liturgy, so lively was the interest they took in the newly made children of holy mother Church, that they joyfully went through the whole of the services of this week. Their hearts were filled with the joy of the Resurrection, and they thought it but right to devote their whole time to its celebration. Councils laid down canons, changing the pious custom into a formal law. The Council of Mâcon, in 585, thus words its decree: 'It behooves us all fervently to celebrate the feast of the Pasch, in which our great High Priest was slain for our sins, and to honour it by carefully observing all it prescribes. Let no one, therefore, do any servile work during these six days (which followed the Sunday), but let all come together to sing the

Easter hymns, and assist at the daily Sacrifice, and praise our Creator and Redeemer in the evening, morning, and mid-day.'

The Councils of Mayence (813) and Meaux (845) lay down similar rules. We find the same prescribed in Spain, in the seventh century, by the edicts of kings Receswind and Wamba. The Greek Church renewed them in her Council in Trullo; Charlemagne, Louis the Good, Charles the Bald, sanctioned them in their Capitularia; and the canonists of the eleventh and twelfth centuries, Burchard, St Ivo of Chartres, Gratian, tell us they were in force in their time. Finally, Pope Gregory IX inserted them in one of his decretals in the thirteenth century. But their observance had then fallen into desuetude, at least in many places. The Council held at Constance, in 1094, reduced the solemnity of Easter to the Monday and Tuesday.

The two great liturgists, John Beleth in the twelfth, and Durandus in the thirteenth century, inform us that, in their times, this was the practice in France. It gradually became the discipline of the whole of the western Church, and continued to be so, until relaxation crept still further on, and a dispensation was obtained by some countries, first for the Tuesday, and finally for the Monday. In order fully to understand the Liturgy of the whole Easter Octave (Low Sunday included), we must remember that the neophytes were formerly present, vested in their white garments, at the Mass and Divine Office of each day. Allusions to their Baptism are continually being made in the chants and lessons of the entire week.

We should ask ourselves, how do we plan to keep the celebration of Easter alive this year throughout the Octave? One custom that we can observe, which is still observed in some parts of Europe, is the Emmaus Walk.

The Emmaus Walk on Easter Monday

As a result of Easter Monday remaining a Holy Day of Obligation until the time of Pope St. Pius X, and a result of it still largely remaining as a paid holiday, the Emmaus Walk is still practiced in places. What is the Emmaus walk? It is first and foremost what it sounds like – a walk. It can take the simple form of a walk with friend and family on a day spent in relaxation and leisure. The name for this custom is inspired by the traditional Gospel read on Easter Monday which is taken from the 24th chapter of St. Luke's Gospel which recounts our Lord appearing to two of His followers who were on the road of Emmaus. In Germany and Austria, children can still be found to play Easter games and sports (Osterspiele) in the Easter field (Osteranger) on Easter Monday. And in the French region of Canada, the Emmaus walk takes the form of a visit to the grandparents.

We can continue this tradition by taking Easter Monday off work and spending the day out in nature with a long walk and a picnic with our families. Spend time enjoying lunch after an end to the fast of Lent, and cherish the company of others around you in the spring air.

Another Easter Monday tradition is found in Hungary where young men will pour buckets of water over young women's heads while asking for a kiss and a red egg in return. This custom relates to the healing and cleansing effects of water, which we see in the Church's blessing of holy water on Holy Saturday. Even throughout Paschaltide we will sing the *Vidi Aquam,* which expresses the healing effect of water instead of the *Asperges,* before Sunday's principal Mass.

Easter Food Customs

As the holiest of all Christian holy days, it is fitting that Easter is rife with customs. While cultures may vary in how they observed Easter, a unifying theme throughout is found in food. After having completed 40 days of fasting and 46 days of abstinence, Easter ushers in a period of fifty days where the faithful celebrate through various meats, eggs, dairy products, and other foods which were forbidden in Lent.

On Holy Saturday, the custom originated for the faithful to bring their Easter foods to church where the priest would bless them. The Roman Ritual provides a beautiful blessing of Easter food in the form of blessings of lamb, eggs, bread, and new produce.

Which foods are found in Easter baskets varied from culture to culture. In Slavic regions, ham was often the main dish because of its richness and serving it was a symbol of joy and abundance at Easter. But lamb and veal were found too. But in any case, the meats were often cooked together so as not to burden the cooks with too much preparation on such a great holy day. In Hungary, Easter is referred to as the "Feast of Meat" (Husvet), because the eating of meat resumes after the long fast of Lent.

As a consequence of having traditionally abstained from all butter, eggs, and cheese, these foods were often found in baskets as well. We see this first and foremost in the continued tradition of Easter Eggs. One truly appreciates Easter Eggs only after having forgone eggs for 46 days. After such a time, having an egg is truly a treat! Russian eggs are traditionally died red due to a story dating back to St. Mary Magdalene, but other cultures have chosen to paint even elaborate symbols on the eggs. (The story is told that St. Mary Magdalene preached the Gospel to a doubter who asked for a miracle – prompting a white egg to turn red. The red egg also symbolizes the Passion, which, after it is broken shows the egg white, which symbolizes the Resurrection.)

And let us not forget cheese. As another item formerly forbidden in Lent, cheese is a great treat to those who have abstained from it for the 46 days of abstinence. The Russians would customarily make a custard type of cheese that was shaped into a ball. Known for its bland but sweet taste, it was meant to indicate that it is fitting that Christians should still engage in moderation and never gluttony even in Eastertide. And on this point, Fr. Goffine expresses similar rationale for why the Church enriches such customs with blessings from the Roman Ritual:

> Why does the Church on this day bless eggs, bread, and meat? To remind the faithful that although the time of fasting is now ended, they should not indulge in gluttony, but thank God, and use their food simply for the necessary preservation of physical strength.

Russian Easter baskets will often feature salt as well as a reminder of our Lord's own words in Matthew 5:13, which remind the Christian of his duty. And alongside these items is sometimes found horseradish, which symbolizes the passion of Christ yet, when mixed with sugar, helps us see how the Resurrection has sweetened the Passion of Christ. Indeed, the details indicate to us how cultures valued and celebrated the Resurrection with intricate attention to detail. Even the butter in some baskets would be shaped into the figure of a small lamb or at least decorated in stick form with the image of a cross on the top.

This year, ask your priest to bless your Easter foods, even if it is a few days after Easter Sunday, and enjoy these worthwhile treats with your family as a reward for your abstinence this Lent.

Agnus Dei Sacramental

Even after Easter Tuesday concludes, the faithful continued to celebrate through customs the reality that priests were still celebrating in the Mass and Office throughout Easter Week – Christ is risen!

One virtually forgotten custom is the blessing of Agnus Dei Sacramentals. The *Catholic Encyclopedia*, written in 1907, explains their connection to Easter Week:

> We learn from an 'Ordo Romanus' printed by Muratori ('Lit. Rom,' II, p. 1,004) that in the ninth century the archdeacon manufactured the Agnus Deis early on Holy Saturday morning out of clean wax mixed with chrism, and that they were distributed by him to the people on the Saturday following (Sabbato in Albis). At a later date the Pope himself generally assisted at both the blessing and the distribution. The great consecration of Agnus Deis took place only in the first year of each pontificate and every seventh year afterwards, which rule is still followed. The discs of wax are now prepared beforehand by certain monks, and without the use of chrism. On the Wednesday of Easter week these discs are brought to the Pope, who dips them into a vessel of water mixed with chrism and balsam, adding various consecratory prayers. The distribution takes place with solemnity on the Saturday following, when the Pope, after the 'Agnus Dei' of the Mass, puts a packet of Agnus Deis into the inverted mitre of each cardinal and bishop who comes up to receive them.

For the Rite of the Blessing of the Angus Dei can be found online.[41] This ceremony shows the splendor and holiness

---

[41] Gregory DiPippo, "The Rite of Blessing of the Agnus Deis," *New Liturgical Movement* (Apr 25, 2020) <https://www.newliturgicalmovement.org/2020/04/the-rite-of-blessing-of-agnus-deis.html>, accessed December 9, 2023.

inherent in the Church's traditional blessings. The last pope to consecrate the wax and make it available was Pope Pius XII, which makes them incredibly hard to find, but to those who have inherited them, they are a true family treasure.

Easter Pilgrimages

As Easter Friday arrives, the faithful in Austria still spend the day in celebration of the Lord's Resurrection by making day pilgrimages called *Osterwallfahrt*. The faithful would walk for hours preceded by a cross and banners – sometimes even 10 hours each way! In some sections of Germany and Austria, the pilgrimage would occur on horseback as the faithful would be accompanied by a band playing Easter hymns in joyous fashion.

Sabbato in Albis

The ancient custom for those who received the Sacrament of Baptism on Holy Saturday was to wear the same white garment throughout the Octave. For this reason, Easter Week was also called "White Week" in the Western Church (it is known as "Bright Week" among Greek Catholics). The neophytes would attend Mass together each day of the Octave and the bishop would address them with special instruction and words of encouragement after Mass. That would continue until Saturday in Easter Week when they would lay aside their white garment for regular clothes and assume their place amongst all the faithful. For that reason, the Saturday in the Octave of Easter was called "Sabbato in Albis" which is Latin for "Saturday in white"

Dom Guéranger writes of this day:

> In Rome, the Station is in the Lateran Basilica, the mother and mistress of all churches. It is close to the baptistery of Constantine, where, eight days back, the neophytes received the grace of regeneration. The basilica, wherein they are now assembled, is that from which

they set out, during the still and dark night, to the font of salvation, led on by the mysterious light of the Paschal torch. It was to this same church that they returned after their Baptism, clad in their white robes, and assisted, for the first time, at the entire celebration of the Christian Sacrifice, and received the Body and Blood of Christ Jesus. No other place could have been more appropriate for the Station of this day, whereon they were to return to the ordinary duties of life. Holy Church sees assembled around her these her new-born children. It is the last time that she will see them in their white garments, and she looks at them with all the affection of a joyful mother. They are most dear to her, as the fruit of heaven's own giving; and during the week she has frequently given expression to her maternal pride, in canticles such as she alone can sing.

The Sunday of Many Names

The Sunday after Easter Sunday is not lacking in names. Known as the Octave of the Pasch, White Sunday, Low Sunday, Quasimodo Sunday, and in the Novus Ordo, as Divine Mercy Sunday, this is the final day of the Octave of Easter. The most common traditional name of "Low Sunday" comes from the practice of counting the octave day as belonging to the feast itself so Easter had two Sundays. Low Sunday is in contrast to Easter Sunday (i.e., High Sunday) from the week before.

Low Sunday had its own customs as well. In the Middle Ages, this was customarily the day on which children would make their First Communion. And in some places, this occurred as the father and mother would kneel beside their child and already receive Holy Communion at the same time. In our times, it reminds us of the importance of hearing Holy Mass as a family every single Sunday of the year.

Easter Duty Reminder

With the disciples, let us celebrate with unparalleled joy the end of the Great Fast and the resurrection of the Redeemer of the world Who really – in the greatest display of His divinity – resurrected Himself. In addition to the customs mentioned, it is important to also fulfill our Easter Duty before Trinity Sunday, if we have not already done so.[42] Do note that in some countries, the time within which the Easter Communion must be received commences on Palm Sunday and terminates on Low Sunday. In the United States, it is between the First Sunday of Lent and Trinity Sunday.

Conclusion

Keep in mind this was just a sampling of the many Easter Week customs. For more information, the *Handbook of Christian Feasts and Customs* by Father Weiser would be a good read as we said.

In the end, Easter Week, a week replete with customs from all Catholic cultures, draws to a close even as the Paschal Season continues. While Lent was observed by fasting for 40 days and abstinence for 46 days, we celebrate Easter for 50 days, not including the Octave of Pentecost. The Saturday following the Octave of Pentecost officially begins the Season After Pentecost. The total length of Paschaltide from Easter Sunday to the end of Whitsuntide is 56 days inclusive. In this way, Holy Mother Church shows us the joy of Easter has eclipsed the time of penance of Lent. Paschaltide is also time for a special daily meal blessing, time for us to pray the Regina Caeli daily (in place of the Angelus), and time for us to greet each other with the special Paschal greeting.[43]

---

[42] Matthew Plese, *loc. cit.*,
<https://acatholiclife.blogspot.com/2020/04/the-easter-duty-receive-holy-communion.html>.

[43] Ibid., <https://acatholiclife.blogspot.com/2020/05/blessings-before-and-after-meals.html>;
<https://acatholiclife.blogspot.com/2006/04/regina-coeli.html>.

Above all, Easter is a call to a new life with Christ. It is a time to put into habitual practice the good habits, the works of charity, and the regular fasting we performed in Lent. One way we can do this is to keep Fridays throughout the year as days of fast, which used to be required in former times, and to keep Fridays and Saturdays as days of abstinence.[44] Even Easter Friday should be kept as a day of abstinence.[45]

May the Good Lord fill our hearts with His love and grace so that the great joy we experience of seeing the sunrise on Easter Sunday morning never fade from our hearts. As Father Goffine reminds us:

> What encouragement does the Resurrection of Christ give us? It encourages us to rise spiritually with Him, and live henceforth a new life, (Rom. VI. 4.) which we do if we not only renounce sin, but also flee from all its occasions, lay aside our bad habits, subdue our corrupt inclinations, and aim after virtue and heavenly things (from Goffine's "The Church's Year").

Let us pray that those changes are permanent so that we who were baptized in Christ's death may rise to new life and live always in the state of sanctifying grace.

---

[44] Matthew Plese, "Saturday Fasting in Honor of the Blessed Virgin Mary," *Fatima Center* (Oct 6, 2020) <https://fatima.org/news-views/saturday-fasting/>, accessed December 9, 2023.

[45] Ibid., "Friday Penance: Still Required in Eastertide," *A Catholic Life* (Apr 8, 2016) <https://acatholiclife.blogspot.com/2016/04/friday-penance-still-required-in.html>, accessed December 11, 2023.

VII

Rogation Days

Liturgies.net summarizes these forgotten elements of our Catholic heritage as follows:

> Rogation Days are the four days set apart to bless the fields and invoke God's mercy on all of creation. The 4 days are April 25, which is called the Major Rogation (and is only coincidentally the same day as the Feast of St. Mark); and the three days preceding Ascension Thursday, which are called the Minor Rogations. Traditionally, on these days, the congregation marches the boundaries of the parish, blessing every tree and stone, while chanting or reciting a Litany of Mercy, usually a Litany of the Saints.

Rogations and Moveable Feasts

As stated, the Major Rogation Day is on April 25th, the Feast of St. Mark. Should it happen that the feast of St. Mark the Evangelist is transferred to another day (e.g., when a day in the Octave of Easter falls on April 25th), the Rogation procession is held nevertheless on April 25th, unless the feast falls on Easter Sunday or Monday, in which case the procession is transferred to Easter Tuesday. April 25th is the latest date that Easter may ever fall on. And as Dom Guéranger states, "If April 25 occur during Easter week, the procession takes place on that day (unless it be Easter Sunday), but the feast of the Evangelist is not kept till after the octave."

Since the Minor Rogation Days are correspond with Ascension Thursday, the date of the Minor Rogation Days varies.

The History of the Major Rogation Day

Major and Minor Rogation Days are also known as the Greater Litanies and Lesser Litanies, respectively, on account of the traditional custom of praying litanies on these days in the form of the Rogation Procession. Dom Guéranger explains more about the characteristic procession on these days and how they originated:

> The Greater Litanies, (or Processions,) are so called to distinguish them from the Minor Litanies, that is, Processions of less importance as far as the solemnity and concourse of the Faithful were concerned. We gather from an expression of St. Gregory the Great, that it was an ancient custom in the Roman Church to celebrate, once each year, a Greater Litany, at which all the Clergy and people assisted. This holy Pontiff chose the 25th of April as the fixed day for this Procession and appointed the Basilica of St. Peter as the Station.
>
> Several writers on the Liturgy have erroneously confounded this institution with the Processions prescribed by St. Gregory for times of public calamity. It existed long before his time, and all that he had to do with it was the fixing it to the 25th of April. It is quite independent of the Feast of St. Mark, which was instituted at a much later period.

The History of the Minor Rogation Days

In 2020, Dom Alcuin Reid gave a monastic conference on the Minor Rogation Days where he said in part:

> Their observance is now similar in format to the Greater Litanies of April 25th, but these three days have a different origin, having been instituted in Gaul in the fifth century as days of fasting, abstinence and abstention from servile work in which all took part in an extensive penitential procession, often barefoot. The procession and litanies only found a place in the Roman liturgy much later (around the beginning of the ninth century) and even then purely as days of rogation – of intercession – rather than as ones of fasting and penance; the latter being deemed incompatible with the nature of Eastertide.[46]

He continued:

> Indeed, this ancient tradition itself is now widely lost in the West. How many Catholics understand what is meant by the greater or lesser litanies, or by the expression "the Rogations" – clergy included?

> …Dom Guéranger himself lamented the lack of appreciation of the Rogations in his own day: "If we compare the indifference shown by the Catholics of the present age for the Rogation days, with the devotion wherewith our ancestors kept them, we cannot but acknowledge that there has been a great falling off in faith and piety. Knowing, as we do, the great importance attached to these processions by the Church, we cannot help wondering how it is that there are so few among the faithful who assist at them. Our surprise increases when

---

[46] Dom Alcuin Reid, "On the Rogation Days," *New Liturgical Movement* (May 17, 2020) <https://www.newliturgicalmovement.org/2020/05/dom-alcuin-reid-on-rogation-days.html>, accessed December 9, 2023.

> we find persons preferring their own private devotions to these public prayers of the Church, which, to say nothing of the result of good example, merit far greater graces than any exercises of our own choosing."

The origin of the Minor Rogation Days that Dom Alcuin Reid alludes to goes back to 470 AD when Bishop Mamertus of Vienne in Gaul instituted an annual observance of penance on the three days immediately before the Feast of the Ascension. He prescribed litanies in the form of processions for all three days. Thereafter they spread to the Frankish part of France in 511, to Spain in the 6th century, and to the German park of the Frankish empire in 813. In 816, Pope Leo III incorporated the lesser litanies into the Roman Liturgy, and during the subsequent centuries the custom of holding these litanies being custom for each year.

While the Lesser Litanies (i.e., Minor Rogation Days) are kept on the three days leading up to Ascension Day, Father Francis Weiser notes an important exception: "Pope Pius XII granted to some Catholic missions in the Pacific Islands the permission to celebrate both the major and minor litanies in October or November" (*Christian Feasts and Customs*, p. 42).

Is Penance Unbefitting for the Paschal Season?

Dom Guéranger answers this question which many liturgically-minded Catholics ask:

> The question naturally presents itself, why did St. Gregory choose the 25th of April for a Procession and Station, in which everything reminds us of compunction and penance, and which would seem so out of keeping with the joyous Season of Easter?
>
> The first to give a satisfactory answer to this difficulty, was Canon Moretti, a learned Liturgiologist of last century. In a dissertation

of great erudition, he proves that in the 5th, and probably even in the 4th, century, the 25th of April was observed at Rome as a day of great solemnity. The Faithful went, on that day, to the Basilica of St. Peter, in order to celebrate the anniversary of the first entrance of the Prince of the Apostles into Rome, upon which he thus conferred the inalienable privilege of being the Capital of Christendom. It is from that day that we count the twenty-five years, two months and some days that St. Peter reigned as Bishop of Rome. The Sacramentary of St. Leo gives us the Mass of this Solemnity, which afterwards ceased to be kept. St. Gregory, to whom we are mainly indebted for the arrangement of the Roman Liturgy, was anxious to perpetuate the memory of a day, which gave to Rome her grandest glory. He, therefore, ordained that the Church of St. Peter should be the Station of the Great Litany, which was always to be celebrated on that auspicious day. The 25th of April comes so frequently during the Octave of Easter, that it could not be kept as a Feast, properly so called, in honor of St. Peter's entrance into Rome; St. Gregory, therefore, adopted the only means left of commemorating the great event.

Hence from ancient times the Church kept these days as days of supplication. And even if fasting, the hallmark of Lent, would be ill suited for Paschaltide, abstinence is still permitted and even obligatory in the Paschal Season. For instance, Friday abstinence is mandatory in the Paschal Season both in the 1983 Code of Canon Law and in all prior times, back to the establishment of Wednesday and Friday fasting and abstinence by the Apostles.

In former times, Rome enjoined abstinence from meat on the faithful during Rogationtide. Other places, however, such as the Churches in Gaul where Rogation Days originated, required fasting. Dom Guéranger explains:

> A day, then, like this, of reparation to God's offended majesty, would naturally suggest the necessity of joining some exterior penance to the interior dispositions of contrition which filled the hearts of Christians. Abstinence from flesh meat has always been observed on this day at Rome; and when the Roman Liturgy was established in France by Pepin and Charlemagne, the Great Litany of April 25 was, of course, celebrated, and the abstinence kept by the faithful of that country. A Council of Aix-la-Chapelle, in 836, enjoined the additional obligation of resting from servile work on this day: the same enactment is found in the Capitularia of Charles the Bald. As regards fasting, properly so-called, being contrary to the spirit of Paschal Time, it would seem never to have been observed on this day, at least not generally. Amalarius, who lived in the ninth century, asserts that it was not then practiced even in Rome.

Fasting was championed as well by St. Charles Borromeo in Milan although Rome has never obligated fasting during the Paschal Season. Fasting during the Paschal Season though is not a sin, just as almsgiving and prayer, the other Lenten pillars, are certainly praiseworthy during Paschaltide.

Abstain from Meat and Join in the Processions

I highly encourage all Catholics to observe these days and spend time praying the Litany of Saints not only for a bountiful harvest but also for mercy and repentance. The Rogation Days are also days we could at least abstain from meat as penance to implore the mercy of God during our present chastisements.

Priests, please offer for the benefit of the faithful public Rogation Day processions. Advertise them. Encourage people to voluntarily abstain from meat and offer it up to implore God's mercy for our nation, our country, and our families. Please make these days known and loved again by the faithful.

For those looking for Rogation Day prayers for the procession, including the Litany, they can be found online.[47] And for those who would like prayers of blessings to be said on one's property, especially appropriate for Rogation Day, we have treated this in another place.[48] These prayers may be said by the laity.

Lastly, Fr. Christopher Smith, a priest of the Diocese of Charleston, South Carolina put together a truly beautiful and excellent illustrated guide explaining both the Rogations and Ember Days, with a number of very useful quotes from various liturgical sources. This is available online for download.[49]

Prayer from the Rogation Mass of the ancient Gallican Rite:

It is from thee, O Lord, we receive the food, wherewith we are daily supported; to thee also do we offer these fasts, whereby, according to thy command, we put upon our flesh the restraint from dangerous indulgence. Thou hast so ordered the changes of seasons, as to afford us consolation: thus, the time for eating gives nourishment to the body, by sober repasts; and the time for fasting inflicts on them a chastisement pleasing to thy justice. Vouchsafe to bless and receive this our offering of a

---

[47] Texts and rubrics:
<https://media.musicasacra.com/sjfm/Eastertide/Easter-Rogations.pdf>, accessed December 11, 2023.
[48] Matthew Plese, *loc. cit.*
<https://acatholiclife.blogspot.com/2020/04/major-rogation-day-april-25th-prayers.html>.
[49] Ibid., <https://acatholiclife.blogspot.com/2014/04/rogation-day-and-ember-day-manual.html>.

three days' penitential fast; and mercifully grant, that whilst our bodies abstain from gratification, our souls also may rest from sin. Through Christ our Lord. Amen.

VIII

Ascensiontide

Ascensiontide as the Forgotten End of Paschaltide

The total length of Paschaltide from Easter Sunday to the end of Whitsuntide is fifty-six days inclusive. In this way, Holy Mother Church shows us the joy of Easter has eclipsed the time of penance of Lent. Ascentiontide lasts for 10 days and is part of the Paschal Season. The first nine days of Ascensiontide include the traditional Octave of the Ascension. The last day of Ascentiontide is the Vigil of Pentecost. Pentecost Sunday, which has its own octave, follows. The Sunday following the Octave of Pentecost (Trinity Sunday) officially begins the Season After Pentecost. Some of these names should be familiar to Catholics, especially those who regularly assist at the Tridentine Mass.

Ascension Thursday Must Be Kept on a Thursday

The Ascension has three principal parts: the departure of Jesus from earth, His going up into heaven, and taking His place at the right hand of the Father. It was precisely on the fortieth day after our Lord's Resurrection that He ascended into Heaven.

According to St. Augustine, the Feast of the Ascension is of Apostolic origin. As early as the fifth century, documentation of this feast is preserved. Since the ninth century during the Pontificate of Pope Leo III (795 – 816) and up until the 1950s, the Ascension had an associated Octave attached to it. Predating this Octave is the long-established practice of having a Vigil for the Ascension, which dates back to the 7th century.

While the Feast of the Ascension – despite its high rank as one of the most important holy days in the year – has fallen into obscurity and lack of observance in many areas (often transferred to the following Sunday post Vatican II), it is still a public holiday in many countries (e.g. Austria, Belgium, Colombia, Denmark, Finland, France, Germany, Haiti, Iceland, Indonesia, Liechtenstein, Luxembourg, Madagascar, Namibia, The Netherlands, Norway, Sweden, Switzerland and Vanuatu). As such, Catholic culture underscores the importance of the Ascension through its customs that precede and follow Ascension Thursday. One of those customs is seen through Ascension Day Processions.

Processions &
the Extinguishment of the Paschal Candle

Father Weiser relates the following:

> From the very beginning of its observance as a separate festival, the Ascension had a distinctive feature in the liturgical procession which went outside the city, and usually to the top of a hill, in imitation of Chris's leading the Apostles "out towards Bethany" (Luke 24, 50). In Jerusalem it was, of course, the original path that Christ took to the summit of the Mount of Olives. In Constantinople the suburb of Romanesia, where Saint John Chrysostom had preached his sermons on the Ascension, was chosen. In Rome, the pope was crowned by the cardinals in his chapel after the morning service, and in solemn procession conducted to the church of the Lateran. From there, after the Pontifical Mass, toward noon, the procession went to a shrine or church outside the walls. The Epistle of the Ascension was read and a prayer service held.

> This custom of the procession was introduced as a fairly universal rite in the Latin Church during the eighth and ninth centuries, but finally was replaced by the non-liturgical pageants of the High Middle Ages. The only relic still extant in our present liturgy is the simple but impressive ceremony in every Catholic church, after the Gospel of the Mass has been sung, of extinguishing the Easter candle. In some sections of Germany and central Europe, however, semi-liturgical processions are still held after the High Mass. Preceded by candles and cross, the faithful walk with prayer and song through fields and pastures, and the priest blesses each lot of ground.

Why Did Our Lord Ascend into Heaven?

Stepping back though, we may ask why the Ascension is even so highly celebrated. The answer to this fundamental question is found in the Preface for the Ascension, a Preface found in the Traditional Roman Rite:

> It is truly meet and just, right and availing unto salvation that we should at all times and in all places give thanks unto Thee, O holy Lord, Father almighty and everlasting God; through Christ our Lord. Who after His resurrection appeared and showed Himself to all His disciples; and while they beheld Him, was lifted up into heaven, so that He might make us partakers of His Godhead. And therefore with angles and archangels, with thrones and dominations, and with all the heavenly hosts, we sing a hymn to Thy glory, saying without ceasing…

The answer to our question is thus: "so that He might make us partakers of His Godhead." Our Lord ascended for us. He ascended so that we might become divine. Dom Guéranger similarly expresses the sublime reason for our Lord's Ascension with the words:

> Jesus ascended into heaven. His Divinity had never been absent; but, by Ascension, His Humanity was also enthroned there, and crowned with the brightest diadem of glory. This is another phase of the mystery we are now solemnizing. Besides a triumph, the Ascension gave to the sacred Humanity a place on the very throne of the eternal Word, to whom it was united in unity of Person. From this throne, it is to receive the adoration of men and of angels. At the name of Jesus, Son of Man, and Son of God—of Jesus who is seated at the right hand of the Father almighty—"Every knee shall bend, in heaven, on earth and in hell."

Dom Guéranger elsewhere reflects as to why the Ascension is always mentioned in the Canon of the Mass. Here he expresses similar noteworthy sentiments:

> The feast of the Ascension shows us the work of God in its completion. Hence it is that the Church, in her daily offering of the holy sacrifice, thus addresses the eternal Father: the words occur immediately after the consecration, and contain the motives of her confidence in the divine mercy: 'Wherefore, O Lord, we Thy servants, as also Thy holy people, calling to mind the blessed Passion of Christ Thy Son our Lord, His Resurrection from the dead, and His admirable Ascension into heaven, offer unto Thy most excellent Majesty a pure, holy, and unspotted Host.'

It is not enough for man to hope in the merits of his Redeemer's Passion, which cleansed him from his sins; it is not enough for him to add to the commemoration of the Passion that of the Resurrection, whereby our Redeemer conquered death; man is not saved, he is not reinstated, except by uniting these two mysteries with a third: the Ascension of the same Jesus who was crucified and rose again.

The Ascension's Connection with the Passion

On the Mount of Olives, the same mount where the Passion began, Our Lord physically ascended into Heaven. At the top of the mount is a chapel in honor of the Ascension and the ground still retains the depressions His sacred feet had left. Thus, there is an intimate connection between the Passion and the Ascension that is not as clearly seen unless the faithful are taught this important historical fact.

It also must be taught of the importance the Ascension had in winning us Heaven. It was fitting that Christ, the conqueror of death, would be the first to open the gates of Heaven. He did so not on the day of His Resurrection but forty days later when He opened Heaven, led the souls of the just from the Limbo of the Fathers (e.g., Adam, Eve, Moses, Isaiah, et cetera) into Heaven, and He took His seat at the right hand of the Father. For the first time in world history, human flesh had entered Heaven. Hence, when our Lord told the Good Thief, "Today you will be with Me in Paradise," He was not speaking of Heaven as we understand it usually.[50]

The Octave of the Ascension

The Mass Propers for the Octave of the Ascension are the same as on the Feast of the Ascension itself with white vestments,

---

[50] Matthew Plese, *loc. cit.*, <https://acatholiclife.blogspot.com/2020/04/today-you-will-be-with-me-in-paradise.html>.

the Gloria, the Paschal Alleluia, the Credo, the Preface of the Ascension and the Proper Communicantes for the Ascension in the Canon. You may find them in a pre-1955 Missal such as the Saint Andrew Daily Missal and the Marian Missal from 1945.

For this season of Ascensiontide, Catholics are welcomed and encouraged to immerse themselves in the devotions appropriate for the season. For example, during this season there are special prayers for the time between Ascension and Pentecost. We should consider printing these out and praying these each day of the Octave (see *Catholic Culture* or the Novena to the Holy Spirit).[51]

While the Novus Ordo calendar unfortunately only has two octaves, traditional Catholics will be familiar with the idea of multiple overlapping Octaves. The practice of celebrating an Octave, while not only traced to the time spent by the Apostles and the Blessed Virgin Mary awaiting the Paraclete, also has its origins in the Old Testament eight-day celebration of the Feast of Tabernacles (Leviticus 23:36) and the Dedication of the Temple (2 Chronicles 7:9). Very truly, Christ did not come to abolish the Old Law but to fulfill it.

By the 8th century, Rome had developed liturgical octaves not only for Easter, Pentecost, and Christmas, but also for the Epiphany and the feast of the dedication of a church. After 1568, when Pope Pius V reduced the number of octaves (since by then they had grown considerably), the number of Octaves was still plentiful. Octaves were classified into several types. Easter and Pentecost had "specially privileged" octaves, during which no other feast whatsoever could be celebrated.

---

[51] "Catholic Prayer: Prayers between Ascension and Pentecost," *Catholic Culture* (no date) <https://www.catholicculture.org/culture/liturgicalyear/prayers/view.cfm?id=937>, accessed December 11, 2023; "Novena to the Holy Spirit for the Seven Gifts," *EWTN* (no date) <https://www.ewtn.com/catholicism/devotions/novena-to-the-holy-spirit-for-the-seven-gifts-309>.

Christmas, Epiphany, and Corpus Christi had "privileged" octaves, during which certain highly ranked feasts might be celebrated. The octaves of other feasts allowed even more feasts to be celebrated.

To reduce the repetition of the same liturgy for several days, Pope Leo XIII and Pope St. Pius X made further distinctions, classifying octaves into three primary types: privileged octaves, common octaves, and simple octaves. Privileged octaves were arranged in a hierarchy of first, second, and third orders. The Octave of the Ascension was a Privileged Octave of the Third Order.

According to Father Weiser, the Sunday within the Octave of the Ascension was, in the Middle Ages, called the Sunday of Roses because it was the custom to strew the pavement of churches with roses, as a homage to Christ who ascended to Heaven.

Feast Day of Our Lady, Queen of The Apostles

During Ascensiontide as we prepare to celebrate the descent of the Holy Ghost upon the Apostles and the Blessed Virgin Mary at Pentecost, there is a lesser known feast day to our Lady on the Saturday after Ascension Thursday.

This is the feast day of Our Lady, Queen of Apostles, is one of the Masses in Some Places that were a part of the Traditional Catholic Missal. This feast day, in addition to being kept on the Saturday within the Octave of the Ascension, is kept annually on September 5th. While not often said, we can make it a point to reflect on the spirituality of our Lady as Queen of the Apostles on this day. Father Lawrence G. Lovasik reflects on this feast day with the following thoughts:

> Mary, Mother of God, at Pentecost you were with the Apostles, preparing for the Holy Spirit the promised Gift of your Son. Prayer was the soul of your preparation, and the Apostles were inspired by your example. When the Holy

Spirit descended, you received the richest outpouring of His graces. Your holiness was due to this Spirit of Love, to Whose guidance you abandoned yourself. All that He could give, He bestowed upon you, His Immaculate Bride. On the day of Pentecost the Apostles' worldly views about the Kingdom of God on earth were banished by the Spirit of God, and holiness replaced their imperfections, but no-taint of the slightest sin had to be removed from your virginal soul. He overshadowed you at the Annunciation and on Pentecost He made your heart a furnace of divine love.

Not only did the Holy Spirit pour into your soul a fullness of grace, but He entrusted to you, the Mother of the human family, the distribution of all grace. What was true of the effusion of the Holy Spirit on that day, is equally true of every outpouring of grace: God gives nothing to earth without causing the gift to pass through your hands.

Ascension Day Food

Finally, no discussion of customs would be appropriate with food. Father Weiser notes why the faithful ate fowl on this day:

> It was a widespread custom in many parts of Europe during the Middle Ages to eat a bird on Ascension Day, because Christ "flew" to Heaven. Pigeons, pheasants, partridges, and even crows, graced the dinner tables. In western Germany bakers and innkeepers gave their customers pieces of pastry made in the shapes of various birds. In England the feast was celebrated with games, dancing, and horse races. In central Europe, Ascension Day is a

> traditional day of mountain climbing and picnics on hilltops and high places.

Yet he continues by noting several superstitions connected with Ascension Day, reminding us that anything we do must be connected with the true Faith and not deviate into superstitions against the First Commandment:

> Popular superstitions threaten dire punishments to anyone who works on Ascension Day in field and garden, but especially to women who do their sewing on the feast. Any piece of garment that has been touched by a needle on the Ascension will attract lightning before long, and many stories are told of how people were killed that way. In some sections of Europe it is said that weddings should not be held on Ascension Day because one of the partners would die soon. Those who go bathing in rivers and lakes are exposed to the danger of drowning more than on other days. It seems that all these superstitions are relics of the pre-Christian lore of the demons of death who were said to roam the earth and kill people around this time of the year

The Mozarabic Breviary provides a fitting and beautiful prayer for this time:

O Jesus! the power and wisdom of God! who coming down from heaven for our sake and for our salvation, deignedst to clothe thyself in human flesh, that, by a most merciful union, thou mightest clothe us with thy divinity, and that, by ascending into heaven, thou mightest enrich with immortality the mortality thou assumedst by descending upon our earth: grant, we beseech thee, by the merit of this day's solemnity, (whereon we rejoice at and desire to imitate thine Ascension) that we may acknowledge the favour of this most loving dispensation, by paying to thy mercy the only homage in our power, the offering of our praise; and awaiting thy second coming which is to console us with joys eternal.

IX

Pentecost

The Forgotten, Yet Ancient Vigil of Pentecost

The Feast of Pentecost (i.e., White Sunday) is one of the principal feasts in the life of the Church. After Pentecost Sunday and its Octave, we will conclude Paschaltide and begin the Season after Pentecost. Consequently, the Vigil of Pentecost has been a day of required fasting and abstinence for centuries and it was kept as such even through the early 1960s. Catholics should fast and partially abstain from meat on the Vigil of Pentecost to better prepare themselves to celebrate Pentecost.

The Vigil of Pentecost used to be celebrated in a manner like the Easter Vigil with Old Testament prophecies, the blessing of the font, the Litany of the Saints, and the Mass. Sadly, the Vigil of Pentecost was suppressed entirely in 1956 and has only recently been re-discovered by Catholics seeking to restore our practices that were lost even in the years preceding Vatican II. MusicaSacra.com has a PDF copy of the prayers and readings for the ancient Pentecost Vigil.[52]

Interestingly, the English name "White Sunday," by which Pentecost is called, refers to the ancient practice of Baptisms associated with the Vigil of Pentecost. As was the case with Easter, the newly baptized would wear white garments to Mass on Pentecost in celebration of their baptisms.

---

[52] See <https://media.musicasacra.com/sjfm/Pentecost/Pentecost-Vigil.pdf>.

Father Weiser comments on some special customs which began on the vigil of Pentecost:

> Like Easter night, the night of Pentecost is considered one of the great 'blessed nights' of the year. In many sections of Europe it is still the custom to ascend hilltops and mountains during the early dawn of Whitsunday to pray. People call this observance 'catching the Holy Ghost.' Thus they express in symbolic language the spiritual fact that only by means of prayer can the divine dove be 'caught' and the graces of the Holy Spirit obtained.
>
> In rural sections of northern Europe superstitions ascribe a special power of healing to the dew that falls during Pentecost night. To obtain these blessings people walk barefoot through the grass on the early morning of the feast. They also collect the dew on pieces of bread which afterward are fed to their domestic animals as a protection against disease and accidents.

Roses From Heaven on Pentecost Sunday

As the Catholic Dictionary of Fr. John Hardon summarizes, this holy day

> commemorat[es] the descent of the Holy Ghost on the Apostles. It takes its name from the fact that it comes about fifty days after Easter. The name was originally given to the Jewish Feast of Weeks, which fell in the fiftieth day after Passover, when the first fruits of the corn harvest were offered to the Lord (Deuteronomy 16:9), and later on the giving of the law to Moses was celebrated.

Our celebration is based on a greater gift than that of the Two Tables of the Law to Moses – today we celebrate the Apostles and Our Lady receiving God Himself – the Holy Ghost. As the Acts of the Apostles, Chapter 1, illustrates, there were 120 people praying for the Holy Ghost. And just as the heavens opened and a dove descended in the Baptism of Jesus, the Holy Ghost descended on the Apostles and the Blessed Virgin Mary at Pentecost. The same Spirit is within those that have been confirmed in the Catholic Church. We have the Holy Ghost, and we have the responsibility to go out and be beacons of the light of Christ, just like the Apostles did. For those who have been confirmed, recalling this reality and thanking God for the gift of our Confirmation should be a hallmark of our annual Pentecost observance.

Dom Guéranger provides us with this account of the liturgy of Pentecost Sunday while mentioning the ancient connection of Pentecost with roses:

> The Christian Pentecost, prefigured by the ancient one of the Jews, is of the number of the feasts that were instituted by the apostles. As we have already remarked, it formerly shared with Easter the honour of the solemn administration of Baptism. Its octave, like that of Easter, and for the same reason, ended with the Saturday following the feast. The catechumens received Baptism on the night between Saturday and Sunday. So that the Pentecost solemnity began on the vigil, for the neophytes at once put on their white garments: on the eighth day, the Saturday, they laid them aside.
>
> In the middle-ages, the feast of Pentecost was called by the beautiful name of 'The Pasch of roses,' just as the Sunday within the octave of the Ascension was termed the 'Sunday of roses.' The color and fragrance of this lovely

flower were considered by our Catholic forefathers as emblems of the tongues of fire, which rested on the heads of the hundred and twenty disciples and poured forth the sweet gifts of love and grace on the infant Church. The same idea suggested the red-colored vestments for the liturgical services during the whole octave. In his Rational (a work which abounds in most interesting information regarding the medieval liturgical usages), Durandus tells us that, in the thirteenth century, a dove was allowed to fly about in the church, and flowers and lighted tow were thrown down from the roof, during the Mass on Whit Sunday; these were allusions to the two mysteries of Jesus' baptism, and of the descent of the Holy Ghost on the day of Pentecost.

In Rome, rose petals would be dropped through the circular "oculus" at the Pantheon (now a minor basilica called "Sancta Maria ad martyres"). The petals would fall to the crowd below reminiscent of the coming of the Holy Spirit like tongues of flame. In keeping this custom alive, this practice still takes place at the end of the Masses on Pentecost Sunday at St. John Cantius Church in Chicago, Illinois.

Rose petals are dropped through the circular opening of the transept of the church during the recessional hymn, "Come Holy Ghost." Some are surprised while others wait expectantly for the rose petals to fall.

Pentecost as a New Springtime

Roses are not the only flowers associated with Pentecost. In the Byzantine Catholic Tradition, green is the vestment color of Pentecost as the Byzantine tradition highlights Pentecost's connection with the new springtime of the Church and the corresponding birth of nature and re-birth of souls in Baptism. Father Weiser alludes to – and expands upon – this:

Some nations have appropriately named the feast after the ancient custom of decorating homes and churches with flowers and boughs. This practice goes back to the nature lore of the Indo-European races. At the time of full spring, when trees stood in their early foliage and flowers blossomed in abundance, our pre-Christian ancestors celebrated a gay festival, with maypole, May Queen, and May dance, during which they adorned their homes with flowers and branches of pale-green tender leaves. This custom was retained in Christian times, and some of its features were transferred to the Feast of Pentecost. Thus, the festival is called the 'Green Holyday' (Zielone Swieta) in Poland and among the Ukrainians, 'Flower Feast' (Blumenfest) in Germany, 'Summer Feast' (Slavnost Letnice) among the Czechs. In the Latin countries a similar term is used: Pascha Rosatum, in Latin, meaning 'Feast of Roses.' The Italian name Pascua Rossa (Red Pasch) was inspired by the color of the liturgical vestments.

The Forgotten Holy Days of Obligation on Whit Monday & Whit Tuesday

When writing about the rank of days in the Catholic Liturgical calendar, there are various ways to label them. In the modern Church, they will use the terms solemnity, feast, memorial, or optional memorial. In the 1962 Missal, we have First, Second, Third, or Fourth Class feast days. But before the 1962 Missal up until the changes made by Pope Pius XII in 1955, there were from least to most important: Simples, Semidoubles, Lesser Doubles or also known as Doubles, Greater Doubles, Doubles of the second class, and lastly Doubles of the first class.

Using the traditional pre-1955 calendar, we notice something very interesting about Whit Monday and Whit Tuesday. Both of these days, like their counterparts in the Easter Octave, are doubles of the first class whereas the rest of the Pentecost Octave is of Double rank. Why the special treatment for Monday and Tuesday in the Octave of Pentecost? It is because they were universal holy days of obligation for a very long time. Father Weiser writes:

> During the early centuries, just the day [of Pentecost Sunday] itself was celebrated in the Western Church. After the seventh century, however, the whole week came to be considered a time of festive observance. Law courts did not sit, and servile work was forbidden during the entire Octave. The Council of Constance (1094) limited this prohibition to three days.

In 1642, Pentecost Monday and Pentecost Tuesday were listed as Holy Days by Pope Urban VIII in *Universa Per Orbem*. In 1771, Pope Clement XIV abolished both Easter Tuesday and Pentecost Tuesday as days of refraining from servile work. By 1778, they ceased being days of obligatory Mass attendance. Pentecost Monday was dropped from the universal list only in 1911 by Pope St. Pius X's significant reduction in Holy Days on the Universal Calendar.[53]

The Monday after Pentecost is still a holiday in Antigua and Barbuda, Anguilla, Austria, The Bahamas, Barbados, Belgium, The British Virgin Islands, Cyprus, Denmark, Dominica, France, Germany, Greece, Grenada, Hungary, Iceland, Ivory Coast, Luxembourg, Monaco, Montserrat, The Netherlands, Norway, Romania, Saint Lucia, Saint Kitts and Nevis, Saint Vincent and the Grenadines, Solomon Islands,

---

[53] Matthew Plese, *loc. cit.*, <https://acatholiclife.blogspot.com/2021/04/how-st-pius-x-1917-code-of-canon-law.html>.

Switzerland, Togo, and Ukraine. Until 1973, it was also a holiday in Ireland, and until 1967 it was a bank holiday in the United Kingdom. And Sweden also continued to observe it as a public holiday until 2004

Whit Embertide: A Joyful Fast

Ember Days are set aside to pray and/or offer thanksgiving for a good harvest and God's blessings. The fasting and abstinence on the Ember Days of Pentecost is unique in the Church as these are the only Ember Days celebrated without violet vestments as the Ember Days of Pentecost are meant to be a joyful fast.[54] As the website *Catholic Culture* writes concerning the Ember Days:

> Since the late 5th century, the Ember Days were also the preferred dates for ordination of priests. So, during these times the Church had a threefold focus: (1) sanctifying each new season by turning to God through prayer, fasting and almsgiving; (2) giving thanks to God for the various harvests of each season; and (3) praying for the newly ordained and for future vocations to the priesthood and religious life.

Join the Church during these three days by fasting, abstaining from meat, and praying for vocations.

The Uniqueness of the Octave of Pentecost

During the Octave of Pentecost, the Church celebrates more especially the glories of the grace of the Holy Ghost and His secret work of sanctification in the Mystical Body of Christ. Originally the feast of Pentecost brought to an end in Rome the fifty days of the Easter celebrations and introduced the fast

---

[54] Michael Foley, "Dubium: Is It Appropriate to Fast during the Pentecost Octave?" *New Liturgical Movement* (Jun 6, 2020) <https://www.newliturgicalmovement.org/2020/06/dubium-is-it-appropriate-to-fast-during.html>, accessed December 11, 2023.

of the Ember Days of the summer quarter.[55] Afterward, it became customary to continue the festivity for two more days, the Monday and the Tuesday, and, finally, after the time of Pope St. Leo the Great, it was extended like the Octave of Easter through the entire week.

In medieval times, families in many parts of Europe would suspend a carved and painted wooden dove over their dining table during this time of Pentecost. Such a custom could be easily revived for the throughout the Octave of the Pentecost – and imagine that dining room table covered with a white tablecloth, sprinkled with red rose petals.

Dom Guéranger insightfully writes:

> The Christian Pentecost, prefigured by the ancient one of the Jews, is of the number of the feasts that were instituted by the apostles. As we have already remarked, it formerly shared with Easter the honor of the solemn administration of Baptism. Its octave, like that of Easter, and for the same reason, ended with the Saturday following the feast. The catechumens received Baptism on the night between Saturday and Sunday. So that the Pentecost Solemnity began on the vigil, for the Neophytes at once put on their white garments: on the eighth day, the Saturday, they laid them aside.

There is a profound connection of the Scripture readings at Mass during the Octave of Pentecost with each of the Sacraments.[56] And the Stational Churches of the Octave of

---

[55] Matthew Plese, *loc. cit.*, <https://acatholiclife.blogspot.com/2013/05/whit-embertide.html>.
[56] Peter Kwasniewski, "Correlations between the Sacraments and the Readings for the Octave of Pentecost," *New Liturgical Movement* (Jun 1, 2020) <https://www.newliturgicalmovement.org/2020/06/correlations-between-sacraments-and.html>, accessed December 11, 2023.

Pentecost have a unique connection to the stations during the Octave of Easter.[57] And in another unusual twist, Pentecost is the only major feast day without an Octave Day. The Sunday following Pentecost is known as the First Sunday after Pentecost which has been kept for several centuries now as the Feast of the Most Holy Trinity.[58]

The *Catholic Encyclopedia* mentions another rather unusual feature for the Octave of Pentecost, which mirrors again Easter's Octave:

> The office of Pentecost has only one Nocturn during the entire week. At Terce the 'Veni Creator' is sung instead of the usual hymn, because at the third hour the Holy Ghost descended. The Mass has a Sequence, 'Veni Sancte Spiritus' the authorship of which by some is ascribed to King Robert of France. The color of the vestments is red, symbolic of the love of the Holy Ghost or of the tongues of fire.

Sadly, Paul VI abolished the Octave in 1969, although he did not even realize it when he signed the authorization, in one sad example of his lack of oversight.[59] Thankfully, Traditional Catholic priests maintain this Octave. And even some priests

---

[57] Gregory DiPippo, "The Feast and Fast of Pentecost," *New Liturgical Movement* (Jun 2, 2020) <https://www.newliturgicalmovement.org/2020/06/the-feast-and-fast-of-pentecost.html>, accessed December 11, 2023.

[58] Matthew Plese, *loc. cit.*, <https://acatholiclife.blogspot.com/2006/06/solemnity-of-most-holy-trinity.html>.

[59] Msgr. Charles Pope, "On Restoring the Lost Emphasis on Pentecost by Restoring the Octave and the Numeration of the Sundays after Pentecost," *Community in Mission* (Jun 9, 2019) <https://blog.adw.org/2019/06/restoring-lost-emphasis-pentecost-restoring-octave-numeration-sundays-pentecost/>, accessed December 11, 2023.

who say the Novus Ordo Mass choose to celebrate Votive Masses in Honor of the Holy Ghost over this week.

Conclusion

While the Octave of Pentecost may not be days of precept anymore, we can certainly in our own prayer lives observe the Octave of Pentecost, hear Mass these days, pray the Divine Office more regularly, observe the Ember Days, and strive to do more than the minimum required by current Church Law. Let us keep these traditions alive.

As a reminder, a plenary indulgence may be gained by anyone who recites "Veni Creator Spiritus," the Hymn for Pentecost on Pentecost Sunday under the usual conditions.

Veni Sancte Spiritus!

X

Corpus Christi

A great solemnity has this day risen upon our earth: a feast both to God and to men: for it is the feast of Christ the Mediator, who is present in the sacred Host, that God may be given to man, and man to God. Divine union—such is the dignity to which man is permitted to aspire; and to this aspiration God has responded, even here below, by an invention which is all of heaven. It is to-day that man celebrates this marvel of God's goodness (Dom Guéranger).

The History of Corpus Christi & Its Forgotten Octave

The Feast of Corpus Christi was instituted in the 13th Century to commemorate the Institution of the Eucharist. Around the early 1200s, Saint Juliana of Mont Cornillon (1192 – 1258) received a vision concerning this feast at a young age. St. Juliana always had a strong devotion to the Blessed Sacrament. In her vision, she saw the Church under the appearance of the full moon. One large, dark spot was in the moon – symbolic of the absence of a solemnity to honor the Holy Eucharist. St. Juliana became an Augustinian nun in Liége, France in 1206. Corpus Christi became a feast for the Diocese of Liege in 1246, and later in 1264, after having seen the Eucharistic Miracle in Orvieto, Pope Urban IV issued "*Transiturus de hoc mundo*" establishing it as a feast for the Universal Church with an Octave. Pope Clement V renewed the decree in his own bull in 1314 and the feast of Corpus Christi then spread rapidly. It remained a day of great importance of centuries and had an Octave attached to it until the elimination of all but three Octaves by Pope Pius XII in 1954.

The Mass Propers for the Octave Day of Corpus Christi in the Roman Rite is the same as the Feast day itself. As *New Liturgical Movement* notes,

> Some of the oldest Roman octaves, such as those of Ss Peter and Paul and St Lawrence, have a Mass on the octave day itself which is different or partly different from that of the main feast; Peter and Paul also have another Mass for the days within the octave. However, by the time the feast of Corpus Christi was promulgated in the mid-13th century, this custom was no longer being developed for new celebrations, and the Mass of the feast was simply repeated though the octave.[60]

What is unique about the Octave of Corpus Christi is that our Lord Himself referred to it. As many Catholics know, the Institution for the Feast of the Sacred Heart was a result of the appearances of our Lord to St. Margaret Mary Alacoque in 1675. St. Margaret Mary suffered contempt from many people who refused to believe the authenticity of the visions. Our Lord said to her, "I ask thee that the first Friday after the octave of Corpus Christi be set apart as a special feast to honor My Heart."

In 1970 the name was changed from Corpus Christi to the "Solemnity of the Body and Blood of Christ" when Corpus Christi and the Feast of the Precious Blood (July 1) were joined. The feast of the Most Precious Blood of Our Lord was suppressed in the Novus Ordo when the new calendar was

---

[60] Gregory DiPippo, "The Parisian Mass for the Octave of Corpus Christi," *New Liturgical Movement* (Jun 10, 2021) <https://www.newliturgicalmovement.org/2021/06/the-parisian-mass-for-octave-of-corpus.html>, accessed December 11, 2023.

promulgated in 1969. The reason for its suppression was the alleged promotion of the understanding of Corpus Christi in terms of both Sacred Species. However, this is highly unfortunate because the feast of the Precious Blood (still observed at all Masses said according to the Liturgical Books of 1962 or previously) was not, strictly speaking, eucharistic in nature, but theological and devotional. It referred more to the Sacred Wounds of Our Lord and the hypostatic union of Our Lord's divine and human natures. The Feast of Corpus Christi has always honored the fullness of Christ – a Body, Blood, Soul, and Divinity – in the Eucharist. This is just another reminder why we should stay clear of the Novus Ordo and remain attached to the Church's Traditional Calendar.

Corpus Christi as a Forgotten Holy Day of Obligation

Corpus Christi is a Holy Day of Obligation in many countries. When the United States were founded, Corpus Christi was a Holy Day of Obligation for Catholics. The United States received permission to transfer the celebration of the Mass to the Sunday after Corpus Christi in 1885 by Pope Leo XIII, in a concession to the modern world.[61] This permission remains; however, those who pray the Divine Office will keep the Divine Office on Thursday.

In the largest change to Holy Days in centuries, Pope St. Pius X in *Supremi disciplinæ* in 1911 drastically reduced the number of Holy Days of Obligation in the Universal Church to only 8: Christmas, Circumcision, Epiphany, Ascension, Immaculate Conception, Assumption of the Blessed Virgin, Ss. Peter and Paul, and All Saints.

In only 269 years, the number of Holy Days on the Universal Calendar had been reduced from 36 under Urban VIII to 8

---

[61] Matthew Plese, "A History of Holy Days of Obligation & Fasting for American Catholics: Part 2," *A Catholic Life* (Jun 3, 2020) <https://acatholiclife.blogspot.com/2020/06/a-history-of-holy-days-of-obligation.html>, accessed December 11, 2023.

under Pius X.[62] Shortly thereafter in 1917, Corpus Christi and St. Joseph were added back, bringing the total to 10. The 10 currently observed on the Universal Calendar are the same as from 1917.

As for the Holy Days observed in the United States, the *Catholic Encyclopedia* states, "Where, however, any of the above feasts has been abolished or transferred, the new legislation is not effective. In the United States consequently the Epiphany and the feast of Ss. Peter and Paul are not days of precept." On a similar note, Corpus Christi when added back as a Holy Day in the Universal Church in 1917 remained transferred to the following Sunday in the United States as a result of Pope Leo XIII's indult from 1885.

Eucharistic Processions

One of the characteristic features of Corpus Christi is the beautiful outdoor processions that serve as a visible testimony to others of our belief in the Real Presence of God in the Eucharist. This custom originated early in the 14th century as noted by Father Weiser. These processions are endowed with indulgences dating back to both Pope Martin V and Pope Eugene IV. And the Council of Trent approved and recommended these processions as a public profession of the Catholic Faith's belief in the Real Presence. These processions have grown in popularity again around the world, as a public manifestation of our worship of the Most Holy Eucharist. Such processions often feature beautiful hymns like the "Ave Verum Corpus," which is ascribed to Pope Innocent VI (1362).

In some European nations, the custom developed of plays that were performed after the procession. While they were common throughout England, Germany, and Spain, the most famous were the "Plays of the Sacrament" written by Father Pedro Calderon de la Barca (1681) in Spain. Father Weiser

---

[62] Ibid., <https://acatholiclife.blogspot.com/2020/05/a-history-of-holy-days-of-obligation.html>.

adds the following account on how even children were very engaged in Corpus Christi Processions:

> Especially favored was the attendance of children dressed as angels. Already in 1496, at the great children's procession in Florence, Savonarola had all of them appear in white or garbed as angels. This custom quickly spread all over Europe in the following centuries. At the Corpus Christi procession in Mainz in 1613 hundreds of children, impersonating the nine choirs of angels, marched before the Blessed Sacrament while many other "angels" strewed flowers in front of the Eucharistic Lord. These manifestations of baroque piety were gradually restricted and most of them suppressed during the second half of the eighteenth century, not without some resistance and much complaining on the part of the population. In some cities even Lutherans protested against the suppression because, not having processions of their own, they had enjoyed watching these features of the Catholic pageant.

Day of Wreaths

In one custom foreign to many in the United States, Corpus Christi is known in central Europe and some areas of France as the "Day of Wreaths." Father Weiser again explains:

> Wreaths and bouquets of exquisite flowers in various colors are attached to flags and banners, to houses, and to the arches of green boughs that span the streets. The clergy and altar boys wear little wreaths on their left arms in the procession; girls carry wreaths on their heads. Even the monstrance containing the Blessed Sacrament is adorned with a wreath of choice flowers on Corpus Christi Day. In

Poland these wreaths are blessed by the priest on the eve of the feast day. After the solemnities people decorate their homes with them. Some are suspended on the walls of the houses or affixed to doors and windows. Others are put up in gardens, fields, and pastures, with a prayer for protection and blessing upon the growing harvest.

Having a wreath blessed by your parish priest and adorning it with flowers and images of the Holy Eucharist would be a wonderful way to incorporate this tradition into your life. And in so doing, it can be an effective evangelization tool for those who will walk past and see on the wreath clear representations of the Catholic Faith.

Indulgences for Corpus Christi

The Church has enriched the celebration of Corpus Christi – as well as devotions to the Blessed Sacrament at other times – with a number of indulgences. For instance, the *Raccolta*, listing the traditional indulgences in place before the changes after Vatican II, stated for the Feast of Corpus Christi and its Octave:

> Pope Urban IV… being desirous that all the faithful should give God due thanks for this inestimable benefit and be excited to meet their Lord's love in this most holy Sacrament with grateful hearts, granted in the said Constitution several Indulgences to the faithful, which were again augmented by Pope Martin V in his Constitution *Ineffabile*, of May 26, 1429. Afterwards Pope Eugenius IV, in his Constitution *Excellentissimum*, of May 20, 1433, confirmed the Indulgences of Martin V, and added others, as follows:
>
> 1. An indulgence of 200 days, on the vigil of the Feast of Corpus Christi to all who, being

truly contrite and having confessed, shall fast, or do some other good work enjoined them by their confessor.

2. An indulgence of 400 days, on the feast itself, to all who, being contrite and having Confessed, shall devoutly assist at or be present at any of the following functions: First or Second Vespers, Matins, and Mass. An indulgence of 160 days for each of the Little hours, Prime, Terce, Sext, None, and Compline.

3. An indulgence of 200 days, during the octave, for each Vespers, Matins, and Mass. An indulgence of 80 days for each of the Little Hours.

4. An indulgence of 200 days for accompanying the procession of the Blessed Sacrament, which takes place on the Feast or during the Octave, to every priest who has said Mass, and to every layman who has gone to Communion on any one of these days, and who shall pray for the Holy Church.

5. An indulgence of 200 days for accompanying the procession made by the Confraternity of the Blessed Sacrament on the third Sunday of the month, and on Holy Thursday.

Such practices such as a voluntary fast on the day before Corpus Christi is virtually forgotten by all. This practice is however still kept by some traditional Carmelites. We would do well to engage in some voluntary fasting and abstinence on the day before Corpus Christi in the spirit of and for the intention of making reparation to the Blessed Sacrament.

Indulgences Year Round on Thursdays

A truly fitting prayer for Corpus Christi – and for any Thursday of the year – is the *Respice, Domine* which was composed by St. Cajetan. The prayer's English translation is as follows:

> Look down, O Lord, from Thy sanctuary, and from Heaven Thy dwelling-place on high, and behold this sacred Victim which our great High-Priest, Thy holy Child, Our Lord Jesus, offers up to Thee for the sins of This brethren; and be appeased for the multitude of our transgressions. Behold the voice of the Blood of Jesus, our Brother, cries to Thee from the Cross. Give ear, O Lord! be appeased, O Lord! hearken, and do not tarry for Thine own sake, O my God, for Thy Name is invoked upon this city and upon Thy people; and deal with us according to Thy mercy. Amen.

The *Raccolta* listed the following indulgences for this prayer:

1. A plenary indulgence to all the faithful who, being contrite, and having confessed and gone to Communion on THE first Thursday in the month, shall on that day visit the Blessed Sacrament, either at Exposition time or when enclosed in the Tabernacle, and say there the following prayer, *Respice, Domine*.

2. An indulgence of seven years and seven quarantines every Thursday in the year, to all who, after Confession and Communion, shall say the above prayer, on their knees, before the Blessed Sacrament.

    o An indulgence of 100 days for saying it, with contrite heart, before the Blessed Sacrament, on any day whatever.

Can we make it a practice to stop into a church each Thursday of the year – even for five minutes – to pray before the tabernacle this prayer? Such a small sacrifice is blessed by the Church, and in so doing, we can help make reparation to our Eucharistic Lord.

Conclusion

On Corpus Christi, we remember and again celebrate a true and lasting miracle. Think about it, we can receive the flesh and blood of Our God! We can truly receive our Creator in a way so that we might have life within us. The Institution of the Eucharist changed the world. We must contemplate this miracle before receiving Our Lord at every single Mass. How can we not share the sentiments of Archbishop Sheen who said, "The greatest love story of all time is contained in a tiny, white Host"?

May our observance of some of these customs bring honor to Almighty God and consolation to His Most Sacred Heart.

XI

Sacred Heart

> Look at this Heart which has loved men so much, and yet men do not want to love Me in return. Through you My divine Heart wishes to spread its love everywhere on earth
>
> –Words of our Lord Jesus Christ
> to St. Margaret Mary Alacoque

The History of the Feast of the Sacred Heart & Its Forgotten Octave

While the entire month of June is devoted to the Sacred Heart of Jesus, the Feast of the Sacred Heart is unique kept to honor the mercy and love of God while making reparation for the serious sins committed against Our Blessed Lord. Traditionally up until 1955, the Feast of the Sacred Heart immediately follows the Octave Day of Corpus Christi. After having celebrated 8 days devoted to the Blessed Sacrament, we immediately turn to the Sacred Heart, which also traditionally had its own octave as well.

The Institution of the Feast of the Sacred Heart was a result of the appearances of our Lord to St. Margaret Mary Alacoque in 1675. St. Margaret Mary suffered contempt from many people who refused to believe the authenticity of the visions. In these appearances, Our Lord told her twelve graces that He would give to anyone devoted to His Sacred Heart. Our Lord said to her, "I ask thee that the first Friday after the octave of Corpus Christi be set apart as a special feast to honor My Heart." He also promised 12 promises to those who are devoted to the Sacred Heart:

1. I will give them all the graces necessary for their state in life.
2. I will give peace in their families.
3. I will console them in all their troubles.
4. They shall find in My Heart an assured refuge during life and especially at the hour of death.
5. I will pour abundant blessings on all their undertakings.
6. Sinners shall find in My Heart the source and infinite ocean of mercy.
7. Tepid souls shall become fervent.
8. Fervent souls shall speedily rise to great perfection.
9. I will bless the homes in which the image of My Sacred Heart shall be exposed and honoured.
10. I will give to priests the power to touch the most hardened hearts.
11. Those who propagate this devotion shall have their name written in My Heart, and it shall never be effaced.
12. The all-powerful love of My Heart will grant to all those who shall receive Communion on the First Friday of nine consecutive months the grace of final repentance; they shall not die under My displeasure, nor without receiving their Sacraments; My Heart shall be their assured refuge at the last hour.

In 1693, three years after the death of St. Margaret Mary, the Holy See imparted indulgences to the Confraternities of the Sacred Heart, and in 1697 granted the feast to the Visitandines with the Mass of the Five Wounds, but refused a feast common to all, with special Mass and Office. The devotion spread, particularly in religious communities. The Marseille plague in 1720 furnished perhaps the first occasion for a solemn consecration and public worship outside of religious communities. Other cities of southern Europe followed the example of Marseille. In 1726 Rome was again asked for a feast with a Mass and Office of its own; this was refused in 1729 but granted in 1765. In that year, at the request of the queen, the feast was received quasi-officially by the episcopate of France. Hence, the Mass and Office in Honor of the Sacred Heart were not approved for any use until 1765 by Pope Clement XIII – one hundred years after the request was made by our Lord!

Finally, in 1856, at the urgent entreaties of the French bishops, Pope Pius IX extended the Feast of the Sacred Heart to the Latin Church under the rite of double major. In 1889 it was raised by the Latin Church to the double rite of first class. In 1928, Pope Pius XI raised the feast to the highest rank, Double of the First Class, and added an octave; the 1955 reforms of the general Roman calendar suppressed this octave and removed most other octaves.

On November 9, 1921, Pope Benedict XV established the Feast of the Eucharistic Heart of Jesus on the Thursday within the Octave of the Sacred Heart, which in a sense, further established the connection of the Sacred Heart with Corpus Christi and its just-concluded Octave.[63]

Devotion to the Sacred Heart Dates Back to the Middle Ages

Long before the apparition to St. Margaret Mary, devotion to the Sacred Heart of Jesus existed. On the December 27th feast day of St. John the Evangelist in 1256 AD, St. Gertrude the Great had a profound vision in which she laid her head near the wound in the side of Jesus and heard the beating of the

---

[63] Matthew Plese, *loc. cit.*, <https://acatholiclife.blogspot.com/2016/06/feast-of-eucharistic-heart-of-jesus.html>.

Sacred Heart. This is especially profound since St. John the Evangelist reclined his head to the heart of the Divine Savior at the Last Supper.

The First Friday Devotion

When Our Lord later appeared to St. Margaret Mary Alacoque in the 1600s, He appeared to her on the feast day of St. John the Evangelist. Our Lord requested three things: frequently receiving Holy Communion, receiving Holy Communion especially on the first Friday of each month, and observing a Holy Hour in front of the Blessed Sacrament, with the aforementioned promises.

Father Weiser writes this short excerpt on Devotions to the Sacred Heart, mentioning this practice:

> As a result of the revelations granted to Saint Margaret Mary Alacoque (1690), the practice developed from the seventeenth century on of devoting the first Friday of every month in a special way to the Sacred Heart of Jesus. Since 1889 a Roman indult has given this custom a liturgical expression through the "Mass of the Sacred Heart" which, under certain conditions, may be celebrated as a solemn votive Mass. Other liturgical devotions, too, have been provided for "First Friday"; they may be held in churches with the approval of the bishop and according to his regulations. Through the pious exercises of the "Nine Fridays" and the "First Fridays," the custom grew in many places of performing on every Friday some devotion in honor of the Sacred Heart of Jesus, partly in church (by attendance at Mass, Communion, evening devotions), partly at home (by family prayer, burning of vigil lights before the Sacred Heart statue.

Hence, priests should be offering extra Masses each Friday in honor of the Sacred Heart and encouraging the faithful to make the nine First Fridays (and repeating it often throughout life). And families should also have statues of the Sacred Heart in their home which are housed on or near our home prayer altars.

Act of Dedication to the Sacred Heart

What is Consecration to the Sacred Heart? Fr. Peter Scott explains:

> Consecration to the Sacred Heart is consequently an act of individuals, of families, of parishes, of nations, and will bring all the more graces as it is clearly understood as an act of returning love for love, and is accomplished fervently by an entire community. What, then, is consecration? It is much more than a formula, a passing pious act to be repeated from time to time. It is a complete gift of oneself, in this case to divine love. It is an interior belonging to Christ, that might be accomplished the words of the Apostle: "it is no longer I that live, but Christ lives within me" (Gal 2:20). It is a donation of our whole being and life, as of a victim, to be immolated to divine love. It is the living of our baptismal vows, by which we renounced entirely Satan and his allurements to serve Christ our King and Him alone.
>
> There is no one act of consecration to the Sacred Heart. St. Margaret Mary in fact requested that her novices write their own, as she herself did. However, in a letter of 1684 to one of her superiors, she describes what it must contain: "If you desire to live for Him alone and to attain to the perfection that He desires from you, you must offer to his Sacred Heart the

entire sacrifice of yourself and all that belongs to you, without any reserve, so that you may no longer like anything but what he likes; may act only according to his inspirations, undertaking nothing without first asking his counsel and his aid, giving unto him the glory of all-glorifying Him for everything… (Cf. J.B. Bainvel SJ).

We can honor Heaven's request to honor the Sacred Heart by making the Act of Consecration as written by St. Margaret Mary:

I, _____, give myself and consecrate to the Sacred Heart of our Lord Jesus Christ, my person and my life, my actions, pains and sufferings, so that I may be unwilling to make use of any part of my being, save to honor, love and glorify the Sacred Heart. This is my unchanging purpose, namely, to be all His, and to do all things for the love of Him, at the same time renouncing with all my heart whatever is displeasing to Him. I therefore take Thee, O Sacred Heart, to be the only object of my love, the guardian of my life, my assurance of salvation, the remedy of my weakness and inconstancy, the atonement for all the faults of my life and my sure refuge at the hour of death.

Be then, O Heart of goodness, my justification before God Thy Father, and turn away from me the strokes of His righteous anger. O Heart of love, I put all my confidence in Thee, for I fear everything from my own wickedness and frailty, but I hope for all things from Thy goodness and bounty. Do Thou consume in me all that can displease Thee or resist Thy holy will; let Thy pure love imprint Thee so deeply upon my heart, that I shall nevermore be able to forget Thee or to be separated from Thee; may I obtain from all Thy loving kindness the grace of having my name written in Thee, for in Thee I desire to place all my happiness and all my glory, living and dying in very bondage to Thee.

We can also pray the Act of Consecration to the Sacred Heart which was written by Pope Leo XIII.[64]

Honor the Sacred Heart as a Family Throughout June

At the Feast of the Sacred Heart, in addition to dedicating ourselves and our families to the Sacred Heart, we can and should make the Act of Reparation to the Sacred Heart (which is an indulged prayer) and having our home enthroned to the Sacred Heart (if it has not already been).[65] Lastly, after we conclude our daily Rosaries, each day of June we can add the Litany of the Sacred Heart. Other less common prayers like the Daily Offering to the Sacred Heart for the Dying are also worth practicing with fervor during this month.[66]

While the Sacred Heart is a newer feast day in the life of the Church and has not developed customs like more ancient feast days, we can nevertheless live out the customs that have arisen in the past few centuries. After all, Our Lord asked for reparation to the Sacred Heart in the form of the nine First Fridays and if God Himself asks it of us, who can dare refuse?

---

[64] Ibid., <https://acatholiclife.blogspot.com/2015/10/prayer-of-consecration-to-sacred-heart.html>.

[65] Ibid., <https://acatholiclife.blogspot.com/2013/06/act-of-reparation-to-sacred-heart.html>; <https://acatholiclife.blogspot.com/2005/11/home-enthronment.html>.

[66] Ibid., <https://acatholiclife.blogspot.com/2006/07/daily-offering-to-sacred-heart-of.html>.

XII

Precious Blood

The History of the Feast

According to the Traditional Catholic Calendar of 1962 and prior, July 1st is the Feast of the Most Precious Blood of Our Lord Jesus Christ. This feast was instituted for the Universal Church in 1849 by Pope Pius IX and was raised to the rank of a double of the first class by Pope Pius XI on the occasion of the nineteenth centenary of our Savior's death in 1933.

This Feast, like so many others, has fallen victim to the post-Vatican II Church's novelties. While only established in 1849, this relatively recent feast day is worth honoring and considering after having completed the month of June, which is dedicated to the honor of the Sacred Heart of Jesus.

Fr. Johann Evalgelist Zollner (1883) relates the following history for this importance feast day:

> On this day, the Church celebrates the feast of the Most Precious Blood of Jesus Christ. This feast, which had been celebrated in some dioceses since the fifteenth century, on Monday after Trinity Sunday, was extended by Pope Pius IX over the whole Christian world, and its celebration prescribed for the first Sunday of July. The time of persecution and suffering had already begun for the Sovereign Pontiff. Compelled by a revolution to leave Rome, he repaired to Gaeta, in the kingdom of Naples, where he lived in exile for seventeen

months, till April 1850. Here it was that on the tenth day of August 1849, he instituted the feast of the Precious Blood.

That most sacred blood is the price of our Redemption and is poured out daily in the Holy Sacrifice of the Mass, whence it flows into the channels of the seven Sacraments, as an atonement for our sins and for our sanctification. For, as in Egypt, God was propitiated by the blood of the paschal lamb, the type and figure of the true Lamb of God, so He is propitiated by the blood of his Son, the true Paschal Lamb, which speaketh better than Abel's. Herein is the strongest evidence of the infinite love of Jesus Christ, who not only once, but seven times, shed his precious blood amidst the most cruel sufferings for our salvation. Let this seven-fold shedding of the precious blood be the subject of our present meditation.

1. The first shedding of blood was at His Circumcision

2. The shedding of blood in the garden of Olives

3. Jesus is scourged. The four Evangelists narrate that Jesus was scourged

4. Jesus shed His blood the fourth time, when he was crowned with thorns

5. Jesus shed his blood the fifth time, carrying the cross

6. Jesus shed his blood the sixth time, when He was crucified

7. The seventh and last time Jesus shed His blood was when His side was opened

Thus Jesus shed His precious blood seven times, and the price of these seven sheddings of blood is found in the seven Sacraments, by which we are cleansed from sin and sanctified. These seven sheddings of blood remind us also of the three theological and the four Cardinal virtues; also of the seven virtues opposed to the seven deadly or capital sins, which are infused into us by baptism; also of the seven gifts of the Holy Ghost, which we receive in confirmation, and finally of the seven days of the week, which we should dedicate to the service of God.

The covenant between God and the Israelites was sealed with blood. The new covenant was sealed with the precious blood of Jesus Christ. The covenant between God and men is sealed again as many times as the Holy Sacrifice of the Mass is offered to God. Assist, whenever you can, at the tremendous Sacrifice of the Mass, and frequently receive holy communion.

Customs in Honor of the Precious Blood

Most customs we have covered in this book have been based in ancient or at least medieval customs which honored the feasts and fasts of the liturgical year. However, due to the relatively recent institution of this feast day, there are not historical customs associated with this feast day in the same way as Corpus Christi, the Assumption, Easter, and other ancient holy days.

However, devotion to the Precious Blood of our Lord stretches back long before the establishment of this July 1st feast day. Devotion to the Precious Blood is connected to devotion to the Passion and Death of Our Lord since through the shedding of His Blood, mankind was redeemed. Consequently, one can say the Church has always honored the Blood of Jesus Christ. Romans 5:9 states, "we are justified by His blood," and

Hebrews 13:12 states, "and so Jesus also, that He might sanctify the people by His blood, suffered outside the gate." 1 John 1:7 also writes of the Precious Blood: "...and the blood of Jesus Christ, His Son, cleanses us from all sin." We would do well to meditate on the seven times Christ shed His Precious Blood for our salvation. As Fr. Peter Scott, SSPX reminds us:

> The veneration of the Precious Blood of Our Divine Saviour is as old as the Passion in which it was shed. It is founded on the simple doctrine of the Incarnation, namely that the Second Person of the Blessed Trinity took a human nature to Himself, and that this human nature is the human nature of God. We call this the hypostatic union. Every part of Christ's human nature is united to the second divine Person. This includes his Precious Blood, to which is consequently owed the adoration that is owed to God Himself, that of *latria*. We consequently do not need any private revelation to tell us about devotion to the Precious Blood, but find it deeply rooted in the deposit of the faith.

Closer to our modern era, devotion to the Precious Blood has been greatly encouraged by St. Gaspar Buffalo, founder of the Congregation of the Precious Blood of Jesus Christ. The feast had been celebrated beforehand by the fathers of the Most Precious Blood on the Friday after the Fourth Sunday of Lent as related by Father Ulrich F. Mueller:

> For many dioceses there are two days to which the Office of the Precious Blood has been assigned, the office being in both cases the same. The reason is this: the office was at first granted to the Fathers of the Most Precious Blood only. Later, as one of the offices of the Fridays of Lent, it was assigned to the Friday

after the fourth Sunday in Lent. In many dioceses these offices were adopted also by the fourth Provincial Council of Baltimore (1840). When Pius IX went into exile at Gaeta (1849) he had as his companion the saintly Don Giovanni Merlini, third superior general of the Fathers of the Most Precious Blood. Arrived at Gaeta, Merlini suggested that His Holiness make a vow to extend the feast of the Precious Blood to the entire Church, if he would again obtain possession of the papal dominions. The pope took the matter under consideration, but a few days later sent his domestic prelate Jos. Stella to Merlini with the message: 'The pope does not deem it expedient to bind himself by a vow; instead, His Holiness is pleased to extend the feast immediately to all Christendom.' This was June 30, 1849, the day the French conquered Rome and the republicans capitulated. The thirtieth of June had been a Saturday before the first Sunday of July, wherefore the pope decreed (August 10, 1849) that henceforth every first Sunday of July should be dedicated to the Most Precious Blood.

We owe the institution of a special feast in honor of the Precious Blood to Pope Pius IX. It was Pope St. Pius X who transferred the feast from the first Sunday of July to July 1st. And it was Pope Pius XI, who raised the rank of the feast day, in commemoration of the 19th centennial of the mystery of the Redemption.

Devotions to the Precious Blood

In honor of the Feast of the Most Precious Blood, and for the month of July which is in a special manner dedicated to the memory of the Precious Blood, the Church has blessed several devotions that we should consider practicing at this time:

1. Chaplet of the Most Precious Blood (approved by Pope Pius VII and enriched with indulgences originating back to 1809 and 1815)

2. Litany of the Most Precious Blood of Jesus (approved by Pope John XXIII on February 24, 1960 and enriched with an indulgence)

3. Offering in Reparation to the Most Precious Blood of Jesus (approved by Pope Pius VII on September 22, 1817, and enriched with an indulgence)[67]

4. An Offering of the Precious Blood for Souls[68]

5. The Seven Offerings of the Precious Blood (approved by Pope Pius VII and enriched with indulgences originating back to 1817)[69]

We may also consider for our summer reading getting a copy of *Devotion to the Most Precious Blood of Our Lord Jesus Christ: The Greatest Devotion of Our Time* produced by the Apostolate for the Precious Blood.

The Forgotten Octaves of St. John the Baptist & Ss. Peter and Paul

Besides being the Feast of the Most Precious Blood of our Lord Jesus Christ, July 1st is traditionally the Octave Day of St. John the Baptist while also still part of the Octave of Ss Peter and Paul.[70] It is worth remembering these forgotten Octaves on this day as well.

---

[67] Ibid., <https://acatholiclife.blogspot.com/2019/07/7-times-christ-shed-his-blood-for-us.html>.
[68] Ibid., <https://acatholiclife.blogspot.com/2006/04/offering-of-precious-blood-for-souls.html>.
[69] Ibid., < https://acatholiclife.blogspot.com/2019/07/7-times-christ-shed-his-blood-for-us.html>.
[70] Ibid., <https://acatholiclife.blogspot.com/2013/07/octave-day-of-st-john-baptist.html>; <https://acatholiclife.blogspot.com/2020/07/within-octave-of-ss-peter-and-paul.html>.

Conclusion

Fr. Frederick Faber in *The Precious Blood* write the following meditation most appropriate for this day and every day of July:

> The Precious Blood was assumed directly to our Blessed Lord's Divine Person from His Immaculate Mother... Mary's blood was the material out of which the Holy Ghost, the Third Person of the Most Holy Trinity, the artificer of Sacred Humanity, fashioned the Blood of Jesus. Here we see how needful to the joy and gladness of our devotion is the doctrine of the Immaculate Conception. Who could bear to think that the matter of the Precious Blood had ever been itself corrupted with the taint of sin, that it had once been part of the devil's kingdom, that what was to supply the free price of our redemption was once enslaved to God's darkest, foulest enemy? Is it not indeed an endless daily jubilee to us, that the church has laid upon us as an article of our faith that sweet truth which the instincts of our devotion had so long made a real part of our belief?

> Moreover, there is some portion of the Precious Blood which once was Mary's own blood, and which remains still in our Blessed Lord, incredibly exalted by its union with His Divine Person, yet still the same. This portion of Himself, it is piously believed, has not been allowed to undergo the usual changes of human substance. At this moment in heaven, He retains something which once was His Mother's...

May Our Lady help us to better honor Her Son's Precious Blood. And may our devotions and prayers in honor of this forgotten feast day help to establish further customs that traditional Catholics will honor and observe each July 1st for centuries.

XIII

Ember Days

The Ancient Institution of Ember Days

Ember days were categorized by three elements: prayers for both thanksgiving and petition, penance in the form of fasting and abstinence, and ordinations. Like Rogation Days, Ember Days developed early times, taking the form that would continue for centuries. The *Catholic Encyclopedia* explains:

> At first the Church in Rome had fasts in June, September, and December; the exact days were not fixed but were announced by the priests. The *Liber Pontificalis* ascribes to Pope Callistus (217-222) a law ordering the fast, but probably it is older. Leo the Great (440-461) considers it an Apostolic institution.

By the time of Pope Gregory I, who died in 601 AD, they were observed for all four seasons though the date of each of them could vary. In the Roman Synod of 1078 under Pope Gregory VII, they were uniformly established for the Wednesday, Friday, and Saturday after December 13th (St. Lucia), after Ash Wednesday, after Pentecost Sunday, and after September 14th (Exaltation of the Cross).

While they were initially observed only in Rome, their observance quickly spread as the *Catholic Encyclopedia* further adds:

> Before Gelasius the ember days were known only in Rome, but after his time their observance spread. They were brought into

> England by St. Augustine; into Gaul and Germany by the Carlovingians. Spain adopted them with the Roman Liturgy in the eleventh century. They were introduced by St. Charles Borromeo into Milan. The Eastern Church does not know them. The present Roman Missal, in the formulary for the Ember days, retains in part the old practice of lessons from Scripture in addition to the ordinary two: for the Wednesdays three, for the Saturdays six, and seven for the Saturday in December. Some of these lessons contain promises of a bountiful harvest for those that serve God.

Guéranger adds that the institution of the Ember Days is further based on the fast ordered by God for the changing of the seasons in the Old Testament. Thus, the Church hallowed that fast and adopted it for the worship of the True God thus fulfilling the Lord's words that He came not to abolish but to complete (cf. Matthew 5:17) what was instituted in the Old Testament:

> We may consider it as one of those practices which the Church took from the Synagogue; for the prophet Zacharias speaks of the fasts of the fourth, fifth, seventh, and tenth months. Its introduction into the Christian Church would seem to have been made in the apostolic times; such, at least, is the opinion of St. Leo, of St. Isidore of Seville, of Rabanus Maurus, and of several other ancient Christian writers. It is remarkable, on the other hand, that the orientals do not observe this fast.

Spirituality of the Ember Days

The purpose of Ember Days is, in the words of the *Catholic Encyclopedia,* to "thank God for the gifts of nature, to teach men to make use of them in moderation, and to assist the needy." As a result, their focus differs from the focus of the Rogation Days to which they are often compared. An article on Liturgies.net explains the separate, specific focus of Rogation Days as such:

Rogation Days are the four days set apart to bless the fields and invoke God's mercy on all of creation… Traditionally, on these days, the congregation marches the boundaries of the parish, blessing every tree and stone, while chanting or reciting a Litany of Mercy, usually a Litany of the Saints.[71]

In addition to the general purpose of thanking God and invoking His blessings, the author of *Barefoot Abbey* provides specific intentions for each of the Ember Days by season so that we can render thanks to Almighty God for the fruits of the earth which specifically become instruments of His grace through the Sacraments:

> Winter or Advent Ember Days are after the Feast of St. Lucy (December 13th): Give thanks for the olives that make holy oils for Unction.
>
> Spring or Lenten Ember Days are after Ash Wednesday: Give thanks for the flowers and bees that make blessed candles as in for Baptism and upon the alter.
>
> Summer or Whit Ember Days are after the Solemnity of Pentecost: Give thanks for the wheat used to make the Eucharist hosts.
>
> Autumn or Michaelmas Ember Days are after the Feast of Exaltation of the Holy Cross

---

[71] Carl Fortunato, "What Are Rogation Days," <http://www.liturgies.net/Rogation/RogationArticle.htm>, accessed December 11, 2023..

(September 14): Give thanks for the grapes that make wine for the Precious Blood of Christ.[72]

By writing these down and recalling them for the Ember Days of each season, we can be more intentional in what we are thanking God for in any given season. In this respect, the Ember Days further distinguish themselves from the Rogation Days.

The Cultural Impact of the Ember Days to Japan

Ember Days would remain obligatory for the faithful until the changes immediately after Vatican II in the mid-1960s. In fact, their observance has led to several long-term cultural implications. For instance, Ember Days are the reason we have "tempura" dishes in Asian cuisine. For instance, shrimp tempura is based on Ember Days, which are known as *quatuor tempora* in Latin.

Portuguese (and Spanish) missionaries to the Far East would invite the converted Japanese to fast during the *quatuor tempora* by eating a dish that consisted of battered and deep-fried seafood and vegetables called "*Peixinhos da Horta*" in Portuguese which literally translated to "little fishes from the garden." It is a dish consisting of bell peppers, squash, and green beans that is fried into a flour-based batter. The term steadily gained popularity in southern Japan and became widely used to refer to any sort of food prepared using hot oil, battered or not. This term would persist even after Catholicism was outlawed by the Japanese and the Church's missionaries were executed or exiled in the late 1500s. It was not until the 1870s that Christianity legally returned to Japan. But the faithful of Japan continued to keep the Faith alive in their

---

[72] Genie Shaw, "Everything You Need to Know about the Ember Days," *Barefoot Abbey* (Mar 11, 2019) <https://barefootabbey.com/2019/03/11/everything-you-need-to-know-about-the-ember-days/>, accessed December 11, 2023.

families, including through the keeping of fast and abstinence days.

Wednesdays, Fridays, and Saturdays

Ember Days are observed on Wednesdays, Fridays, and Saturdays in keeping with the ancient weekly devotional fast that originated with the Apostles. On the rationale for fasting on these days, St. Peter of Alexandria, Patriarch of Alexandria until his death in 311 AD, explains: "On Wednesday because on this day the council of the Jews was gathered to betray our Lord; on Friday because on this day He suffered death for our salvation." Likewise, the 1875 Catechism of Father Michael Müller adds: "This practice began with Christianity itself, as we learn from St. Epiphanius, who says: 'It is ordained, by the law of the Apostles, to fast two days of the week.'" Some places added Saturday fasting as well, as noted by St. Francis de Sales who writes, "The early Christians selected Wednesday, Friday and Saturday as days of abstinence."[73]

Father Slater notes in "A Short History of Moral Theology" published in 1909 how these weekly devotional fasts gradually ended but were retained for the Ember Days:

> The obligation of fasting on all Wednesdays and Fridays ceased almost entirely about the tenth century, but the fixing of those days by ecclesiastical authority for fasting, and the desire to substitute a Christian observance at Rome for certain pagan rites celebrated in connection with the seasons of the year, seem to have given rise to our Ember Days... About the tenth century the obligation of the Friday fast was reduced to one of abstinence from flesh meat, and the Wednesday fast after being

---

[73] St. Francis de Sales, *Introduction to the Devout Life*, Chapter 23.

similarly mitigated gradually disappeared altogether.[74]

Ember Days in the Early 1900s

The days of obligatory fasting as listed in the 1917 Code of Canon Law were the forty days of Lent (including Ash Wednesday, Good Friday, and Holy Saturday until noon); the Ember Days; and the Vigils of Pentecost, the Assumption of the Blessed Virgin Mary, All Saints, and Christmas. Partial abstinence, the eating of meat only at the principal meal, was obligatory on all weekdays of Lent (Monday through Thursday). And of course, complete abstinence was required on all Fridays, including Fridays of Lent, except when a holy day of obligation fell on a Friday outside of Lent. Saturdays in Lent were likewise days of complete abstinence. Fasting and abstinence were not observed should a vigil fall on a Sunday as stated in the code: "If a vigil that is a fast day falls on a Sunday the fast is not to be anticipated on Saturday but is dropped altogether that year."

Canon 1006 of the 1917 Code further stated men were to be ordained only on Ember Saturdays, Holy Saturday and the Saturday before Passion Sunday, but the Code added "if a serious cause intervenes, the bishop can have them even on any Sunday or feast day of the order." Episcopal consecration was reserved for Sundays and for Feasts of the Apostles. Thus, even the 1917 Code kept the ancient practice of holding Ember Days as privileged days for ordinations.

Many changes though would continue through the 20th century. In one such change, on January 28, 1949, the United States bishops issued modified regulations on abstinence in America again after receiving a ruling from the Sacred Congregation of the Council. Partial abstinence replaced complete abstinence for Ember Wednesdays, Ember

---

[74] Father Thomas Slater, *A Short History of Moral Theology* (Benzinger Brothers, 1909), p. 24, 27.

Saturdays, and the Vigil of Pentecost. Previously, all Ember Days were days of complete abstinence.

Changes to Ember Days in the Early 1960s

By 1962, the laws of fasting and abstinence were as follows as described in *Moral Theology* by Father Heribert Jone and adapted by Father Urban Adelman for the "laws and customs of the United States of America" copyright 1961:

> Complete abstinence is to be observed on all Fridays of the year, Ash Wednesday, the Vigils of Immaculate Conception and Christmas. Partial abstinence is to be observed on Ember Wednesdays and Saturdays and on the Vigil of Pentecost. Days of fast are all the weekdays of Lent, Ember Days, and the Vigil of Pentecost. If a vigil falls on a Sunday, the law of abstinence and fasting is dispensed that year and is not transferred to the preceding day.[75]

1960 also saw a change to the calculation of how the autumnal Ember Days can follow as the *Barefoot Abbey* website explains:

> Autumn Ember Days are unique in their scheduling. With the 1960 revisions to the breviary rubrics and the newly instituted system of counting Sundays from August to December, Pope John XXIII added that the September Ember Days should not only follow the Feast of the Exaltation of the Cross as they had historically done, but also fall after the 3rd Sunday of September.[76]

---

[75] Father Herbert Jone, *Moral Theology* (The Newman Press, 1961), p. 261 – 262.
[76] Barefoot Abbey, *op cit.*

Gregory DiPippo explains in more detail how the counting of Sundays changed at this time:

> The first Sunday of each of these months is the day on which the Church begins to read a new set of scriptural books at Matins, with their accompanying antiphons and responsories; these readings are part of a system which goes back to the sixth century...The 'first Sunday' of each of these months is traditionally that which occurs closest to the first calendar day of the month, even if that day occurs within the end of the previous month... In the 1960 revision, however, the first Sunday of the months from August to November is always that which occurs first within the calendar month.[77]

Thus, not only did fasting change before Vatican II but the possible dates of the Ember Days were changed as well.

The Abandonment of Our Heritage

Shortly after the close of the Second Vatican Council, Pope Paul VI issued an apostolic constitution on fasting and abstaining on February 17, 1966, called *Paenitemini*, whose principles were later incorporated into the 1983 Code of Canon Law. *Paenitemini* allowed the commutation of the Friday abstinence to an act of penance at the discretion of the local ordinaries and gave authority to the episcopal conferences on how the universal rules would be applied in their region. Abstinence which previously began at age seven was modified to begin at age fourteen. Additionally, the obligation of fasting on the Ember Days and on the remaining vigils was abolished.

---

[77] Gregory DiPippo, "The Calculation of the September Ember Days," *New Liturgical Movement* (Aug 29, 2015) <https://www.newliturgicalmovement.org/2015/08/the-calculation-of-september-ember-days.html>, accessed December 11, 2023.

Father Lew, commenting on the post-conciliar changes, admonishes priests accordingly:

> True, modern canon law is silent about the Ember Days. But tucked away in an obscure corner of the 1970 missal is a reference to 'the Four Times, in which the Church is accustomed to pray to our Lord for the various needs of men, especially for the fruits of the earth and human labours, and to give him public thanks' (*Normæ Universales de Anno Liturgico*, 45). The same words remain in the 3rd *editio typica* of this missal, published in 2002. However, the 'adaptation' of these days is left to Bishops' Conferences: they can decide how many are to be observed, and when, and with what prayers. A couple of 'fast days' are duly marked on each year's Ordo for the church in England and Wales, one in Lent and one in October, with the suggestion of celebrating a votive Mass of a suitable kind. Surely so ancient a tradition as the Ember Days must not be allowed to fade away.[78]

May we all return to the practice and observance of the Ember Days for the glory of God and for reparation for sin. Offering up our fasts for vocations and for the priests who are ordained on – or around the Ember Days – would be a meritorious and charitable work we can do. And we can spend more time learning about this part of our heritage. Like Ember Days, so much of our history of fasting and abstinence has been forgotten.[79]

---

[78] Father Lawrence Lew, "Rekindling the Embers," *New Liturgical Movement* (Sep 21, 2012) <https://www.newliturgicalmovement.org/2012/09/rekindling-embers.html>, accessed December 11, 2023.

[79] For more on this see this work by the author: *The Definitive Guide to Catholic Fasting & Abstinence* (Our Lady of Victory Press, 2023).

XIV

Octave of Christian Unity

> That all may be one: as thou, Father art in me, and I in thee, that they also may be one in us (John 17:21).

Known as the "Octave of Christian Unity" as well as the "Chair of the Octave of Christian Unity" this period of time which lasts from January 18th through January 25th has been virtually forgotten even while it is kept as a more informal "Week of Christian Unity" in the modern Church. Sadly, the aftermath of Vatican II has obscured the primary purpose of this Octave: to pray and work for the conversion of those outside of the True Faith (i.e., the Catholic Faith).

From Episcopalian Beginnings to Catholic Unity

In 1898, Lewis Thomas Wattson would establish the Society of the Atonement, an Episcopalian religious community whose purpose would be to bring the Franciscan life to the Anglican Church. Working with Luraran Mary White, they would eventually in 1909 convert to the Catholic Faith, after having preached the primacy of the Roman pontiff for several years. In fact, the Vatican took at that time an unprecedented step to accept the members of their society as a corporate body, allowing the friars and sisters to remain in their way of life.

Father Paul Wattson, as he was then known, would continue to labor for the Franciscan Friars of the Atonement and for Christian Unity until his death on February 8, 1940. The same is true of Mother Lurana who would labor for this purpose until her death on April 15, 1935 at age 65. A lasting legacy of their work is the establishment of the Octave of Christian Unity observed each January since first established by Father Wattson in 1908.

The Intentions for the Octave of Christian Unity

While we do pray for the conversion of all who are separated from the Unity of the True Faith at this time, the Church does denote a special focus on certain days to certain particular groups. The traditional delineation is as follows:

- 18 January: The union of all Christians in the one true faith and in the Church
- 19 January: The return of separated Eastern Christians to communion with the Holy See
- 20 January: The reconciliation of Anglicans with the Holy See
- 21 January: The reconciliation of European Protestants with the Holy See
- 22 January: That American Christians become one in union with the Chair of Peter
- 23 January: The restoration of lapsed Catholics to the sacramental life of the Church
- 24 January: That the Jewish people come into their inheritance in Jesus Christ
- 25 January: The missionary extension of Christ's kingdom throughout the world

The Chair of Unity Octave Prayers

For each day of this Octave, make it a point to say this prayer. A printable version is available online.[80]

---

[80] Matthew Plese, *loc. cit.*,
<https://acatholiclife.blogspot.com/2016/01/chair-of-octave-of-christian-unity.html>.

Ant. That they all may be one, as Thou, Father, in me and I in Thee, that they also may be one in us; that the world may believe that Thou has sent me.

℣. I say to thee, that thou art Peter,
℟. And upon this rock I will build my Church.

Let us pray: Lord Jesus Christ, Who didst say to Thine Apostles: peace I leave with you, my peace I give unto you, look not upon my sins, but upon the faith of Thy Church; and vouchsafe unto Her that peace and unity which is agreeable to Thy will: Who livest and reignest God forever and ever. Amen.

This prayer has been blessed with indulgences issued by the Holy See. Specifically, a plenary indulgence on the usual conditions at the end of the octave of prayers for the unity of the Church from January 18th to January 25th.[81]

For those of us who pray the Divine Office, this can easily be added at the end of our prayers. For those who do not, we can print out this prayer and say it each morning before Mass or at least during our morning prayers at home.

In addition to this prayer, we can spend extra time praying for the conversion of various groups. The following prayers can be a great aid to that as they are all taken from official Catholic sources and express the traditionally missionary yearnings of Holy Mother Church.[82]

- o Prayer for Pagans
- o Prayer for Jews
- o Prayer for Muslims

---

[81] Apostolic Brief: Feb. 25, 1916; S. P. Ap., Nov. 15, 1927, and Dec. 10, 1946.
[82] For the texts of these prayers, see Plese, *loc. cit.*

- Prayer for Schismatic Orthodox Christians
- Prayer for Protestant Sects
- Prayer for Freemasons
- Prayer for Lapsed Catholics
- Prayer for Anglicans
- Prayer for the True Faith

The Forgotten Two Feast days in Honor of the Chair of St. Peter

A reason why this Octave has become forgotten in practice among Catholics stems from the changes to the Feast of St. Peter's Chair. Traditionally January 18th is the Feast of St. Peter's Chair at Rome and Feb 22 is St. Peter's Chair at Antioch. Pope Paul IV in 1558 instituted this Feast on January 18th to confound the errors of the Protestants who sought to discredit that St. Peter actually lived and died in Rome. The two feasts were included in the Tridentine Calendar with the rank of Double, which Pope Clement VIII raised in 1604 to the newly invented rank of Greater Double.

In 1960 John XXIII removed from the General Roman Calendar the January 18th feast of the Chair of Peter, along with seven other feast days that were second feasts of a single saint or mystery.[83] The February 22 celebration became a Second-Class Feast. This calendar was incorporated in the 1962 Roman Missal. For those Catholics who follow the pre-1955 Missal and Office, they will keep January 18th as the Feast of St. Peter's Chair at Rome. And the spiritually associated with this day naturally lended well to the Octave of Christian Unity. It was a fitting beginning to the Octave while the Conversion of St. Paul, celebrated on January 25th, served

---

[83] Matthew Plese, "Honoring Saints Twice: St. John, St. Michael, and the Eastertide Feast of St. Joseph," *Fatima Center* (May 12, 2022) <https://fatima.org/news-views/catholic-apologetics-165/>, accessed December 11, 2023.

as a poignant and appropriate ending to a week of prayer for those separated from the Ark of Salvation.

There is No Salvation Outside of the Catholic Church

The Church has always taught that there is no salvation outside of the Church (*Extra Ecclesiam nulla salus*). We are called to bring all people into the One Church of salvation, the Catholic Church. Our efforts to spread the Faith are centered on saving the souls of others. This is of supreme charity.

Perhaps Pope Eugene IV said it best in *Cantate Domino* when he unambiguously affirmed:

> The most Holy Roman Church firmly believes, professes and preaches that none of those existing outside the Catholic Church, not only pagans, but also Jews and heretics and schismatics, can have a share in life eternal; but that they will go into the eternal fire which was prepared for the devil and his angels, unless before death they are joined with Her; and that so important is the unity of this ecclesiastical body that only those remaining within this unity can profit by the sacraments of the Church unto salvation, and they alone can receive an eternal recompense for their fasts, their almsgivings, their other works of Christian piety and the duties of a Christian soldier. No one, let his almsgiving be as great as it may, no one, even if he pours out his blood for the Name of Christ, can be saved, unless he remain within the bosom and the unity of the Catholic Church.

Year-Round Efforts for the Propagation of the Faith

Hence rediscovering these customs is essential to countering the false ecumenism of our era.[84] Make it a point to pray the prayers of Christian Unity between January 18 and January 25th, in addition to offering other prayers for groups separated from the Faith. We would do well to request priests to offer Masses for this intention and to offer Rosaries for those separated from Catholic Unity, including those who have fallen away from regular Sacramental life. In fact, the Church has attached indulgences in the *Raccolta* to pious practices for the propagation of the Faith. We should make it a point to do so throughout the year.

---

[84] Matthew Plese, *loc. cit.*, <https://fatima.org/news-views/catholic-apologetics-1>.

XV

St. Valentine

February 14th is widely known as Valentine's Day. But were you fully aware that the day is named after St. Valentine, making it *St.* Valentine's Day? And even if you were aware that it was named after St. Valentine, do you know who the ancient saint is and why we send cards in his honor?

Who is Saint Valentine?

St. Valentine's Day is based on the life of St. Valentine, a Roman martyr who was beheaded in c. 269 – 273 AD. For a short period, Emperor Claudius II outlawed marriage to keep men available as soldiers for the Roman army. However, St. Valentine refused to accept this error and the saintly priest continued to marry young couples. Claudius attempted to convert St. Valentine to paganism, but St. Valentine resisted and attempted to bring Claudius to the Church and Jesus Christ. For this, the emperor had St. Valentine beheaded.

In prison, he helped imprisoned, soon-to-be martyrs. The jailer saw that Valentine was a man of learning, so he brought his daughter Julia to Valentine for lessons. Julia was a young girl, who had been blind since her birth. During the lessons, St. Valentine would read to her about the history of Rome. And he taught her about God. The following is one account of St. Valentine:

> "Valentinus, does God really hear our prayers?" Julia asked one day.
>
> "Yes, my child, He hears each one."

"Do you know what I pray for every morning and every night? I pray that I might see. I want so much to see everything you've told me about!"

"God does what is best for us if we will only believe in Him," Valentinus said.

"Oh, Valentinus, I do believe! I do!" She knelt and grasped his hand.

They sat quietly together, each praying. Suddenly there was a brilliant light in the prison cell. Radiant, Julia screamed, "Valentinus, I can see! I can see!"

"Praise be to God!" Valentinus exclaimed, and he knelt in prayer.

On the eve of his death Valentinus wrote a last note to Julia, urging her to stay close to God. He signed it, "From your Valentine." His sentence was carried out the next day, February 14, 270 A.D., near a gate that was later named Porta Valentini in his memory.

He was buried at what is now the Church of Praxedes in Rome. It is said that Julia planted a pink-blossomed almond tree near his grave. Today, the almond tree remains a symbol of abiding love and friendship. On each February 14, Saint Valentine's Day, messages of affection, love, and devotion are exchanged around the world."

After her healing, the jailer too was converted to the Catholic Faith.

Having almonds (even almond cake), while telling this story, would be a great way to keep the story of St. Valentine alive hopefully for generations to come.

High Praise for a Low Ranking Feast day

St. Valentine is commemorated each year in the Mass and the Office on February 14th when his feast day falls during Lent (as it usually does). What is rather remarkable is the impact his life has had on cultural and liturgical customs even when his feast day before 1954 was kept only as a simple (i.e., the lowest rank). It was reduced to a commemoration by 1962 and sadly in the Novus Ordo Calendar, his feast day was removed from the Liturgy entirely. However, at least in one silver lining, the Novus Ordo rubrics authorize liturgical veneration of him on February 14th in any place where that day is not devoted to some other obligatory celebration, in accordance with the rule that on such a day the Mass may be that of any saint listed in the Martyrology for that day (cf. *General Instruction of the Roman Missal*, 355). However, as his feast day often falls during Lent, such an option would not exist in many years.

How Authentic is the Life of St. Valentine?

Some have suggested that Saint Valentine's Day emerged as an attempt to supersede the pagan holiday of Lupercalia, but most academics reject that theory. The liturgical celebration of St. Valentine was established by Pope Gelasius I in 496 AD, long before the Middle Ages. If the stories most asserted regarding the life of St. Valentine were invented in the Middle Ages and widely diffused through Chaucer's *Canterbury Tales*, the historical existence of such a saint is nonetheless certain. Today the skull of St. Valentine is on display for public veneration in Rome in the Basilica of Saint Mary in Cosmedin, which is also the home of La Bocca della Verità (The Mouth of Truth).

The Roman Martyrology lists seven other saints named "Valentine" who died on days other than February 14th, of which a few are also from Roman times: a priest from Viterbo (November 3); Valentine of Passau, papal missionary bishop to Raetia, who died in 475 AD (January 7); a 5th-century priest and hermit (July 4); a Spanish hermit who died in c. 715 AD (October 25); Valentine Berrio Ochoa, who was martyred in 1861 (November 24); and Valentine Jaunzarás Gómez, who was martyred in 1936 (September 18).

Sending Love on February 14th and Beyond

One way we can keep St. Valentine's Day permeated with a Catholic ethos is to call it as such: *Saint* Valentine's Day. In just a few generations, the memory of the saint could be completely forgotten if we cease reminding everyone that this day is named after a great saint is not secular in origin.

The most common custom associated with St. Valentine's Day is the sending of cards, flowers, and candies to those we love. This custom existed in some form since the Middle Ages as St. Valentine's Day has been associated since then with romance. It was however not until the 18th century in England and America that the popularity of sending gifts began to accelerate by the aristocratic class. This trend continues to this day even more than a century after Ester Howland created the first St. Valentine's Day card in the 1840s.

But where did the custom of sending random cards originate? While that is debated, the Sophienburg Museum shares the following story:

> There are as many versions as to how Valentine's Day started as there are valentines. The history is both interesting and bazaar. Here's one: In Roman Empire days, the Romans engaged in a pagan practice of putting the names of teenage girls in a box and adolescent boys would draw a name at random. The girls were then assigned to live with the boys for a year, celebrating a young man's rite of passage.
>
> Early church leaders, objecting to this practice and determined to replace this pagan

> Lupercalia festival on February 14th, substituted St. Valentine, a bishop who had been martyred two hundred years earlier for secretly marrying couples after Emperor Claudius II banned marriage. February 14th then became St. Valentine's Day in his honor. The box idea lived on, and with time, into the box were put names of saints. Both men and women drew a name and in turn promised to live like that saint. St. Valentine was the most popular saint. Valentine boxes have changed dramatically over the years![85]

An interesting custom not commonly known is the Bohemian custom of engagements on Laetare Sunday, and not on February 14th. Father Weiser relates the following:

> In Germany, Austria, and among the Western Slavs, Laetare Sunday used to be the day of announcing the engagements of young people (Liebstatt Sonntag; Druzebna). In Bohemia the boys would send messengers to the homes of their girlfriends to deliver the solemn proposal. In Austria the girls of the village lined up in front of the church after Mass; their boyfriends would take them by the hand and lead them back into the house of God, and thus "propose" to them by a silent act of religious import. After having prayed together, the couple would seal their engagement with a special meal. It is a curious fact that these engagement customs were called "Valentine," although they did not take place on Saint Valentine's day. The name is explained by the fact that Saint Valentine

---

[85] Myra Lee Adams Goff, "Customs of St. Valentine's day changed over the years," Sophienburg (Feb 9, 2010) <https://sophienburg.com/customs-of-st-valentines-day-changed-over-the-years>, accessed December 11, 2023.

was the heavenly patron of young lovers and engaged couples.

We can do our part to keep this day Catholic by buying cards that call it *Saint* Valentine's Day or in the very least, to add the title *St.* to the cards we do buy. And can likewise invoke St. Valentine for those we know who are engaged. And we can ask God through his intercession to help us safeguard the sanctity of marriage and tighten up the annulment criteria which attack the sanctity of marriage.[86]

---

[86] Matthew Plese, "Annulments: The 'Get Out of Marriage Card' for Catholics," *A Catholic Life* (Sep 19, 2015) <https://acatholiclife.blogspot.com/2015/09/annulments-get-out-of-marriage-card-for.html>, accessed December 11, 2023.

XVI

St. Patrick

Like St. Valentine's Day, St. Patrick's Day has unfortunately become a secularized holiday. But rather than remarking on leprechauns and good luck, Catholics have a moral responsibility to reclaim St. Patrick's Day for the honor of one of the greatest of all saints. And like other great saints, unique customs have emerged to honor his feast day.

Who is Saint Patrick?

St. Patrick was born around 370 AD in Scotland, and at the age of 16, he was kidnapped and sent as a slave in Ireland. St. Patrick was not profoundly religious as a child, but in Ireland when he was sent to work as a shepherd, he began to pray. After six years of service and fervent prayer, St. Patrick received a dream where he was commanded to return to Britain. St. Patrick escaped Ireland and returned to Britain. In Britain, he entered the Catholic Church like his father and grandfather before him.

St. Patrick was ordained a priest by Saint Germanus in 432 and later made a bishop. He later returned to Ireland to convert his people to Christianity. Pope Saint Celestine sent him to evangelize England, then Ireland. St. Patrick's chariot driver was Saint Odran, and Saint Jarlath was one of his students. He advocated against slavery, idolatry, sun worship, and paganism! Shortly after his death, slavery was abolished in Ireland.

Some reports claim he built between 300-600 churches and countless schools and hospitals. In his 33 years in Ireland, he converted nearly the entire country. He taught the Trinity by using a three-leaf clover. Because of his work, Ireland became known as the Land of Saints. St. Patrick died around 461 AD in Ireland, where he worked for years to evangelize.

The Traditional Roman Breviary relates the following powerful account of his life, including the often-untold penance he performed nightly:

> Patrick, called the apostle of Ireland, was born in Great Britain. His father's name was Calphumius. Conchessa, his mother, is said to have been a relation of St. Martin, bishop of Tours. He was several times taken captive by the barbarians, when he was a boy, and was put to tend their flocks. Even in that tender age, he gave signs of the great sanctity he was afterwards to attain. Full of the spirit of faith, and of the fear and love of God, he used to rise at the earliest dawn of day, and, in spite of snow, frost, or rain, go to offer up his prayers to God. It was his custom to pray a hundred times during the day, and a hundred during the night. After his third deliverance from slavery, he entered the ecclesiastical state and applied himself, for a considerable time, to the study of the sacred Scriptures. Having made several most fatiguing journeys through Gaul, Italy, and the islands of the Mediterranean, he was called by God to labour for the salvation of the people of Ireland. Pope Saint Celestine gave him power to preach the Gospel, and consecrated him bishop. Whereupon, he set out for Ireland.
>
> It would be difficult to relate how much this apostolic man had to suffer in the mission thus entrusted to him: he had to bear with extraordinary trials, fatigues, and adversaries. But, by the mercy of God, that land, which

heretofore had worshipped idols, so well repaid the labour wherewith Patrick had preached the Gospel, that it was afterwards called the island of saints. He administered holy Baptism to many thousands: he ordained several bishops, and frequently conferred Holy Orders in their several degrees; he drew up rules for virgins and widows, who wished to lead a life of continency. By the authority of the Roman Pontiff, he appointed Armagh the metropolitan See of the whole island, and enriched that church with the saints' relics, which he had brought from Rome. God honoured him with heavenly visions, with the gift of prophecy and miracles; all which caused the name of the saint to be held in veneration in almost every part of the world.

Besides his daily solicitude for the churches, his vigorous spirit kept up an uninterrupted prayer. For it is said, that he was wont to recite every day the whole psalter, together with the canticles and the hymns, and two hundred prayers: that he every day knelt down three hundred times to adore God; and that at each canonical hour of the day, he signed himself a hundred times with the sign of the cross. He divided the night into three parts: the first was spent in the recitation of a hundred psalms, during which he genuflected two hundred times: the second was spent in reciting the remaining fifty psalms, which he did standing in cold water, and his heart, eyes, and hands lifted up to heaven; the third he gave to a little sleep, which he took laid upon a bare stone. Being a man of extraordinary humility, he imitated the apostles, and practised manual labour. At length, being worn out by his incessant fatigues in the cause of the Church, powerful in word and work, having reached an extreme old age he slept in the Lord, after being refreshed with the holy mysteries. He was buried at Down, in Ulster, in the fifth century of the Christian era.

A Holy Day of Obligation in Ireland

While it is unfortunate and even deplorable that so many in the secular world reduce this day to gluttony and drunkenness, the Church keeps today as a Holy Day. In fact, in Ireland today it is a Holy Day of Obligation. Up until the 1970s, bars were closed in Ireland on this day in observance of the fact that it was a Holy Day of Obligation, a day when Mass attendance is required and mundane affairs such as shopping are forbidden.

Throughout the world, those of Irish descent should rejoice today in the missionary work of the great St. Patrick who bore many sufferings in order to rid Ireland of paganism and plant the Gospel of Christ in the Irish peoples. In fact, the growing presence of Irish immigrants throughout early America not only on the East Coast but heavily in places like modern day Colorado helped make St. Patrick one of the most common names for parishes in the United States.[87]

Fasting and Abstinence on St. Patrick's Day

Since St. Patrick's Day falls during Lent, it coincides with the traditional Lenten fast which traditionally required 40 days of fasting and abstinence from meat as we have said. Even in Ireland where it is a Holy Day of Obligation, the fast and abstinence on Holy Days of Obligation is not abrogated in Lent without a specific dispensation.[88] In fact, the Irish

---

[87] Ibid., <https://acatholiclife.blogspot.com/2022/03/the-most-and-least-common-catholic.html>.
[88] Ibid., <https://acatholiclife.blogspot.com/2021/03/is-fasting-or-abstinence-required-on.html>.

people kept the strictness of abstinence even from animal products during Lent longer than many other nations.[89]

Yet the custom developed of such dispensations. With the growing number of Irish immigrants to America in the early 1800s, for instance, special attention was given to dispense from the law of abstinence when St. Patricks' Day fell on a Friday. This was done for the members of the Charitable Irish Society of Boston in 1837 and would become customary in the United States.[90] Yet it must be clearly stated there is no incompatibility between fasting and abstaining and celebrating liturgical solemnities. Even Sundays of Lent used to be required days of abstinence (but not fast). Let us fast and abstain always on St. Joseph's Day, Annunciation Day, and St. Patrick's Day each year during Lent. Our adherence to and preservation of the Traditional Catholic Faith requires this.

Even with the fast, it is possible to honor St. Patrick's Day with a loaf of traditional Irish soda bread. Check your local bakery or grocery store and get a loaf to have at dinner.

Hail, Glorious Saint Patrick

The great love of St. Patrick has transpired into songs and celebrations in his honor. For instance, those looking to honor St. Patrick this year may want to listen to Hail Glorious St. Patrick. The version sung by Frank Patterson, freely available on YouTube, is especially moving for those of Irish ancestry.

St. Patrick and the Easter Fire

In one interesting story, St. Patrick in defiance of and in opposition to the cannibalistic Druid religion started the practice of large bonfires on Holy Saturday night. Father Weiser states:

---

[89] Ibid., <https://acatholiclife.blogspot.com/2021/02/abstinence-from-meat-animal-products-on.html>.
[90] Mike Cronin and Daryl Adair, *The Wearing of Green* (Taylor & Francis, 2004), 11.

Irish bishops and monks who came to the European continent in the sixth and seventh centuries brought with them an ancient rite of their own: the setting and blessing of big bonfires outside the church on Holy Saturday night. Saint Patrick himself, the Father and Founder of the Church in Ireland, had started this tradition, to supplant the Druidic pagan spring fires with a Christian and religious fire symbol of Christ, the Light of the World.

That tradition continues to this day.

All Irish Saints

Ireland is home to over 300 canonized saints. On St. Patrick's Day, let us honor them and pray for Ireland and the Irish people, especially that they rekindle their Catholicity and ever stand firm in the Church's teachings and in the Faith. This is especially true in regards to the nation's laws on life. To this end, praying the Litany of All Irish Saints would be an appropriate custom to observe each year on March 17th.[91] No matter if we live in Ireland or not, all Catholics rejoice today in the life and example of St. Patrick.

O Holy St. Patrick, pray for us who have recourse to thee!

---

[91] See chapter 25 for more on this.

XVII

St. Joseph

Along with St. Patrick, St. Thomas Aquinas, and the Annunciation, the feast of St. Joseph, foster father of our Lord Jesus Christ and patron of the Universal Church, falls during Lent. Yet, despite the necessity of maintaining Lenten penance in the form of fasting and abstinence, St. Joseph's Day still provides amble opportunities for celebrating our Catholic heritage.

The Church celebrates St. Joseph a few times during the year: March 19th, Wednesday preceding the Third Sunday after Easter (up until the 1955 changes), and May 1st (starting with the 1955 changes).

Who is Saint Joseph?

St. Joseph is one of the greatest saints. His life is recorded partially in Scripture, where we see a man dedicated to the Lord, a man eager to do the will of God.

What we know of St. Joseph comes from the Gospel accounts of Matthew and Luke. And what the Scriptures tell us is that St. Joseph was a silent servant of God. St. Joseph owned little possessions, but he was a descendant of David and full of the grace of God. There is not one recorded sentence spoken by St. Joseph, but the Gospels are clear that he acted kindly towards Mary and Jesus. He cared for them when Herod sought to kill Our Lord, and after the threat passed, he quietly passed away. For that reason, he is frequently recognized as the patron of a peaceful death. In the words of Pope Leo XIII: "Workman and all those laboring in conditions of poverty will have reasons to rejoice rather than grieve, since they have in common with the Holy Family daily preoccupations and cares."

According to tradition, St. Joseph, the foster father of Jesus, watches over and guards the Church. Numerous saints also had devotions to St. Joseph, including Saint Bernard, Saint Thomas Aquinas, Saint Gertrude, Saint Bridget of Sweden, Saint Alphonsus and Saint Teresa of Avila.

St. Joseph is truly the universal protector of the Church. In *The Man Nearest to Christ: The Nature and Historic Development of Devotion to Saint Joseph*, Fr. Francis L Filas recounts the origin of devotion in the United States to St. Joseph. As you will see, this devotion predates the foundation of the country:

> On the North American missions, the name of Saint Joseph appeared frequently. In Canada, he was regarded as patron of the land ever since it was called New France. In 1633, Saint John de Brebeuf founded the first mission among the Hurons and dedicated it to Saint Joseph. The first Algonquin mission was likewise placed under his care. Both the Recollect Fathers and the Jesuits often named islands and rivers in his honor. In 1675, Fr. Allouez called Lake Michigan Lake Saint Joseph. At Montreal the Sulpician Fathers followed in the steps of their founder, Fr. Olier, by inspiring the faithful to turn to the spouse of Mary in their need. The Ursulines and Grey Nuns always paid him exceptional veneration[.]

Why have a Devotion to St. Joseph?

St. Teresa of Avila answered it best:

> To the other Saints it appears that the Lord may have granted power to succor us on particular occasions; but to this Saint, as experience

proves, He has granted power to help us on all occasions. Our Lord would teach us that, as he was pleased to be subject to Joseph upon the earth, so He is now pleased to grant whatever this Saint asks for in heaven. Others whom I have recommended to have recourse to Joseph, have known this from experience. I never knew any one who was particularly devout to him, that did not continually advance more and more in virtue. For the love of God, let him who believes not this make his own trial. And I do not know how any one can think of the Queen of Angels, at the time when she labored so much in the infancy and childhood of Jesus, and not return thanks to Joseph for the assistance which he rendered both to the Mother and to the Son.

It is piously believed that the following eight promises are granted to all who have a devotion to St. Joseph.[92]

1. God will grant special graces to those that do not know me, to have a great devotion to me.
2. God will bless all who are married and the blessing in their family will be without limit.
3. Those married and without children will be blessed with offspring.
4. God will give special graces to be delivered from temptations and the attacks of the devil.
5. They shall have a good and happy death.
6. They shall overcome their trials and tribulations.

---

[92] For texts regarding this pious belief, see <http://www.catholictradition.org/Joseph/joseph-txt2.htm>, accessed November 26, 2024.

RESTORING LOST CUSTOMS OF CHRISTENDOM

7. God shall grant them immediate help when they invoke my intercession, for the demons have extreme dread of the invocation of my name.

8. For all those who embrace a St. Joseph cenacle, they shall obtain a more fervent love for Jesus and a true devotion to Most Holy Mary.

St. Joseph's Day as A Holy Day of Obligation

The first catalog of Holy Days comes from the Decretals of Gregory IX in 1234, which listed 45 Holy Days. In 1642, His Holiness Pope Urban VIII issued the papal bull *"Universa Per Orbem"* which altered the required Holy Days of Obligation for the Universal Church to consist of 35 such days as well as the principal patrons of one's one locality. St. Joseph's Day is on that list.

However, due to dispensations, differences ranged drastically as to which days were kept as holy days throughout the world. In some parts of the world, St. Joseph's Day on March 19th was a Holy Day of Obligation whereas in others it was not. For instance, St. Joseph's Day was a Holy Day of Obligation in Quebec in the late 1600s and also in the British Colonies in what is now the United States of America.[93] It was also a holy day of Obligation in what is now Florida, among other places. But changes abounded as the number of holy days gradually weakened over the centuries.

At America's birth, the Holy Days of Obligation, in addition to every Sunday, were as follows: the feasts of Christmas, Circumcision, Epiphany, Annunciation, Easter Monday, Ascension, Whitsun Monday, Corpus Christi, Ss. Peter and Paul, Assumption, and All Saints. St. Joseph's Day had ceased

---

[93] Matthew Plese, "A History of Holy Days of Obligation & Fasting for American Catholics: Part 1," *A Catholic Life* (May 27, 2020) <https://acatholiclife.blogspot.com/2020/05/a-history-of-holy-days-of-obligation.html>, access November 26, 2024.

being a Holy Day of Obligation in the United States. However, it remained a holy day in some other parts of the world.

In 1911, Pope St. Pius X issued *Supremi disciplinæ* which drastically reduced the number of Holy Days of Obligation in the Universal Church to only eight. St. Joseph's Day did not make the list. Shortly thereafter in 1917, however, Corpus Christi and St. Joseph were added back by his successor, bringing the total to ten. The ten currently observed on the Universal Calendar are the same as from 1917. Yet not in the United States.

As for the Holy Days observed in the United States, the Catholic Encyclopedia in referencing *Supremi disciplinæ* noted, "Where, however, any of the above feasts has been abolished or transferred, the new legislation is not effective. In the United States consequently the Epiphany and the feast of Sts. Peter and Paul are not days of precept." The same is true of St. Joseph's Day in the changes in 1917. While the 1917 change did not add St. Joseph's Day back to the list of Holy Days of Obligation in the United States, it did elsewhere.

Presently, Indonesia, Lebanon, Malta, Spain, and the Diocese of Lugano in Switzerland keep St. Joseph's Day as a Holy Day.

Fasting and Abstinence on St. Joseph's Day

Since St. Joseph's Day falls during Lent, it coincides with the traditional Lenten fast which traditionally required 40 days of fasting and 46 days of abstinence from meat. Per the 1917 Code of Canon Law, Friday abstinence is still required on St. Joseph's Day even where it is kept as a Holy Day of Obligation. And would the fast of Lent still be observed? The answer is unequivocally yes.

The question of whether Holy Days of Obligation abrogate the requirement of Friday abstinence outside of Lent is mentioned in the 1917 Code:

> On [Sundays] or feasts of precept, the law of abstinence or of abstinence and fast or of fast only ceases, except during Lent, nor is the vigil anticipated; likewise it ceases on Holy [Saturday] afternoon (1917 Code, Canon 1252 § 4).[94]

The 1917 Code is explicit – feasts of precepts do not remove the requirement to fast or abstain during Lent. The only way that the obligation would be removed during the season of Lent would be if a dispensation would be specifically offered by the lawful Church authorities for a particular day.

It must be further noted that the removal of the obligation of penance on Holy Days of Obligation outside of Lent only applies to areas that observe the day of precept. It is not based on the Roman calendar, as affirmed by the Commission on the Code in a 1924 article in the *American Ecclesiastical Review*. Hence, when January 6th, the Feast of the Epiphany, falls on a Friday, it is still a mandatory day of abstinence in America and France and other places where it is not a Holy Day of Obligation. In contrast, Canada, Rome, and places that keep it as a Holy Day do not have to observe fasting and/or abstinence on that particular Friday. This, however, only applies to Holy Day of Obligation *outside* of Lent. And this change only started with the 1917 Code – beforehand, it was still a day of abstinence on Fridays regardless if it was a day of precept or not, unless a specific dispensation was issued by the Pope himself.

In 1954, Pope Pius XII issued such a decree granting bishops the permission to dispense from Friday abstinence for the Feast of St. Joseph which that year fell on a Friday. A March 26, 1954, article of *The Guardian* elaborates: "Bishops throughout the world have been granted the faculty to dispense

---

[94] Emphasis added. Translation taken from THE 1917 OR PIO-BENEDICTINE CODE OF CANON LAW in English Translation by Dr. Edward Peters.

their faithful from the law of abstinence on the Feast of St. Joseph, Friday, March 19. The power was granted in a decree issued by the Sacred Congregation of the Council, which said it acted at the special mandate of His Holiness Pope Pius XII. The decree published in *L'Osservatore Romano* made no mention of a dispensation from the Lenten fast."

As such, St. Joseph's Day did not permit the faithful to eat meat on Fridays in Lent unless such a specific dispensation were offered, which was very rarely done. Likewise, to those who maintain the 1917 Code's requirement to also fast all forty weekdays of Lent – which was observed since the Early Church – St. Joseph's Day remains a day of fast. Surely St. Joseph would want us to produce worthy fruits of penance during this holiest season as we prepare for the Pascal mystery.

Unfortunately, the 1983 Code of Canon Law which aligns with the many Modernist changes in the Church weakly states:

> The penitential days and times in the universal Church are every Friday of the whole year and the season of Lent. Abstinence from meat, or from some other food as determined by the Episcopal Conference, is to be observed on all Fridays, unless a solemnity should fall on a Friday. Abstinence and fasting are to be observed on Ash Wednesday and Good Friday (1983 Code, Canons 1251 – 1252).

Italian Cultural Customs for March 19th

St. Joseph's Day on March 19th, despite being in Lent, is full of cultural customs in honor of St. Joseph. *Fish Eaters* explains:

> St. Joseph's Day is a big Feast for Italians because in the Middle Ages, God, through St. Joseph's intercessions, saved the Sicilians from a very serious drought. So in his honor, the

custom is for all to wear red, in the same way that green is worn on St. Patrick's Day.

Today, after Mass (at least in parishes with large Italian populations), a big altar (*"la tavola di San Giuse"* or "St. Joseph's Table") is laden with food contributed by everyone (note that all these St. Joseph celebrations might take place on the nearest, most convenient weekend). Different Italian regions celebrate this day differently, but all involve special meatless foods: minestrone, pasta with breadcrumbs (the breadcrumbs symbolize the sawdust that would have covered St. Joseph's floor), seafood, *Sfinge di San Giuseppe,* and, always, fava beans, which are considered "lucky" because during the drought, the fava thrived while other crops failed[.]

The table – which is always blessed by a priest – will be in three tiers, symbolizing the Most Holy Trinity. The top tier will hold a statue of St. Joseph surrounded by flowers and greenery. The other tiers might hold, in addition to the food: flowers (especially lilies); candles; figurines and symbolic breads and pastries shaped like a monstrance, chalices, fishes, doves, baskets, St. Joseph's staff, lilies, the Sacred and Immaculate Hearts, carpentry tools, etc.; 12 fishes symbolizing the 12 Apostles; wine symbolizing the miracle at Cana; pineapple symbolizing hospitality; lemons for "luck"; bread and wine (symbolizing the Last Supper); and pictures of the dead. There will also be a basket in which the faithful place prayer petitions.[95]

It should be noted that traditionally St. Joseph's Tables, even when transferred to Sunday, were always meatless. For centuries, even Sundays in Lent were days of abstinence – just not fasting.[96]

The Zeppole

Zeppole, also known as *sfinge* or St. Joseph's Day pastry, is a traditional Italian pastry that is often associated with the celebration of St. Joseph's Day on March 19th. Zeppole come in various forms, but the most common type is a deep-fried dough ball or ring, resembling a small doughnut. The dough is typically made with flour, water, eggs, sugar, and sometimes ricotta cheese, resulting in a light and airy texture. After frying, zeppole are often coated with powdered sugar or drizzled with honey, providing a sweet and indulgent flavor. A vegan alternative can also be made in keeping with the ancient Lenten fast.

On St. Joseph's Day, zeppole are a popular treat enjoyed by families and communities. It is a customary practice to set up temporary stalls or visit pastry shops where zeppole are sold. Some regions have their own variations of zeppole, with specific ingredients or shapes unique to the local tradition.

The way zeppole are eaten on St. Joseph's Day can vary, but the most common practice is to share them with family and friends. They are often served as a dessert during festive meals or as a snack throughout the day. Families may also participate in the "lucky fava bean" tradition, where a dried fava bean is

---

[95] "Feast of St. Joseph," *Fish Eaters* (n.d.) <https://www.fisheaters.com/customslent5.html>, accessed November 26, 2024.
[96] Matthew Plese, "Abstinence from Meat & Animal Products on Sundays in Lent," *A Catholic Life* (Feb 27, 2021) <https://acatholiclife.blogspot.com/2021/02/abstinence-from-meat-animal-products-on.html>, accessed November 26, 2024.

hidden in one of the zeppole. The person who finds the bean is believed to receive good luck.

In addition to the sweet zeppole, there is also a savory version known as *"zeppole di San Giuseppe"* (St. Joseph's fritters). These savory zeppole are typically filled with ricotta, anchovies, or other savory ingredients, providing a contrast to the sweet versions commonly associated with the celebration.

The Eastertide Solemnity of St. Joseph's Patronage

While many Catholics should be familiar with the annual Solemnity of St. Joseph, Foster Father of Jesus Christ, celebrated annually on March 19th, fewer are likely familiar with the Eastertide Solemnity of St. Joseph. Instituted by Pope Pius IX's decree of September 10, 1847, the Eastertide Solemnity of St. Joseph is celebrated on the second Wednesday after the Octave of Easter.

According to Father Francis X. Lasance, it was instituted during the hostile occupation of Rome by the troops of the Italian King, Victor Emmanuel II. The Pope proclaimed St. Joseph the Patron of the oppressed Household of the Faith, entrusting to St. Joseph the defense of Holy Mother Church.

When Pope St. Pius X reformed the liturgical calendar to restore the Sunday Offices to prominence over those of the Saints, the second Feast of St. Joseph was moved to the Wednesday preceding the Third Sunday after Easter. In 1911, the Feast was raised to a Double of the First Class and later assigned an Octave. It is a Common Octave, so the Octave may or may not be commemorated on the intra Octave days depending on the rank of the feasts that occur during the Octave. While this feast day is not in the 1962 Missal, it is still kept by priests who celebrate Holy Mass according to the pre-1955 reforms.

However, the Eastertide Joseph celebration had also a third placement. At the time of the writing of his illustrious Liturgical Year 15 volume set, Dom Guéranger observed that the feast of St. Joseph during Eastertide was said on the Third Sunday after Easter. Here is an excerpt from this feast:

> The Easter mysteries are superseded today by a special subject, which is offered for our consideration. The holy Church invites us to spend this Sunday in honouring the Spouse of Mary, the Foster-Father of the Son of God. And yet, as we offered him the yearly tribute of our devotion on the 19th of March, it is not, properly speaking, his Feast that we are to celebrate today. It is a solemn expression of gratitude offered to Joseph, the Protector of the Faithful, the refuge and support of all that invoke him with confidence. The innumerable favours he has bestowed upon the world entitle him to this additional homage. With a view to her children's interests, the Church would, on this day, excite their confidence in this powerful and ever ready helper.

St. Joseph the Worker

With the advent of the 1955 Calendar, Pope Pius XII instituted the feast of "St. Joseph the Worker" on May 1 (moving the feast of "Saints Philip and James" from May 1, where it had been since the sixth century, to May 11th). Instead of adding this as a third annual celebration of St. Joseph, Pius XII suppressed the aforementioned Eastertide Solemnity of St. Joseph. The May 1st feast presents an excellent opportunity to recall St. Joseph as a worker who labored for good despite trials. May 1st is also May Day, the obligatory Communist holiday. Thus St. Joseph's feast under the title of Workman is very much set against the Communists so that we may have a heavenly patron, guide, and father who himself knew hard work and discipline and yet who would never have approved of Atheistic Communism. In this, Pius XII was following his immediate predecessor, Pius XI, who placed the Church's whole struggle against what he called in *Divini Redemptoris* the "Satanic scourge" (Communism) under the Patronage of St. Joseph.

We too must become holy and remember to offer up our prayers, works, joys, and sufferings each day in a Morning Offering Prayer. This is worthwhile to also call to mind on the Eastertide Feast of St. Joseph.

We can also recall and share why Communism is always incompatible with Catholicism.

The St. Joseph Scapular

While many Catholics are hopefully familiar with, and enrolled in, the Brown Scapular, most are likely unaware that there are many other Scapulars in the Church (e.g. the Red Scapular, the Black Scapular, the Green Scapular, etc.). All of these scapulars have specific requirements, promises, and symbolic meanings.

The St. Joseph Scapular is a gold and violet-colored scapular with a white cord. On the front is an image of Joseph holding the child Jesus in one arm and a staff of lilies in the other. Underneath are the words, "St. Joseph, patron of the Church, pray for us." On the back of the scapular is the papal crown under a dove, symbolizing the Holy Ghost. Underneath those are the Cross, the keys of Peter, and the inscription: *"Spiritus Domini ductor eius"* (The Spirit of the Lord is his Guide).

The scapular is to remind us of St. Joseph's virtues (humility, modesty, purity); to remind us to pray to St. Joseph, asking him to pray for the Church; and to assist the dying since St Joseph is the patron of a happy death.

In addition to the above benefits, there is a plenary indulgence for those who confess, receive Holy Communion and pray for the intentions of the Holy Father on the following feast days: 25 December, the day of investment of the scapular, 1 January, 6 January, 2 February, 19 March, 25 March, Easter, Feast of the Ascension, 15 August, 8 September, 8 December, 3rd Sunday after Easter, and at the time of death. It is recommended also to say 5 Our Fathers, 5 Hail Marys and 5 Glorias before the Blessed Sacrament at these times.

Prayer to St. Joseph for the Observance of Sundays and Feast Days as taken from the 1910 Raccolta:

Most Glorious Patriarch, St. Joseph, obtain, we beseech thee, from Our Lord Jesus Christ a most abundant blessing on all who keep festival days holy; obtain for us that those who profane them may know, in time, the great evil they commit, and the chastisements which they draw down upon themselves in this life and in the next, and may be converted without delay.

O Most blessed St. Joseph, thou who on the Lord's day didst cease from every labour of thy craft, and with Jesus and Mary didst fulfill the duties of religion with most lively devotion, bless the pious work of the sanctification of feast-days, erected under thy most powerful patronage; cause it to spread to every home, office, and workshop, so that the day may soon come when all the Christian populace may on feast-days abstain from forbidden work, seriously attend to the salvation of their souls, and give glory to God, who liveth and reigneth, world without end. Amen.

XVIII

May – Month of Mary

> May Mary adorn your soul with the flowers and the fragrance of ever new virtues and place her maternal hand on your head. Always stay close to this heavenly Mother, because she is the sea to be crossed to reach the shores of eternal splendors in the Kingdom of dawn (St. Padre Pio).

Catholic Monthly Devotions

Under the Old Law in the Old Testament, God's people observed annual ceremonies commemorating important events in salvation history which prefigured the completion of the Old Law through Christ. Similarly, the Catholic Church commemorates important mysteries, events, and persons, using in an annual cycle of prayers, Scriptures, hymns, and various spiritual disciplines. In the same way, as we have already mentioned above, each of the 12 months has a unique focus, and each day of the week has a unique focus as well. Even in a single day, the hours of the day are divided up into the canonical hours. In so doing, all time is, in a manner of speaking, consecrated to God since He alone created all time and redeemed all of time.

Here is a listing of the most common associations of devotions per calendar month:

1. January is devoted to the Holy Name and the Childhood of Our Lord.

2. February is devoted to the Holy Family and the Purification of Our Lady.

3. March is devoted to St. Joseph and the Passion of Our Lord.

4. April is dedicated to the Blessed Sacrament, the Resurrection, and the Holy Ghost.

5. May is in honor of the Blessed Virgin Mary.

6. June is devoted to the Sacred Heart of Our Lord.

7. July is dedicated to His Most Precious Blood.

8. August is in honor of the Immaculate Heart of Mary and the Assumption.

9. September is dedicated to the Seven Sorrows of Mary and the Exaltation of the Cross.

10. October is in honor of both the Holy Rosary and the Holy Angels.

11. November is dedicated to praying for the Poor Souls in Purgatory.

12. December is dedicated to the Immaculate Conception and the Nativity of Our Lord.

However, the particular focus assigned to each month is not dogmatically defined by the Church's solemn authority. Rather, these devotions have been practiced by the faithful and grown as popular piety over the centuries. They have varied according to both region and local custom. Thus, it is not uncommon for one to find lists that differ somewhat.

Such variations should not cause us any concern, but rather serve to highlight the richness of our Catholic Faith which unites diverse believers from every corner of the earth. There are so many wondrous mysteries which we can meditate upon throughout the months of the year. Over time, such a practice can greatly increase your spiritual arsenal of novenas and meditations and should draw you into a more profound union with the Blessed Trinity and Communion of Saints.

As we enter the month of May, those of us in the northern hemisphere celebrate the return of springtime as evident in creation emerging from winter, just as Our Lord has emerged from the tomb on Easter Sunday. The time of winter is now passed. And in a similar fashion, the month of May brings us the joy of celebrating in a special manner the Blessed Virgin Mary. This month features a number of Marian feast days and, with the celebration of Mother's Day in May in dozens of countries, it is a fitting time for us to recall the maternal protection of our Heavenly Mother and live out this devotion through long established Catholic customs.

The Litany of Loreto

One way that we can better honor the Blessed Virgin Mary this May is to add the Litany of Loreto to the end of our Rosary. This Litany is one of six approved public litanies and its history is particularly rich.[97]

This litany was most likely composed in or around Paris between the years 1150 and 1200. In 1558, it was formally adopted for public use at the famous Marian shrine at Loreto. This Italian city on the Adriatic coast is where the Holy House of Nazareth was miraculously transported by angels after infidels overran the Holy Land. Pope Sixtus V approved its use for public worship in 1587 and urged it to be prayed. This litany carries a partial indulgence for all who recite it.

May Crowning

One of the most memorable aspects of Catholic life in May is the crowning of a statue or an image of the Blessed Virgin Mary as Queen.

---

[97] Ibid., <https://acatholiclife.blogspot.com/2018/01/public-vs-private-litanies.html>.

In addition to attending our parish's May crowning, in our own homes, we can crown a statue of Our Lady also as queen. If we do not have a statue, we can easily place before an image of our Lady a beautiful bouquet of flowers while reciting the Rosary and the Litany of Loreto. This would be a fitting celebration for Mother's Day, allowing the family to be together and to honor the Mother of God in addition to all earthly mothers.

Fish Eaters notes a unique astronomical coincidence worth noting in May:

> In the Northern hemisphere, if you go outside early in May, face East, and look directly up overhead, you will see a relatively faint "L" in the sky (assuming the sky is clear enough). This is the constellation Coma Berenices, a constellation that was named after a Queen... the second brightest star in this constellation is called 'Diadem,' crown of royalty. So take your children outside, point out the star Diadem to them, and think of Our Lady, crowned in Heaven, our Queen Mother who wants nothing more than for us to love her Son.

First Saturday Devotion

May is also a fitting month to begin the First Saturdays Devotion if you have fallen out of this habit. On December 10, 1925, Our Blessed Lady's appeared again to Sr. Lucia of Fatima to request the First Saturday Devotion. In this apparition, She said:

> Look, my daughter, at my Heart encircled by these thorns with which men pierce it at every moment by their blasphemies and ingratitude. You, at least, strive to console me, and so I announce: I promise to assist at the hour of death with the grace necessary for salvation all those who, with the intention of making

> reparation to me, will, on the first Saturday of five consecutive months, go to confession, receive Holy Communion, say five decades of the beads, and keep me company for fifteen minutes while meditating on the fifteen mysteries of the Rosary.

The First Saturday Devotion consists of offering the First Saturday of the month for five consecutive months in reparation for the many and grievous sins committed in our world. A further explanation of our Lady's request is below:

- You must go to the Sacrament of Confession. Your reception of the Sacrament may be 8 days before the Saturday as long as you stay in a state of grace.
- You must receive the Holy Eucharist and as always, it must be in the state of grace or risk the most grievous sin of sacrilege
- You must pray 5 decades of the Holy Rosary of our Lady, including the Fatima Prayer.
- Finally, the last requirement consists of "keeping Mary company" for 15 minutes while meditating on all of the Mysteries of the Rosary with the intention of making reparation to her. This can be done by reading Scripture or other writings relevant to the Mysteries, meditating on pictures of the Mysteries, or simple meditation. Materials for meditation and education on each of the Rosary mysteries is available online.

On May 29, 1930, Our Lord Jesus Christ Himself appeared to Sr. Lucia and explained why Heaven requested five First Saturdays:

> My daughter, the reason is simple. There are five types of offenses and blasphemies committed against the Immaculate Heart of Mary: 1. Blasphemies against the Immaculate Conception; 2. Blasphemies against her

virginity; 3. Blasphemies against her divine maternity, in refusing at the same time to recognize her as the Mother of men; 4. Blasphemies of those who publicly seek to sow in the hearts of children, indifference or scorn or even hatred of this Immaculate Mother; 5. Offenses of those who outrage her directly in her holy images. Here, my daughter, is the reason why the Immaculate Heart of Mary inspired Me to ask for this little act of reparation…

Learn about Regional Feast days of Mary

While Catholics are generally familiar with the feast days on the Universal Calendar, there are dozens of Marian feast days throughout the year celebrated only at the regional level. Our Lady of Power is celebrated on May 12th in Aubervillers, France, one day after Our Lady of Aparecida is celebrated as patroness in Brazil. A few days later, Our Lady of Tears is celebrated in Spoleto, Italy and on May 30th, Mexico keeps the Feast of Our Lady of the Sacred Heart. Spend some time learning about these regional feast days of Mary and look up these titles to learn more about these ancient titles and apparitions of the Blessed Virgin Mary.[98]

Marian Pilgrimages

To travel to a sacred site is to go "on pilgrimage." This is an opportunity for renewal and spiritual healing. There are many well known sites in Europe – Lourdes, Fatima, Loreto – as well as Mexico City, which has Our Lady of Guadalupe, Empress of the Americas. There are also some worthy places to travel to across even in the United States. They include The National Shrine of the Immaculate Conception, in Washington, D.C.

---

[98] "The Feasts of Our Lady," *Catholic Tradition* (no date) <http://www.catholictradition.org/Mary/marian-feasts.htm>, accessed December 11, 2023.

which is the largest Church in the United States and one of the ten largest in the world.

The National Shrine of Our Lady of Consolation, in Carey, Ohio is a place of peace where pilgrims can pray and pay homage to the Blessed Mother. Across the street from the Basilica stands the original Shrine Church. Construction on this, the first church in Carey, began in 1868. When construction was slow, the local priest asked parishioners to pray to Our Lady of Consolation. When the new Church was completed and ready to be dedicated, a statue of Our Lady was carried in procession for seven miles. As parishioners walked a storm came up and the rain fell all around them, but the statue and pilgrims remained dry.

The Central Miraculous Medal Shrine in Philadelphia, PA and the National Shrine of Our Lady of the Miraculous Medal in Perryville, Missouri are both worth visiting. And the Shrine of St. Bernadette and Our Lady of Lourdes located in Albuquerque, NM includes a bronze replica of the saint's incorrupt body and a replica of the Shrine in Lourdes where Our Lady appeared to Bernadette 18 times. The Shrine includes a font with holy water from Lourdes.

Shrine of Our Lady of La Leche in St. Augustine, FL is the first shrine dedicated to Our Blessed Mother in the United States. The history of the devotion to the Blessed Mother as Our Lady of La Leche has roots in a 4th Century grotto in Bethlehem. And there is the Grotto of Our Lady of Sorrows in Portland Oregon is a 62-acre shrine and botanical garden. Work on the shrine began in September 1923. A cave was carved out of the 110-foot basalt cliffside, and a stone altar built. The shrine contains a replica of Michelangelo's Pietà. This grotto, administered by the Order of Friars Servants of Mary, received a special Apostolic Blessing from Pope Pius XI.

As such, May is an ideal time to take a road trip with the family to the closest Marian shrine. Journeying to holy places has great value for the entire Church. Therefore, the Church offers special blessings for pilgrims, special prayers and in many cases, it is possible to gain a Plenary Indulgence. Pilgrimages to a Cathedral Church, to the Holy Land, to Rome, or to other sacred sites as designated by the Church, may gain for the pilgrim a plenary Indulgence (complete remission of the temporal punishment due to sin) when certain conditions are met such as:

> Attending Mass, participation in pious exercises such as the Rosary, Stations of the Cross, recitation of the Akathistos Hymn in honor of the Mother of God, Eucharistic Adoration or other pious meditation ending with the Our Father, a profession of faith and prayer to the Blessed Mother.[99]

Conclusion

There are many opportunities for living out the joy of Paschaltide this May while keeping a Marian focus. If you do not already do so, pray the Rosary every day this May. Wear the Brown Scapular at all times and encourage your family members to wear it too. And of course, if someone has not been properly enrolled in the Brown Scapular by a priest, that is necessary to receive the promises of the Scapular.[100]

Other customs to observe this May include visiting a Marian shrine in your area, consecrating yourself and your family to

---

[99] Directory on Popular Piety and the Liturgy issued December 2001 by the Congregation for the Divine Worship and Discipline of the Sacraments.
[100] Matthew Plese, *loc. cit.*,
<https://acatholiclife.blogspot.com/2006/07/our-lady-of-mt-carmel-brown-scapular.html>.

the Immaculate Heart of Mary, and attending your parish's May crowning.[101]

Nos cum Prole pia benedicat Virgo Maria (*May the Virgin Mary bless us with her dear Child*).

---

[101] "Shrines in the United States," *University of Dayton* (no date) <https://udayton.edu/imri/mary/s/shrines-in-united-states.php>, accessed December 11, 2023; Matthew Plese, *loc. cit.*, <https://acatholiclife.blogspot.com/2012/08/more-about-fatima-and-immaculate-heart.html>.

XIX

St. John the Baptist

Born to Saints Zechariah and Elizabeth, St. John the Baptist's birth was miraculous due to his parents' advanced age. Leading an ascetic lifestyle in the wilderness, St. John wore camel's hair, ate locusts and wild honey, and preached repentance and the imminent Kingdom of God. His recognition of Jesus as the Messiah and his act of baptizing Jesus in the River Jordan marked the beginning of Our Lord's public ministry. St. John proclaimed, "Behold the Lamb of God, who takes away the sin of the world" (John 1:29). He was the final prophet before Our Lord's coming.

St. John the Baptist's condemnation of Herod Antipas' unlawful marriage to Herodias led to his imprisonment and eventual beheading, as requested by Herodias' daughter, Salome. Speaking of him, the Savior Himself said: "Amen I say to you, there hath not risen among them that are born of women a greater than John the Baptist..." (Matthew 11:11). Hence, given his importance, customs have arisen over the centuries in connection with the liturgical celebrations of St. John the Baptist.

St. John the Baptist Was Born (But Not Conceived) Without Original Sin

Did you know that tradition says St. John the Baptist, the Precursor of Christ, was cleansed from original sin in his mother's womb? Many Catholics are often surprised to learn – since it is not often taught – that St. John the Baptist was cleansed from sin in his mother's womb. This is what we celebrate on the Feast of the Visitation.

It is not a dogma, but most theologians agree with this. And it makes sense. To be a forerunner of Christ, St. John the Baptist should have been freed of Original Sin. So while not an Immaculate Conception, like the Blessed Mother, St. John the Baptist was purified in the womb and born without Original Sin, though he was still conceived with Original Sin. This is mentioned in the Catholic Encyclopedia:

> Then was accomplished the prophetic utterance of the angel that the child should 'be filled with the Holy Ghost even from his mother's womb'. Now as the presence of any sin whatever is incompatible with the indwelling of the Holy Ghost in the soul, it follows that at this moment John was cleansed from the stain of original sin.

The Church only celebrates the birthdays of those who were born without original sin – St. John the Baptist, the Blessed Virgin Mary, and Our Lord Jesus Christ. Hence, the Feast of the Nativity of St. John the Baptist on June 24th is celebrated just as is the Nativity of the Blessed Virgin Mary on September 8th or Our Lord's Nativity on December 25th. All other saints are generally honored on the date of their death or in some cases their episcopal consecration – for bishops – or sometimes a separate date close to their date of death if the actual date itself is already impeded by an existing feast day. But with these three, we honor their birthdays as well.

Fasting on the Vigil of St. John the Baptist

June 23rd is the Vigil of the Nativity of St. John the Baptist, which used to be a day of fasting and abstinence. And we may certainly keep it as such to prepare. Dom Guéranger, writing in the mid-1800s on the great Feast of the Nativity of the Lord's forerunner, relates the following:

On the Lateran Piazza (or Square) the faithful Roman people will keep vigil to-night, awaiting the hour which will allow the eve's strict fast and abstinence to be broken, when they may give themselves up to innocent enjoyment, the prelude of those rejoicings wherewith, six months hence, they will be greeting the Emmanuel. St John's vigil is no longer of precept. Formerly, however, not one day's fasting only, but an entire Lent was observed at the approach of the Nativity of the Precursor, resembling in its length and severity that of the Advent of our Lord.

The more severe had been the holy exactions of the preparation, the more prized and the better appreciated would be the festival. After seeing the penance of St. John's fast equaled to the austerity of that preceding Christmas, is it not surprising to behold the Church in her liturgy making the two Nativities closely resemble one another, to a degree that would be apt to stagger the limping faith of many nowadays?

By 1893, the only fasting days kept in Rome were the forty days of Lent, the Ember Days, and the Vigils of the Purification, of Pentecost, of St. John the Baptist, of Ss. Peter and Paul, of the Assumption, of All Saints, and of Christmas. This is summarized from *The Handbook to Christian and Ecclesiastical Rome*.[102] In just a few years after this, Rome would abrogate the fast on the Vigil of the Purification and on the Vigil of St. John the Baptist. But we can keep this long-established penance as a pious custom.

---

[102] M.A.R. Tuker, *Handbook to Christian and Ecclesiastical Rome: The liturgy in Rome* (A & C Black, 1897), 204.

St. John's Eve Bonfires

In addition to fasting and abstaining from meat, we can also keep the venerable practice of having St. John Eve bonfires on the night of June 23rd. Even today, the Vigil of the Nativity of St. John the Baptist is celebrated with bonfires in many Catholic nations. Describing this ancient custom, *Fish Eaters* writes:

The temporal focal point of the festivities, though, is the building of fires outdoors in which to burn worn out sacramentals and to serve as a symbol of the one Christ Himself called "a burning and shining light" (John 5:35). These fires used to be huge, communal bonfires, and this still occurs in parts of Europe, but smaller, "family-sized" fires will do, too. The fire is built at dusk, with this blessing from the Roman Ritual, and allowed to burn past midnight:

P: Our help is in the name of the Lord.
All: Who made heaven and earth.

P: The Lord be with you.
All: May He also be with you.

Let us pray. Lord God, almighty Father, the light that never fails and the source of all light, sanctify + this new fire, and grant that after the darkness of this life we may come unsullied to Thee Who art light eternal; through Christ our Lord. All: Amen.

The fire is sprinkled with holy water; after which the clergy and the people sing the "Ut queant laxis":

O for your spirit, holy John, to chasten
Lips sin-polluted, fettered tongues to loosen;
So by your children might your deeds of wonder
Meetly be chanted.

Lo! a swift herald, from the skies descending,
Bears to your father promise of your greatness;
How he shall name you, what your future story,
Duly revealing.

Scarcely believing message so transcendent,
Him for a season power of speech forsaketh,
Till, at your wondrous birth, again returneth,
Voice to the voiceless.

You, in your mother's womb all darkly cradled,
Knew your great Monarch, biding in His chamber,
Whence the two parents, through their offspring's merits,
Mysteries uttered.

Praise to the Father, to the Son begotten,
And to the Spirit, equal power possessing,
One God Whose glory, through the lapse of ages,
Ever resounding.

P: There was a man sent from God.
All: Whose name was John.

Let us pray. God, Who by reason of the birth of blessed John have made this day praiseworthy, give Thy people the grace of spiritual joy, and keep the hearts of Thy faithful fixed on the way that leads to everlasting salvation; through Christ our Lord. All: Amen.

After the blessing, a decade of the Rosary is prayed while walking sunwise — clockwise, not widdershins — around the fire, the old Sacramentals are reverently burned, and then the party begins. In most places, brave souls leap over the flames of the bonfire — an act which is given different meanings in different places, with most saying it is an act to bring blessings.

If you're in a farming family, it is customary to carry torches lit from this fire through your fields to bless them. Whether you're a farmer or not, tend the fire as late as you can go (at least until after midnight) and have fun. If you have a fireplace, light a fire in it with flames from the bonfire to bless your home. Note that it is customary, too, to save some of the ashes from this fire to mix with water to bless the sick.[103]

One of the greatest ways we can honor St. John the Baptist is by observing this ancient custom with our family, friends, and neighbors. This is a public way to bear witness to the Faith. Additionally, we can learn about the custom of St. John's wort and make wreaths as *Fish Eaters* further adds:

> Make a wreath of flowers that dry well and hang in your home all year to be replaced next St. John's Day. Alternatively, flowers can be tied together in bunches with beautiful ribbons and hanged upside-down to decorate your home all year. Swedish girls will pick seven flowers from seven different fields, and place them under their pillows on this night so they will dream about their future husbands, and in Slavic countries, such as Poland, floral wreaths are floated down the river in honor of Christ's Baptism by St. John in the Jordan.

Another interesting fact is that our musical scale (solfège, i.e. "do, re, mi") took its names from the tones of the Vespers Hymn for St. John, *Ut queant laxis*, mentioned above. Use that as trivia sometime and mention the importance of St. John the Baptist, the last and greatest of the prophets.

---

[103] "St. John's Eve & St. John's Day," *Fish Eaters* (n.d.) <https://www.fisheaters.com/customstimeafterpentecost3.html>, accessed November 26, 2024.

The Nativity of St. John the Baptist as a Holy Day of Obligation

On June 24th, six months before the birth of Our Lord, we celebrate the birth of St. John the Baptist to Zechariah and Elizabeth, Mary's cousin. It was St. John the Baptist that prepared the way for Our Lord and bore witness to Him. Today was for some time a Holy Day of Obligation.

Father Weiser writes of the importance of the Feast of St. John's Nativity:

> The Council of Agde, in 506, listed the Nativity of Saint John among the highest feasts of the year, a day on which all faithful had to attend Mass and abstain from servile work... In 1022, a synod at Seligenstadt, Germany, prescribed a fourteen-day fast and abstinence in preparation for the Feast of the Baptist. This, however, was never accepted into universal practice by the Roman authorities.

By the time of the changes to the Holy Days of Obligation in 1642, Pope Urban VIII kept the Nativity of St. John the Baptist as a day of precept. Why the importance? Father Weiser explains:

> The days of all the Apostles were raised to the rank of public holy days in 932. The feasts of Saint Michael, Saint Stephen, Saint John the Baptist, and other saints of the early centuries were celebrated in the past as holy days among all Christian nations.

By the time of Father Weiser's writing in the 1950s, regarding the feasts of saints (i.e., not feasts of Our Lord), only St. Joseph, Ss. Peter and Paul, All Saints, and the Marian feasts of the Assumption and the Immaculate Conception remained as days of precept. And of these, Saint Joseph and Ss. Peter and Paul were exempt from obligation in the United States as they had been previously abrogated in the 1800s.

In Ireland, the Nativity of St. John the Baptist remained as a day of full precept longer than many other holy days. When changes were made to the Irish holy days in 1755 under Pope Benedict XIV and in 1778 under Pope Pius VI, the Nativity of St. John remained as a day of double precept, even when the feasts of the Apostles were reduced to a single precept.[104] It was not abolished as a day of precept until 1831 in Ireland.

Dom Guéranger writes of how special this day used to be for our forefathers in the Faith:

> The Nativity of St John, like that of our Lord, was celebrated by three Masses: the first, in the dead of night, commemorated his title of Precursor; the second, at daybreak, honoured the baptism he conferred; the third, at the hour of Terce, hailed his sanctity. The preparation of the bride, the consecration of the Bridegroom, his own peerless holiness: a threefold triumph, which at once linked the servant to the Master, and deserved the homage of a triple sacrifice to God the Thrice-Holy, manifested to John in the plurality of his Persons, and revealed by him to the Church.
>
> In like manner, as there were formerly two Matins on Christmas night, so, in many places, a double Office was celebrated on the feast of St John, as Durandus of Mende, following Honorius of Autun, informs us. The first Office began at the decline of day, it was without Alleluia, in order to signify the time of the Law and the Prophets which lasted up to St. John. The second Office, begun in the middle of the night, terminated at dawn; this was sung with

---

[104] Matthew Plese, "Feasts of Single vs. Double Precept," *A Catholic Life* (July 15, 2020) <https://acatholiclife.blogspot.com/2020/07/feasts-of-single-vs-double-precept.html>, accessed November 26, 2024.

Alleluia, to denote the opening of the time of grace and of the kingdom of God.

St. John the Baptist's Nativity is a public holiday in Quebec and Puerto Rico as well as in Catalonia (where Barcelona is). Yet, how many of us honor this day in a special way?

The Octave of St. John the Baptist

Further illustrating the great importance of his Nativity, the Church kept it as an Octave up until the changes to Octaves by Pope Pius XII in 1955. This is a Common Octave, meaning that the Mass and Office of St. John the Baptist during the Octave days gives way to any feast day above the level of Simple. In practice, the only intra-octave day where the Mass of St. John would be celebrated, rather than merely commemorated, would be on June 27th. The other intra-octave days would be outranked by the liturgical feasts already on the Calendar of Saints.[105]

We can live out this forgotten Octave by adding to our daily prayers the Collect from the Nativity of the Lord's Precursor:

O God, Who hast made this day worthy of honor by the birth of blessed John: grant to Thy people the grace of spiritual joys, and direct the minds of all the faithful into the way of eternal salvation. Through Our Lord, etc..

The Martyrdom (i.e. Decollation) of St. John the Baptist

Along with his nativity, the Church commemorates on August 29th the martyrdom of St. John the Baptist when he was beheaded for defending the sanctity of God's law. According to Father Pius Parsch's *The Church's Year of Grace*, this day commemorates "the second finding of his most venerable head." As he writes: "In the year 362 pagans desecrated the grave and burned his remains. Only a small portion of his relics were able to be saved by monks and sent to St.

---

[105] Matthew Plese, "Catholic Feast Days," *A Catholic Life* (Sep 7, 2005) <https://acatholiclife.blogspot.com/2005/09/catholic-feast-days.html>, accessed November 26, 2024.

Athanasius at Alexandria. The head of the saint is venerated at various places."

Dom Guéranger describes what may have happened to Herod and the dancing girl in the years following:

> The sacred cycle itself seems to convey to us too a similar lesson; for, during the following days, we shall see its teaching as it were tempered down, by the fewness of the feasts, and the disappearance of great solemnities until November. The school of the holy liturgy aims at adapting the soul, more surely and more fully than could any other school, to the interior teaching of the Spouse. Like John, the Church would be glad to let God alone speak always, if that were possible here below; at least, towards the end of the way, she loves to moderate her voice, and sometimes even to keep silence, in order to give her children an opportunity of showing that they know how to listen inwardly to Him, who is both her and their sole love. Let those who interpret her thought, first understand it well. The friend of the Bridegroom, who, until the nuptial-day, walked before Him, now stands and listens; and the voice of the Bridegroom, which silences his own, fills him with immense joy: 'This my joy therefore is fulfilled,' said the precursor.
>
> Thus the feast of the Decollation of St. John may be considered as one of the landmarks of the liturgical year. With the Greeks it is a holiday of obligation. Its great antiquity in the Latin Church is evidenced by the mention made of it in the martyrology called St. Jerome's, and by the place it occupies in the Gelasian and Gregorian sacramentaries. The precursor's blessed death took place about the

feast of the Pasch; but, that it might be more freely celebrated, this day was chosen, whereon his sacred head was discovered at Emesa.

The vengeance of God fell heavily upon Herod Antipas. Josephus relates how he was overcome by the Arabian Aretas, whose daughter he had repudiated in order to follow his wicked passions; and the Jews attributed the defeat to the murder of St. John. He was deposed by Rome from his tetrarchate, and banished to Lyons in Gaul, where the ambitious Herodias shared his disgrace. As to her dancing daughter Salome, there is a tradition gathered from ancient authors, that, having gone out one winter day to dance upon a frozen river, she fell through into the water; the ice, immediately closing round her neck, cut off her head, which bounded upon the surface, thus continuing for some moments the dance of death.

One interesting point is that some of the Eastern Catholic Rites (e.g. the Melkite Catholic Church) the feast of the Beheading of St. John the Baptist is a day of fast and strict abstinence where neither wine nor oil are allowed.

The Litany of St. John the Baptist

To honor the Lord's Precursor, we can pray the Litany of St. John the Baptist to ask for his powerful intercession with God.[106] This is a private (i.e. not public) litany.[107]

Conclusion

Say a prayer for St. John the Baptist's intercession that he might lead us closer to Jesus Christ, Our Lord, and Master.

---

[106] Ibid., *loc. cit.* <https://acatholiclife.blogspot.com/2006/08/martyrdom-of-john-baptist.html>, accessed November 26, 2024.
[107] Ibid., *loc. cit.* <https://acatholiclife.blogspot.com/2018/01/public-vs-private-litanies.html>.

And like St. John, may we be willing to stand true to Catholic faith and morality even if it means our own martyrdom. For his honor, and the glory of God, let us honor and observe these customs of our forefathers this year.

XX

Saints Peter and Paul

The Ancient, Yet Forgotten Apostles Fast

The observance of a fast leading up to the Feast of Ss. Peter and Paul likely originated in the Early Church. While this fasting period fell out of observance in the Roman Catholic Church, the Eastern Catholic Church still observes this fast to some extent. Fr. R. Janin summarizes the Traditional Byzantine Fast and Abstinence observance for the Apostles Fast:

> This varies from 9 to 42 days depending on the feast of Easter. It begins on the first Monday after Pentecost until the feast of Saints Peter and Paul. This Lent has the same rules as Great Lent but oil and fish are tolerated (in some places) except on Wednesdays and Fridays.[108]

Even in the Eastern Churches, there is a little divergence on the date when the Fast begins. The Coptic and Old Syrian traditions keep the fast on the First Monday after Pentecost (as noted above), yet in the current Byzantine tradition, the fast begins on the Second Monday after Pentecost (i.e., the day following All Saints Sunday in their calendar).

---

[108] "Traditional Byzantine Rite Fast and Abstinence," *Holy Unia* (Aug 15, 2010) <https://holyunia.blogspot.com/2010/08/traditional-byzantine-rite-fast-and.html>, accessed December 11, 2023.

The Vigil of Ss. Peter and Paul

While the Apostles Fast fell out of observance in the West, the Roman Church retained two fasting Vigils around this time: the Vigil of Pentecost and the Vigil of Ss. Peter and Paul. In addition, the Ember Days also remained during the Octave of Pentecost. As a result, only a fragment of the fasting that was originally practiced during the early summer months persisted in the Roman Rite.

The Vigil of Ss. Peter and Paul ceased being a fast day in America by 1842.[109] In Great Britain, Ireland, Australia, and Canada the Vigil of Ss. Peter and Paul remained a day of fasting and abstinence up until the 1917 Code of Canon law. In 1902, the Holy Father granted a special dispensation for Catholics in England from fasting on the Vigil of Ss. Peter and Paul in honor of the coronation of King Edward VII, illustrating historical proof of its observance in the early part of the 20th century.[110]

Per the 1917 Code, fasting and abstinence were not observed should a vigil fall on a Sunday as stated in the code: "If a vigil that is a fast day falls on a Sunday the fast is not to be anticipated on Saturday but is dropped altogether that year." However, beforehand, the fast was transferred to the Saturday previous. As a result, in years when the Vigil of Ss. Peter and Paul (June 28th) falls on a Sunday, we can observe the fast and abstinence on Saturday. Other years, we can observe June 28th as a day of fasting and abstinence to prepare for the Feast in honor of Ss. Peter and Paul.

The wisdom of Dom Guéranger, written in the late 1800s, can apply to us even today:

> Let us, then, recollect ourselves, preparing our hearts in union with holy Church, by faithfully observing this vigil. When the obligation of

---

[109] *The United States Catholic Almanac* (Myers, 1842), 174.
[110] *The Tablet* (Apr 26, 1902).

thus keeping up certain days of preparation previous to the festivals is strictly maintained by a people, it is a sign that Faith is still living amongst them; it proves that they understand the greatness of that which the holy liturgy proposes to their homage. Christians in the West, we who make the glory of Saints Peter and Paul our boast, let us remember the Lent in honor of the Apostles begun by Greek schismatics on the close of the Paschal solemnities, and continued up to this day. The contrast between them and ourselves will be of a nature to stir softness and ingratitude hold too large a share. If certain concessions have, for grave reasons, been reluctantly made by the Church, so that the fast of this vigil is no longer observed, let us see therein a double motive for holding fast to her precious Tradition. Let us make up by fervor, thanksgiving and love, for the severity lacking in our observance, which is yet still maintained by so many Churches notwithstanding their schismatic separation from Rome.

Ss. Peter and Paul Are Always Mentioned Together

Ss. Peter and Paul is an interesting feast day as it honors both St. Peter and St. Paul. Interestingly, in the Church's rubrics, any collect of St. Paul is always followed by one for St. Peter, and vice versa. This custom extends back to the Middle Ages. The rubrics for the Roman Breviary and Mass, published in 1960, state the following as rubric #110:

> The commemoration of St. Paul is always made in the Office and Mass of St. Peter, and vice versa. This commemoration is termed *inseparable* and the two prayers are considered to be united in such a way that, in counting the

number of prayers, they are reckoned only as one.

It should be noted that this rubric is a 1960 innovation as beforehand there was always a separate commemoration made. But the point remains that Ss. Peter and Paul are intricately united in the Church's Liturgy.

The Feast of Ss. Peter and Paul as a Universal Holy Day of Obligation

All of the feasts of the Apostles were Holy Days of Obligation on the Universal Calendar from 932 AD as cited by Father Weiser. However, most localities did not observe all of these feast days as Holy Days. Yet, the Feast of Ss. Peter and Paul was the most commonly observed Holy Day among the feasts of the apostles. The Liturgical celebration of Ss. Peter and Paul dates back to ancient times with this particular feast of the Apostles being a Holy Day of Obligation, according to Father Weiser, since the 5th century. Even after the changes to Holy Days of Obligation in Ireland in the mid-1700s, Ss. Peter and Paul remained a day of double precept.

At the time of America's formation, the holy days of obligation, in addition to every Sunday, were as follows for the new country: the feasts of Christmas, Circumcision, Epiphany, Annunciation, Easter Monday, Ascension, Whitsun Monday, Corpus Christi, Ss. Peter and Paul, Assumption, and All Saints. But even though these were the "official" holy days, practices varied across the dioceses in the United States as there was no uniformity until 1885.

In 1722, Bishop Giffard, the Vicar Apostolic of London, approved a dispensation "on behalf of the mission of Maryland for the ease and quiet of poor Catholics of that Mission" to sanction a dispensation of holy days. He granted the Maryland Superior the faculties to dispense Catholics from holy days and fasting obligations. As *American Catholic Quarterly Review* notes,

> Bishop Giffard permitted the Jesuits to dispense Catholics in Maryland, Virginia and Pennsylvania from the obligations of all holy days for just cause, e.g. getting in crops at harvest, between May 1 and September 30, respect for the feasts of Ascension, Easter Monday, Corpus Christi, and Assumption.[111]

On March 9, 1777, Pope Pius VI "dispensed all Catholics in the kingdom of Great Britain from the precept of hearing Mass and abstaining from servile works on all holydays except the Sundays of the year, the feasts of Christmas, Circumcision, Epiphany, Annunciation, Easter Monday, Ascension, Whitsun Monday, Corpus Christi, St Peter and St Paul, Assumption, and All Saints." As the *Catholic Directory* of 1861 further states:

> The Vigils of the Feasts thus abrogated his Holiness transferred to the Wednesdays and Fridays of Advent, on which he ordered that fast should be kept as in Lent or Embertide, 'although it is an English custom to keep fasts and vigils on Friday.' The pope adds a power to the Vicars Apostolic to dispense from the precept of abstaining from servile works on SS. Peter and Paul falling in the hay-harvest, and the Assumption in the wheat-harvest, provided Mass has been previously heard, if possible.[112]

And Ss. Peter and Paul seemed to have been dispensed for those Catholics in the Archdiocese of Baltimore, America's first Archdiocese. An 1818 Ordo for the Metropolitan Archdiocese of Baltimore does not list Ss. Peter and Paul as a required day of precept.

---

[111] *The American Catholic Quarterly Review* (Hardy and Mahony, 1886), 469.
[112] *The Catholic Directory* (Burns & Lambert, 1861), 21.

Before 1885, holy days varied within various jurisdictions in the United States. Those formerly French colonies (which followed the Holy Days as set by Quebec) differed from the English. This disunity continued for the young United States since new territories (e.g., Florida, Texas, and Oregon) did not follow the same holy days of obligation and the same fasting days.

Even after the significant changes made by Pope St. Pius X to the list of Holy Days in 1911, Ss. Peter and Paul remained a Holy Day of Obligation in the Universal Church, though it was not reestablished as such in the United States: "Where, however, any of the above feasts has been abolished or transferred, the new legislation is not effective. In the United States consequently the Epiphany and the feast of Saints Peter and Paul are not days of precept" (*Catholic Encyclopedia*).

European Customs in Honor of Ss. Peter and Paul

Father Weiser relates some of the following customs associated with June 29th:

> In Hungary, grains are blessed by the priest after Mass on Peter and Paul's Day. People weave crowns, crosses, and other religious symbols from straw, have them blessed, and carry them on wooden poles in procession around the church. Afterward they take them home and keep them suspended from the ceiling over the dinner table. Bread is also blessed in a special ceremony on this day in Hungary.
>
> A moving custom is practiced in rural sections of the Alpine countries. On June 29, when the church bells ring the "Angelus" early in the morning, people step under the trees in their gardens, kneel down and say the traditional prayer the "Angel of the Lord." Having finished the prayer they bow deeply and make

the sign of the cross, believing that on Saint Peter's Day the blessing of the Holy Father in Rome is carried by angels throughout the world to all who sincerely await it.

Sadly, as with most customs associated with the liturgical era, these faded into history when devotion faded from modern man's life.

Priests Obliged to Solemnize the Feast on the Following Sunday

In 1840, Pope Gregory XVI dispensed the remaining dioceses then in the United States from keeping Ss. Peter and Paul as a Holy Day of Obligation. Permission however was granted to the United States on December 19, 1840, to solemnize the Feast of Ss. Peter and Paul the Sunday following June 29th. Such permission had been given for this Feast day in addition to Epiphany, Corpus Christi, and the patrons of the place to the French by Pope Pius VI on April 9, 1802.

In fact, it was a requirement for priests in the United States to continue to solemnize the feast on the following Sunday – a requirement that continued even through the 1962 Missal. *Matters Liturgical* from 1959 notes:

> The external solemnity of the feast of Corpus Christi must be transferred in the United States and celebrated on the Sunday following; this is also prescribed for the feast of SS. Peter & Paul (June 29), when this feast falls on a week day (Indult of Nov. 25, 1885). Hence, where on Sundays the principal Mass is usually a sung Mass, on the Sundays following these feasts this sung Mass in churches and public oratories must, and in semi-public oratories may, be of the transferred external solemnity (S.R.C. 2974, IV; 4269, IX). This Mass shall be celebrated as on the feast, with only those occurring Offices to be commemorated as are

noted in n. 209 f, even if the Mass is one of two or more different sung Masses, the rubrics in M.R.: ADD., v, 4 being now abrogated.

Its observance as an external solemnity in other nations (e.g., France) is optional. As such, liturgists who are often quoted like Father J.B. O'Connell do not mention this requirement in his rubrics for Votive Masses as he did not write from an American perspective.

Despite these changes over the centuries, the fact that so many observed Ss. Peter and Paul as a Holy Day for so long underscore our own need to keep this day holy, to attend the External Solemnity of Ss. Peter and Paul and our need to keep the Vigil of Ss. Peter and Paul as a day of fasting and abstinence.

Commemoration of St. Paul

Each year on June 30th, the Church commemorates St. Paul. Why this ancient commemoration the day after he is already celebrated? Father Weiser comments on the history of this liturgical Commemoration, showing that it dates back to ancient times:

> According to ancient tradition these two Apostles were put to death by Emperor Nero (64). Peter died by crucifixion in the public circus or amphitheater at the Vatican hill; Paul was beheaded outside the city. The special celebrations which the Christians in Rome held in honor of the "Princes of the Apostles" are known from earliest times. At the end of the fourth century the faithful thronged the streets on June 29 going in pilgrimage to the Vatican (Saint Peter's) and from there to the Church of Saint Paul's "outside the walls," praying at the shrines and attending the pontifical Mass which the pope celebrated first at Saint Peter's, then at Saint Paul's.

> Since the great distance between the two churches made it quite inconvenient, both for the pope and for the people, to perform the two services on the same morning, the liturgy of the feast was divided in the sixth century, and the Mass in honor of Saint Paul was henceforth celebrated on the following day. This "commemoration of Saint Paul" has remained a liturgical feast on June 30 ever since.

Likewise, New Liturgical Movement expands upon this and mentions several customs present in the Middle Ages for the day after Ss. Peter and Paul:

> The following day, therefore, the whole of the liturgy is dedicated to St Paul, and is not called a day within the octave of the Apostles, but rather "the Commemoration of St Paul." The variable texts of the Mass all refer to him, but a commemoration of St Peter is added to the feast, in accordance with the tradition that the two are never entirely separated in the veneration paid them by the Church. (The same is done on the feast of St Paul's Conversion, and commemorations of him are added to the feasts of St Peter's Chairs and Chains.) The Office is likewise dedicated entirely to him; both the Mass and Office, however, make use of St Paul's own testimony in Galatians 2 to the mission of the two Apostles: "For he who worked in Peter for the apostleship of the circumcision, worked in me also among the gentiles; and they knew the grace of God that was given to me." In the 1130s, a canon of St Peter's Basilica named Benedict writes that it was still the custom in his time for the Pope to keep the feast of St Peter at the Vatican, but then celebrate Vespers at the tomb of St Paul in

the great Basilica on the Ostian Way, "with all the choirs" of the city.[113]

The Octave of Ss. Peter and Paul

The Octave of Ss. Peter and Paul, like so many other Octaves, was another casualty in 1955 that few people spiritually celebrate anymore. This is a Common Octave meaning that the days within (i.e., Days 2-7 which are Semidouble) yield to all Double and Semidouble feasts but have precedence over Simple feasts. The Octave is commemorated daily at Lauds, Mass, and Vespers when a higher feast occurs except if the feast is a Double of the First or Second class in which case the Octave is not commemorated. In practice, as laypeople, we can add to our morning and evening prayers (in either the Divine Office or in personal prayer) the collect from Ss. Peter and Paul which asks:

O God, Who hast consecrated this day to the martyrdom of Thine apostles Peter and Paul, grant to Thy Church in all things to follow their teaching from whom it received the right ordering of religion in the beginning. Through our Lord Jesus Christ, Thy Son, Who liveth and reigneth with Thee in the unity of the Holy Ghost, God, Forever and ever.

In practice, the only intra octave day where the Mass of Ss. Peter and Paul could be celebrated would be July 4th. The other intra octave days would be outranked by the liturgical feasts already on the Universal Calendar of Saints. Yet July 4th is Our Lady of Refuge in the Diocese of San Diego and in some places, such as Los Angeles and Brooklyn, it is the Commemoration of All Holy Popes.

---

[113] Gregory DiPippo, "Liturgical Notes on the Commemoration of St Paul," *New Liturgical Movement* (Jun 30, 2017) <https://www.newliturgicalmovement.org/2017/06/liturgical-notes-on-commemoration-of-st.html>, accessed December 11, 2023.

The Commemoration of All Holy Popes

Listed in the pre-1962 Missal is an often-unknown feast for November 5th – The Sacred Relics. This Mass was a "Mass in Some Places" and was not universally celebrated. It is unfortunate that a quick internet search also reveals that few English websites have any information on this feast at all. In fact, the only substantial reference is to the 1960 Breviarium general norms which state, "124. Likewise, red is used in the office and Mass of feasts: ... d) of the commemoration of all holy popes..."

Why celebrate this feast on July 4th? An Italian source from 1719 describes it as the result of the Octave of Ss. Peter and Paul:

> On Sunday after the Octave of the Holy Apostles Peter and Paul is solemnly celebrated as a double in the Vatican Basilica the Universal commemoration of all of the holy Popes of the Roman Church with its proper office granted by the Sacred Congregation of Rites on March 20, 1683...[114]

For our part, we can pray a litany to all canonized popes on July 4th, offering it up especially for the conversion of our nation.[115]

Conclusion

The Vigil of Ss. Peter and Paul was kept as a fasting day until the time of St. Pius X, and the Vigil of Pentecost was kept as a fasting day until the changes post Vatican II. Like the Ember Days which also fell by the wayside, the end of the fast on the Vigil of the feast removed the last vestiges of "Summer Lent."

---

[114] Translation of *Emerologio Di Roma Cristiana, Ecclesiastica, e Gentile* by Claudio Salvucci via Facebook.
[115] Matthew Plese, *loc. cit.*, <https://acatholiclife.blogspot.com/2012/07/all-holy-popes-mass-in-some-places.html>.

Let us not allow these days to pass without using them to perform penance and make satisfaction for sin.

And as it concerns the feast day itself, let us celebrate it fittingly and pray for union with all separated Christians – especially those in the East with valid Sacraments but who are separated from Catholic unity. May we, one day very soon, be united in the same profession of Faith, with the same Sacraments, and under the same hierarchy.

Ss. Peter and Paul, orate pro nobis!

XXI

St. Anne

What we know about the Blessed Virgin Mary's parents, Saints Joachim and Anne, comes from the *Protoevangelium Jacobi* (The Gospel of James). It is not part of the inerrant Word of God, but the document, which was written c. 170 AD gives insight into the life of Mary and her parents. St. Joachim was a prominent and respected man; however, he had no children, and he viewed this as a punishment from God. The Protoevangelium of St. James describes how St. Anne was even mocked for her barrenness, and how her husband was shamed for not being a father.

In an answer to his prayers, he and St. Anne, his wife, were given the daughter Mary, who was conceived without sin, in her womb. She remained sinless, ever-virgin, and would receive the unparalleled honor of being the Mother of God. Their prayers were answered greater than they could have ever imagined!

St. Anne's Day as a Former Holy Day of Obligation

Father Weiser in *Christian Feasts and Customs* recounts the history of liturgical devotion to St. Anne:

> Since the Fathers of the Church rejected the use of such legendary sources, the faithful in Europe had no feast in honor of our Lord's grand-parents. In the Middle East, however, the veneration of Saint Anne can be traced back to the fourth century.

The Crusaders brought the name and legend of Saint Anne to Europe, and the famous Dominican Jacobus de Voragine (1298) printed the story in his Golden Legend. From that time on the popular veneration of the saint spread into all parts of the Christian world. It was encouraged by the religious orders of the Franciscans, Dominicans, Augustinians, and Carmelites. In southern France a Feast of Saint Anne was celebrated as early as the fourteenth century. Pope Urban VI in 1378 extended it to England at the king's request. Not until 1584, however, did the feast become universal, when Pope Gregory XIII prescribed it for the whole Church.

The feast of St. Anne was made a holy day of obligation under Pope Gregory XV who reigned from 1621 to 1623 as Dom Guéranger relates: "Gregory XV, after having been cured of a serious illness by St. Anne, had ranked her feast among those of precept, with the obligation of resting from servile work." The Feast of St. Anne was listed as a Holy Day in Pope Urban VIII's 1642 *Universa Per Orbem*, and it remained as such in some places like Quebec for some time.

Dom Guéranger also adds that Gregory XIII ordered the celebration of this feast universally "with the rite of a double. Leo XIII in recent times (1879), raised it, together with that of St. Joachim, to the dignity of a solemnity of the second class."

The Patronage of St. Anne

St. Anne has long been depicted in art as part of a tradition of Catholic art that stretches back at least to the Middle Ages. In medieval art, St. Anne is often depicted teaching her little daughter to read. Medieval depictions of Mary's birth often place the scene in a richly decorated chamber, with St Anne and her newborn baby being tended by midwives – images of domestic life, of women's work and care.

Images of Mary's childhood show her as the object of her parents' love, holding her mother's hand, or being taught to read. St Anne was a maternal saint in whom medieval mothers could see themselves reflected and she is accordingly honored as a patron saint for cabinetmakers, carpenters, childless couples, equestrians, grandmothers, grandparents, homemakers, housewives, lace makers, mothers, old-clothes dealers, pregnant women, horse riders, seamstresses, and women in labor, among other causes.

St. Anne is also a patron for women who are seeking a husband, as expressed in the popular old prayer: "Good St. Anne, send me a man!" Why? Father Weiser explains this long standing custom: "According to legend, she was married three times, first to Joachim, after his death to Cleophas, and finally to Salomas. This detail of the ancient story inspired young women to turn for help in finding a husband." For this end, praying a Novena in honor of St. Anne was widely practiced in former times when the Faith was more widely known and loved. Women today who are seeking a spouse should likewise be familiar with calling on Good St. Anne for this intention!

Father Weiser also adds an interesting custom:

> Her patronage of fertility was extended also to the soil. Thus she became a patron of rain. It is a popular saying in Italy that "rain is St. Anne's gift," in Germany, July rain is called "Saint Anne's Dowry."

Thus, for farmers and those experiencing drought, do not hesitate to call on the prayers of St. Anne!

The Popularity of St. Anne's Name for Girls

St. Anne, whose name means "grace" became one of the most popular names for gifts in the 18th century. Hence, customs arose for girls celebrating their name days on St. Anne's Day. Father Weiser again explains:

From the eighteenth century on, Anne, which means "grace," was used more and more as a favorite name for girls. At the beginning of the nineteenth century it was the most popular girls' name in central Europe, surpassing even that of Mary. This preference was based on a famous saying of past centuries, "All Annes are beautiful." Naturally, parents wanted to assure this benefit for their baby daughters by calling them Anne or by adding Anne to a first name. Thus we have the many traditional names containing Anne or Ann (Mary Ann, Marianne, Marian, Ann Marie, Joanne, Elizabeth Ann, Lillian, Martha Ann, Louise Ann, Patricia Ann).

A hundred years ago there still remained the custom in many parts of Europe of celebrating Saint Anne's Day as a festival "of all Annes," meaning all beautiful girls. Dressed in their finery the bevy would parade through the streets with their escorts, bands would serenade them in parks and squares, balls would be held (both Johann Strausses composed "Anne Polkas" for this festival).

Saint Anne's Eve was the day of receptions for debutantes at court and in private homes. Public amusements, including fireworks, entertained the crowds. The warm summer night was alive with laughter, beauty, music, and lights. And all of it was still connected in the hearts and minds of the participants with a tribute to Saint Anne, whose feast day shed its radiance upon this enchanting celebration.

St. Joachim, Father of the Mother of God

In the Protoevangelium of James, St. Joachim is described as a rich and pious man of the house of David who regularly gave to the poor and to the temple. However, as his wife was barren, the high priest rejected Joachim and his sacrifice, as his wife's childlessness was interpreted as a sign of divine displeasure. Joachim consequently withdrew to the desert where he *fasted and did penance for forty days*. Angels then appeared to both Joachim and Anne to promise them a child. Some believe it was the Archangel St. Gabriel who also appear to him.

St. Joachim later returned to Jerusalem and embraced Anne at the city gate. The cycle of legends concerning Joachim and Anne were included in the Golden Legend and remained popular in Christian art until the Council of Trent restricted the depiction of apocryphal events.

No liturgical celebration of Saint Joachim was included in the Tridentine Calendar. It was added to the General Roman Calendar in 1584, for celebration on March 20, the day after the feast day of Saint Joseph. In 1738, it was transferred to the Sunday after the Octave of the Assumption of Mary. As part of his effort to allow the liturgy of Sundays to be celebrated, Pope St. Pius X transferred it to August 16, the day after the Assumption, so that Joachim may be remembered in the celebration of Mary's triumph. It was then celebrated as a Double of the 2nd Class, a rank that was changed in 1960 to that of 2nd Class Feast. Dom Guéranger elaborates on the history of Feast of St. Joachim and how it also came to be highly ranked in the Roman Rite:

> From time immemorial the Greeks have celebrated the feast of St. Joachim on the day following our Lady's birthday. The Maronites kept it on the day after the Presentation in November, and the Armenians on the Tuesday after the Octave of the Assumption of the Mother of God. The Latins at first did not keep

his feast. Later on it was admitted and celebrated sometimes on the day after the Octave of the Nativity, September 16, sometimes on the day following the Conception of the Blessed Virgin, December 9. Thus, both East and West agreed in associating St. Joachim with his illustrious daughter when they wished to do him honor.

About the year 1510, Julius II placed the feast of the grandfather of the Messias upon the Roman Calendar with the rank of double major; and remembering that family, in which the ties of nature and of grace were in such perfect harmony, he fixed the solemnity on March 20, the day after that of his son-in-law, St. Joseph. The life of the glorious patriarch resembled those of the first fathers of the Hebrew people; and it seemed as though he were destined to imitate their wanderings also, by continually changing his place upon the sacred cycle.

Hardly fifty years after the Pontificate of Julius II the critical spirit of the day cast doubts upon the history of St. Joachim, and his name was erased from the Roman breviary. Gregory XV, however, re-established his feast in 1622 as a double, and the Church has since continued to celebrate it. Devotion to our Lady's father continuing to increase very much, the Holy See was petitioned to make his feast a holiday of obligation, as it had already made that of his spouse, St. Anne. In order to satisfy the devotion of the people without increasing the number of days of obligation, Clement XII in 1738 transferred the feast of St. Joachim to the Sunday after the Assumption of his daughter, the Blessed Virgin, and restored to it the rank of double major.

On August 1, 1879, the Sovereign Pontiff, Leo XIII, who received the name of Joachim in baptism, raised both the feast of his glorious patron and that of St. Anne to the rank of doubles of the second class.

Home Customs for St. Anne and Joachim

For those looking to add something special to the table on the feast of either of the grandparents of Our Lord, a great choice would be the Italian dessert known as *Torta della nonna*, which is Italian for "grandmother's cake." It is a classic Tuscan pastry characterized by a short crust pastry base filled with a rich, creamy custard and typically flavored with lemon zest and sometimes vanilla. The top of the tart is usually covered with a layer of pine nuts and dusted with powdered sugar.

Their feast days are also ideal opportunities for us to honor our grandparents with our visits (if they are alive) or our prayers (whether they have passed on to the next world or not). And conversely, if you are a grandparent, these are ideal days to consider what you should do now to help further pass down and transmit the Faith to your grandchildren.

Likewise, the Litany of St. Anne is an ideal prayer to add on her feast day, July 26th.[116]

Pilgrimage Sites in Honor of St. Anne and St. Joachim

Lasty, for those in close proximity to one of the great shrines of St. Anne, it would be an ideal day to make a pilgrimage to one of these shrines. For instance, there is a great shrine to St. Anne in Canada – Ste. Anne de Beaupré. The St. Anne Basilica is more than just one of the four major shrines in Québec and

---

[116] Ibid. *loc. cit.* <https://www.fisheaters.com/feastofstanne-litany.html>, accessed November 26, 2024.

the oldest pilgrimage site in North America. It is a site of constant miracles. Cripples have entered the shrine on crutches and left by walking through the door because they were completely healed. Another shrine is Ste. Anne d'Auray in Britanny, France. There is also a church of St. Anne in Jerusalem, and the church is believed to have been built on the location where Ss. Joachim and Anne lived.

Finally, for those in Rome, about six blocks north of the Castel Sant'Angelo, there is a church built in honor of St. Joachim – San Gioacchino ai Prati Castello. It too would be a worthy destination for those seeking to honor one of the grandparents of the Son of God.

XXII

St. Lawrence

While St. Lawrence is one of the greatest deacons in the Church's history, his feast day has over time fallen into obscurity and most average Catholics are unfamiliar with the customs and practices associated with his feast day. The Feast of St. Lawrence was of such importance it was a Holy Day of Obligation for a long time. It remained a holy day in the modern-day United States until 1777 and in Ireland until 1778. The Vigil preceding the Feast of St. Lawrence was as a day of fasting in times past as well. Rediscovering some of these lost practices and learning the life of St. Lawrence can help us to live out an authentic Catholic life.

The Life of St. Lawrence

St. Lawrence was born in Huesca, Spain in the third century. He was an archdeacon of Rome whose job was to care for the goods of the Church and distribute alms. On August 6, 258, Pope St. Sixtus II and six deacons were martyred. This left St. Lawrence as the highest-ranking Church official in Rome. Just before then, Pope St. Sixtus II foretold St. Lawrence that he would join him in martyrdom for the faith in four days because St. Lawrence wished to die with the Pope.

St. Lawrence said: "Father, where are you going without your son? Where are you hastening, O priest, without your deacon? Never before did you offer the holy Sacrifice without assistants. In what way have I displeased you? In what way have you found me unfaithful in my office? Oh, try me again and prove to yourself whether you have chosen an unworthy minister for the service of the Church. So far you have been trusting me with distributing the Blood of the Lord." To this Pope Sixtus II replied, "I am not forsaking you, my son; a severer trial is awaiting you for your faith in Christ. The Lord is considerate toward me because I am a weak old man. But for you, a most glorious triumph is in store. Cease to weep, for already after three days you will follow me"

St. Lawrence, under the command of the pope, began to give all of the Church's goods to the poor. While he was doing this task, a blind man named Crescentius asked him to heal his blindness by laying hands on him. St. Lawrence made the Sign of the Cross over him, and his vision was restored. Lawrence was soon arrested and in prison still healed many blind men. The guard, named Hippolytus, was so impressed by the Faith that he accepted it and also died as a martyr.

On August 10, 258, Lawrence was told to bring along the treasure entrusted by the pope to his execution. After being given two days' time to collect the goods, St. Lawrence arrived with a multitude of Rome's crippled, blind, and sick. St. Lawrence announced to the judge: "Here are the treasures of the Church!" Before he was arrested, though, he had dispersed the material wealth of the Church including many documents, which saved years of early Church history.

He was tortured, scourged, and scorched with glowing plates. In the midst of it, he prayed: "Lord Jesus Christ, God from God, have mercy on Your servant!" A solider named Romanus exclaimed: "I see before you an incomparably beautiful youth. Hasten and baptize me." Romanus had observed during this torture how an angel dried the wounds of Lawrence with a linen cloth.

As he was taken back to the judge he said, "My God I honor and Him alone I serve. Therefore I do not fear your torments; this night shall become as brightest day and as light without any darkness."

St. Lawrence was grilled to death on August 10, 258. As he died, he prayed for the conversion of Rome so that from it the

Faith of Christ would spread. Following his death, idolatry began to decline throughout Rome. He also said, "Now you may turn me over, my body is roasted enough on this side." Then he said, "At last I am finished; you may now take from me and eat." He turned to God and exclaimed: "I thank You, O Lord, that I am permitted to enter Your portals." His body was buried in the cemetery of Saint Cyriaca on the road to Tivoli. The gridiron that is believed to have been his deathbed is in San Lorenzo in Lucina.

The Connection of St. Lawrence and St. Sixtus' Feast days

St. Lawrence's Feast day appropriately falls on the date of his death and entrance into Heaven – August 10th. Three days beforehand, the Church celebrates the Feast of St. Sixtus II and his companions. Pope Sixtus II was one of the first victims of the persecutions by Emperor Valerian I. Four deacons, Januarius, Vincentius, Magnus, and Stephanus, were apprehended at the same cemetery as Pope Sixtus II. Pope Sixtus II was beheaded in his chair, which was later enshrined behind his tomb. Two other deacons, Felicissimus and Agapitus, were martyred the same day as the other four deacons.

The Vigil of St. Lawrence on August 9th

August 9th is a liturgical oddity in many respects in the 1962 Calendar and Divine Office. Whereas in the pre-1955 Office, August 9th is the Feast day of St. John Vianney with a Commemoration of the Vigil of St. Lawrence and a Commemoration of St. Romanus, in the 1962 Office it is the Vigil of St. Lawrence with a Commemoration of St. Romanus. St. Romanus was a soldier converted to Christ by the preaching of Lawrence, who baptized him while in jail awaiting execution. St. Romanus was beheaded the day before Lawrence was martyred.

While nearly all Vigils were removed between 1954 and 1962 from the Calendar (e.g., Vigil of the Immaculate Conception, Vigils for the Apostles feast days, Vigil of All Saints), the

Vigil of St. Lawrence alone remained. And what is unique is that in the 1962 Office Vespers is of the Vigil of St. Lawrence and not the First Vespers for St. Lawrence. This is a true oddity as New Liturgical Movement discussed in a 2018 article.[117]

Many of our forefathers in the Faith kept August 9th as a day of penance in preparation for St. Lawrence's Feast day. In Texas, New Mexico, Arizona, and California which were included in the ecclesiastical province of Mexico, the feasts and were regulated by the Third Council of Mexico in 1585, and the fast days for Catholics in those initial colonies in the modern day United States consisted of "all days in Lent except Sunday; eves of Christmas, Whit Sunday, St Mathias, St John the Baptist, St Peter and St Paul, St James, St Lawrence, Assumption, St Bartholomew, St Matthew, St Simon and St Jude, All Saints, St Andrew, and St Thomas" (*The American Catholic Quarterly Review*, Volume 11).

In keeping with the ancient custom for this Vigil, let us observe it as a day of fasting and abstinence. In years when the Vigil falls on a Sunday, the fasting and abstinence were anticipated on Saturday prior to the changes under Pope St. Pius X.

The Feast of St. Lawrence as a Holy Day of Obligation

In 1642, His Holiness Pope Urban VIII issued the papal bull *Universa Per Orbem* which altered the required Holy Days of Obligation for the Universal Church to consist of 35 such days as well as the principal patrons of one's locality. St. Lawrence was on that list for the Universal Church.

The Diocesan Synod held in 1688 by Bishop Palacios of Santiago de Cuba fixed as holy days for that diocese, which

---

[117] Gregory DiPippo, "Liturgical Notes on the Vigil of St Lawrence," *New Liturgical Movement* (Jul 15, 2020) <https://www.newliturgicalmovement.org/2018/08/liturgical-notes-on-vigil-of-st-lawrence.html>, accessed December 11, 2023.

included modern day Florida, a number of days including the Feast of St. Lawrence. And the same was true for colonies in other parts of the New World. Quoting from the archives of the Archdiocese of Quebec, the *American Catholic Quarterly Review* lists the Holy Days in place there as of 1694:

> The holy days of obligation as recognized officially in 1694 were Christmas, St Stephen, St John, the Evangelist, Circumcision, Epiphany, Candlemas, St Matthew, St Joseph 'patron of the country,' Annunciation, St Philip and St James, St John the Baptist, St Peter and St Paul, St James, St Anne, St Lawrence, Assumption, St Bartholomew, St Louis 'titular of the Cathedral of Quebec,' Nativity of the Blessed Virgin, St Matthew, St Michael, St Simon and St Jude, All Saints, St Andrew, St Francis Xavier, the Conception of the Blessed Virgin 'titular the Cathedral,' St Thomas, Easter Monday and Tuesday, Ascension, Whitsun Monday and Tuesday, Corpus Christi, and the patronal feast of each parish.

These holy days were likewise in force in many current American states under Quebec's jurisdiction as the journal elaborates:

> These were the holy days observed in the French settlements in Michigan, Wisconsin, Indiana, and Illinois, as well as in Louisiana, Mobile, and the country west of the Mississippi till that district passing under the Spanish rule was reclaimed about 1776 as part of the diocese of Santiago de Cuba. East of the Mississippi they continued to be in force certainly till the Holy See detached those parts of its territory from the diocese of Quebec and annexed them to the newly erected diocese of Baltimore.

Before 1777, British Catholics in the colonies and in Great Britain itself kept St. Lawrence as a Holy Day as well. It was not until March 9, 1777, that Pope Pius VI "dispensed all Catholics in the kingdom of Great Britain from the precept of hearing Mass and abstaining from servile works on all holy days except the Sundays of the year, the feasts of Christmas, Circumcision, Epiphany, Annunciation, Easter Monday, Ascension, Whitsun Monday, Corpus Christi, St Peter and St Paul, Assumption, and All Saints." At that time, the precept of hearing Mass on the Feast of St. Lawrence ceased.

While modern Catholics will have no memory of St. Lawrence's Day as a Holy Day of Obligation, only a few centuries ago our ancestors kept his feast as a day of obligatory Mass attendance. And in Ireland, it also remained as such a day until 1778. By the time of St. Pius X and the 1917 Code, it – along with many other days – was universally abolished as Holy Day of Obligation.

Octave of St. Lawrence

It should also be recalled that the Feast of St. Lawrence had an Octave associated with it that stretched back to around the 7th century. By the mid-1950s before it was abolished, it was commemorated on August 17th in the Mass of St. Hyacinth. New Liturgical Movement writes:

> Like all of the most important feasts, that of St. Lawrence was traditionally celebrated with an octave; the octave day has a proper Mass, like the octave of Ss. Peter and Paul, sharing only the Epistle and Gospel with the feast day. The introit of this Mass is taken from Psalm 16, which is also said at Matins of St. Lawrence: 'Thou hast proved my heart, and visited it by night, thou hast tried me by fire: and iniquity hath not been found in me.' The words 'visited (my heart) by night' refer to the Emperor's threat to torture Lawrence for the length of the

night, to which the great Levite answered, 'My night hath no darkness, but in it, all things shine brightly in the light.'[118]

Sundays Named in Terms of Time After St. Lawrence

In one interesting fact, the Feast of St. Lawrence was of such importance that in some old liturgical books Sundays were named as "after St. Lawrence" as we would refer to a numbered Sunday "after Pentecost" as Fr. Weiser relates:

> In the calendar of the Western Church each Sunday has its own Mass formula. The oldest Masses are those of the Easter season, from the first Sunday of Lent to Pentecost. They are found in Sacramentaries (liturgical books) of the seventh century, and probably are of earlier origin. In subsequent centuries were added the Mass texts for the Sundays after Epiphany and the Sundays of Advent and pre-Lent. The twenty-four Sundays after Pentecost were first introduced in smaller groups (four after Pentecost, five after Peter and Paul, five after Lawrence, and six after Michael).

Conclusion

Besides fasting and abstaining on August 9th, and hearing Holy Mass on August 10th, we should reflect on our own charity for the poor at this time. St. Lawrence gave his life for Christ, preached, brought about conversions, and cared for the spiritual and physical demands of the poor. We should pray often for the poor when we see them. And at the same time, we should find concrete ways the help alleviate their physical suffering. Since giving outright money to the homeless is not

---

[118] Gregory DiPippo, "The Feasts of Saint Lawrence," *New Liturgical Movement* (Aug 10, 2011)
<https://www.newliturgicalmovement.org/2011/08/feasts-of-saint-lawrence.html>, accessed December 11, 2023.

always the best answer, finding Catholic homeless shelters, soup kitchens, and outreach programs grounded in authentic Catholicism is the best we can be help them. See how you can impact both the physical and spiritual lives of the poor in your own area in honor of St. Lawrence who remarked, in reference to the sick and poor, before his death: "Here are the treasures of the Church!"

St. Lawrence, ora pro nobis!

XXIII

Assumptiontide

> You have crowned the year with your bounty, and your paths overflow with a rich harvest; The untilled meadows overflow with it, and rejoicing clothes the hills. The fields are garmented with flocks and the valleys blanketed with grain. They shout and sing for joy.
> –Blessing of Herbs on Assumption Day

Fasting on the Vigil of the Assumption

It is only fitting that before any feast, there be a fast. We see this most clearly manifested at Easter with the conclusion of Great Lent, the forty days fast. Other traditional periods of fasting throughout the Church's history included the Advent Fast, the Apostles Fast in June, the Assumption Fast in August, and other devotional fasts like St. Michael's Lent—championed by the Franciscans—for forty days leading up to Michaelmas.

As fasting has consistently waned throughout the centuries, even in the decades before Vatican II, only a small remnant of those days remained in practice by the time the Code of Canon Law was codified in 1917. In general, fasting was required on Ember Days, Vigils, and Lent. The number of Vigils changed over time and many localities observed their own fasting rules as dispensations and indults varied considerably not only over time but from region to region.

Yet, despite this, the Vigil of the Assumption was observed as a fasting day for centuries. For American Catholics in particular, the 1909 *Catholic Encyclopedia* mentions: "In the United States only four of these vigils are fast days: the vigils of Christmas, Pentecost, the Assumption, and All Saints."

On July 25, 1957, Pope Pius XII commuted the fast in the Universal Church from the Vigil of the Assumption to the Vigil of the Immaculate Conception on December 7, even though he had a few years prior abrogated the Mass for the Vigil of the Immaculate Conception. Despite this recent change, its observance as a fast day is ancient, which the *Catholic Encyclopedia* affirms: "Pope Nicholas I (d. 867), in his answer to the Bulgarians, speaks of the fast on the eves of Christmas and of the Assumption ... The Synod of Seligenstadt in 1022 AD mentions vigils on the eves of Christmas, Epiphany, the feast of the Apostles, the Assumption of Mary, St. Laurence, and All Saints, besides the fast of two weeks before the Nativity of St. John."

The Vigil of the Assumption can, of course, still be observed as a fast day by the faithful even if it has not been listed as obligatory since 1957. To have a greater appreciation for Our Lady's Assumption, it is fitting that we should fast and abstain in her honor.

The Blessing of Herbs

God, who on this day raised up to highest heaven the rod of Jesse, the Mother of your Son, our Lord Jesus Christ, that by her prayers and patronage you might communicate to our mortal nature the fruit of her womb, your very Son; we humbly implore you to help us use these fruits of the soil for our temporal and everlasting welfare, aided by the power of your Son and the prayers of his glorious Mother; through Christ our Lord.[119]

---

[119] Taken from Philip T. Weller, S.T.D. *The Roman Ritual* (The Bruce Publishing Company, Milwaukee, WI, 1964).

Illustrating the great harmony in Catholic life between seasonal customs and the liturgical year, the Church instituted at this time of year the blessing of Herbs in connection with Our Lady's glorious Assumption into Heaven. This blessing found in the *Rituale Romanum* was only to be offered on this particular day and was observed for centuries before the dogma of the Assumption was infallibly defined by Pope Pius XII in 1950. Gregory DiPippo in a 2015 article at *New Liturgical Movement* wrote:

> The blessing originated in Germany and is first attested in the 10th century; one version of it or another is found in a great many of the liturgical books which contain blessings of this sort. In the 1614 Roman Ritual of Pope Paul V, it consists of a psalm, a series of versicles and responses, three prayers, and the blessing, after which the flowers are sprinkled with holy water; the blessing is supposed to be done before the principal Mass of the day.[120]

Why the blessing of Herbs? It is connected with an ancient tradition that states that after Our Lady's Assumption into Heaven, beautiful and sweet-smelling flowers began to grow out of the stone sarcophagus, confirming to the Apostles that she had truly been assumed by her divine son. Regardless of whether this manifestation of flowers actually occurred, our custom for keeping Assumption Day as a day for blessing herbs helps unite us to the Apostles and centuries of Catholics who knew of and believed in her triumph over death. Like Our Lady, we too look forward to our eventual Resurrection, confident in the mercy of God if we preserve in the state of sanctifying grace until death.

---

[120] Gregory DiPippo, "The Blessing of Herbs on the Feast of the Assumption," *New Liturgical Movement* (Aug 15, 2015) <https://www.newliturgicalmovement.org/2015/08/the-blessing-of-herbs-on-feast-of.html>, accessed December 11, 2023.

Herbs also show a connection with the life of the average agrarian Catholic who would at this time be observing the fall harvest. Father Weiser notes this connection especially led Hungary and Poland to observe Assumption Day as a celebration of God's blessings upon the harvest:

> In the Christian era the custom of celebrating a thanksgiving harvest festival began in the High Middle Ages. For lack of any definite liturgical day or ceremony prescribed by the Church, various practices came to be observed locally. In many places, as in Hungary, the Feast of the Assumption included great thanksgiving solemnities for the grain harvest. Delegates from all parts of the country came for the solemn procession to Budapest, carrying the best samples of their produce. A similar ceremony was observed in Poland, where harvest wreaths brought to Warsaw from all sections were bestowed on the president in a colorful pageant. These wreaths (*wieniec*), made up of the straw of the last sheaf (*broda*), were beautifully decorated with flowers, apples, nuts, and ribbons, and blessed in churches by the priests.

The blessing of herbs is preserved in the 1962 and 1964 *Rituale Romanum* (which are nearly identical aside from some alterations to the Rite of Marriage). A PDF of the 1962 *Rituale* may be found online and the blessing of herbs may be said by any priest. Ask your priest in advance to publicly bless herbs on Assumption Day and invite the faithful to bring their own herbs from home for this unique tradition.

Forty Hours Devotion

The Blessing of Herbs is not the only custom associated with Assumption Day. The Forty Hours Devotion—which we often associate with the days leading up to Ash Wednesday—

were previously kept especially around Easter, Pentecost, Christmas Day, and Assumption Day. On this, Father Weiser notes the following:

> Usually, the origin of the Forty Hours' Devotion is ascribed to the city of Milan, where, in 1527, in a time of war and calamities, the faithful were invited to visit the exposed Blessed Sacrament four times a year and to pray to the Eucharistic Lord, imploring His mercy and help. The dates for this devotion, which was called *Forty Hours' Prayer*, were Easter, Pentecost, Feast of the Assumption, and Christmas.

Priests, help us rediscover the customs in honor of Our Blessed Lady's Assumption. Bless herbs for us. Offer the Forty Hours Devotion. Preach a sermon after First Vespers on August 14th in honor of her Assumption highlighting that her physical Assumption into Heaven was believed for centuries before the dogmatic proclamation in 1950. Encourage everyone to fast and abstain on August 14.[121]

Together may we restore the Church's venerable customs and traditions brick by brick and in so doing give greater honor to God.

---

[121] In years when August 14th falls on a Sunday, the fasting can be observed on the Saturday beforehand (i.e. August 13th). This is in keeping with the practice that was observed right up until the codification of the 1917 Code of Canon Law.

XXIV

Marymas

> Thy birth, O Virgin Mother of God, proclaimed joy to the whole world; for from Thee arose the sun of righteousness, Christ our God; who released us from the curse, and gave us blessing; and confounding death, He granted us eternal life.
>
> –Greek antiphon chanted at the Magnificat for Vespers II September 8th

The Liturgical Feast of Our Lady's Nativity

We know little about Mary's birth and youth with most of our information coming from the apocryphal Gospel of the Nativity of Mary (translated from the Hebrew by St. Jerome, A.D. 340-420), the Protevangelium of St. James (dated to ca. A.D. 125), and the visions of various mystics through the years.

This feast, like that of the Assumption of Mary, originated in Jerusalem. It began in the fifth century as the feast of the *Basilica Sanctae Mariae ubi nata est*, now called the Basilica of Saint Anne. In the seventh century, the feast was celebrated by the Greeks and at Rome as the feast of the Birth of the Blessed Virgin Mary. In the East, Mary's birthday is celebrated as one of the twelve great liturgies. The title for the liturgy in the East: "The Birth of Our Exalted Queen, the Birthgiver of God and Ever-Virgin Mary." The feast is also celebrated by Syrian Christians on September 8th and by Coptic and Ethiopian Orthodox Christians on May 9th.

In the Roman Rite, the Feast of the Nativity of the Blessed Virgin Mary was granted an Octave by Pope Innocent IV in 1243. In 1913, with the *Divino Aflatu* reforms of the Breviary under Pope St. Pius X, the Octave was downgraded to a simple octave and the Octave Day itself, September 15th, was replaced by the Feast of Our Lady of Sorrows. The presence of the Octave though illustrates just how important this day was in the life of Catholics for centuries.

Our Lady's Nativity as A Former Holy Day of Obligation

The papal bull *Altitudo Divini Concilii* of Pope Paul III in 1537 reduced the days of penance and those of hearing Mass for Native Americans out of pastoral concern due to the physically demanding lifestyle that they lived and also largely due to the fact that they fasted so much already. As a result, the natives were required to only hear Mass on a much smaller number of days: Sundays, Christmas, Circumcision, Epiphany, Candlemas, Annunciation, Sts Peter and Paul, Ascension, Corpus Christi, the Assumption, and the Nativity of the Blessed Virgin.

When the number of days of precept were reduced by Pope Urban VIII in 1642 to only 35 Holy Days of Obligation, including the principal patrons of one's locality, this feast day remained as such. It remained as a Holy Day of Obligation in certain areas longer than in others. In Ireland, it remained as a Holy Day of Obligation until 1778 when Pope Pius VI abolished it as a day of precept.

Likewise, it remained as a Holy Day in parts of the New World for some time. The Diocesan Synod of Santiago de Cuba in 1688, which included present-day Florida and Louisiana, listed it as a Holy Day as did the Diocese of Quebec which had affirmed it as a day of precept in 1687. Catholics in the British Colonies kept Our Lady's Nativity as a Holy Day of Obligation until Pope Pius VI dispensed a number of days for them, including this feast day, in March 1777. Most Catholics are unfamiliar with these changes but by keeping sacred the days that our forefathers honored and cherished, we better live out the same Faith they knew and loved.

The End of Summer

For Catholics in the era of western Christendom (1000-1400), the birthday of our Blessed Mother marked an unofficial end of summer and the beginning of harvest season. While this has been lost through the passage of time, we can honor her birthday by reliving some of these seasonal customs. Father Francis Weiser writes:

> Since September 8th marks the end of summer and beginning of fall, this day has many thanksgiving celebrations and customs attached to it. In the Old Roman Ritual there is a blessing of the summer harvest and fall planting seeds for this day. The winegrowers in France called this feast "Our Lady of the Grape Harvest." The best grapes are brought to the local church to be blessed and then some bunches are attached to the hands of the statue of Mary. A festive meal which includes the new grapes is part of this day. In the Alps section of Austria this day is "Drive-Down Day" during which the cattle and sheep are led from their summer pastures in the slopes and brought to their winter quarters in the valleys. This was usually a large caravan, with all the finery, decorations, and festivity. In some parts of Austria, milk from this day and all the leftover food are given to the poor in honor of Our Lady's Nativity.

Family Customs

Today, parents can easily relive this tradition by having grapes on the table and at the meal. Recall as a family the Providence of God who year by year sends us the rains, protects our farmers, and provides us with the fruits of the earth.

Likewise, it is highly encouraged to have a birthday cake in honor of our Blessed Mother! Have the children light candles, sing her happy birthday, and recite the Rosary or at least a few chanted *Ave Marias* in her honor. Take this opportunity to teach children this prayer in Latin. To this end, the prayer cards put out by PrayLatin.com would be a great aid for anyone seeking to learn and practice prayers in the language of Roman Rite Catholics.

Today would also be an ideal day to learn about the story of the Miraculous Image of Maria Santissima Bambina and to make a donation to a worthwhile Catholic cause, in keeping with the Austrian custom of donating to the poor on this day in Our Lady's honor.

Suggestions for Priests & Blessing of Grapes

Priests, encourage the faithful to keep holy and honored the Nativity of our Blessed Mother. Help the faithful recover the spirit of devotion to our Blessed Mother on this day. And help us to better live out the liturgical year's forgotten seasonal customs. To this end, offer to bless for the faithful on her Nativity any grapes using the 1962 Roman Ritual's Blessing of Grapes which, in English, is as follows:

P: Our help is in the name of the Lord.
All: Who made heaven and earth.

P: The Lord be with you.
All: And with your spirit.

Let us pray.
Lord, bless this new fruit of the vineyard, which in your benevolence you have ripened by heavenly dew, an abundance of rainfall, gentle breezes, and fair weather; and have given us to use with gratitude in the name of our Lord Jesus Christ, who lives and reigns with you, in the unity of the Holy Spirit, God, forever and ever, Amen.

They are sprinkled with holy water.

XXV

Roodmas

> But it is fitting that we should glory in the cross of our Lord Jesus Christ, in whom is salvation, life, and resurrection for us, by whom we are saved and delivered. May God have mercy on us and bless us; may He let His face shine upon us; and may He have mercy upon us.
>
> Introt of the Feast of the Exaltation of the Holy Cross

Two Feast Days in Honor of the True Cross

Each year the Church celebrates the Feast of the Exaltation of the Holy Cross on September 14th. Originally, this feast day commemorated the day after the consecration of the church on September 13, 335, which was built by Macarius and St. Helena when the good bishop was prevailed upon to elevate the True Cross publicly for the faithful to venerate. It also now commemorates the recovery of the True Cross from King Chosroes of Persia by Emperor Heraclius in 629 AD. As Heraclius attempted to carry the True Cross along the Via Dolorosa to Calvary back to Calvary, a seemingly invisible force prevented him from advancing any further. Commenting on this miracle, Bishop Zachary of Jerusalem, pointed to his luxurious clothing and declared, "Attired in these rich robes, you are far from imitating the poverty of Jesus Christ and His humility in bearing His Cross." The Emperor cast aside his royal garments and, clad only in a simple cloak, he ascended Mount Calvary barefooted until he ultimately brought the True Cross to the Basilica on Calvary. Providentially, the Exaltation of the Holy Cross also occurs 40 days after our Lord's Transfiguration, a connection which the abbot Father Peter Funk reflected upon a few years ago.[122]

Traditionally, up until the mid-1950s, there was a second day each year on May 3rd to celebrate the Cross – this feast day was the Finding of the True Cross, also called by some as the "Invention of the Holy Cross." The second nocturn of Matins for May 3rd in the pre-1955 Roman Breviary recounts how St. Helena used a sick person to discern which of several crosses found buried in the earth was indeed the True Cross of Our Lord. The sick man was healed instantly upon touching the True Cross. In fact, the Feast of the Finding of the Holy Cross was listed in 1642 by Pope Urban VIII in *Universa Per Orbem* as a Holy Day of Obligation for the Universal Church, though it was not kept as such in all localities.

Despite the liturgical changes of the 1950s and 1960s that saw this feast day dropped even in the 1962 Missal, the Latin Rite Catholics in the Church of the Holy Sepulcher in Jerusalem still observe this feast. Priests who offer the 1962 Missal may also choose to say the Votive Mass for the Finding of the True Cross on May 3rd.

The Use of the Sign of the Cross in Catholic Life

> Let the sign of the cross be continually made on the heart, on the mouth, on the forehead, at table, at the bath, in bed, coming in and going out, in joy and sadness, sitting, standing, speaking, walking. In short, in all our actions. Let us make it on our breasts and all our members, that we may be entirely covered with this invincible armor of Christians.
>
> –St. Gaudentius

---

[122] Matthew Plese, *loc. cit.*, <https://acatholiclife.blogspot.com/2016/08/the-transfiguration-to-holy-cross.html>.

The uses of this sacred sign in the life of a Catholic are practically without limit, and this feast is an ideal day to reflect on how often we think about and make the sign of our salvation. We should also reflect on whether our homes have enough crucifixes – ideally every bedroom should have one.[123] In some European traditions, the focal point of the kitchen is also a crucifix which is mounted in the corner of the room. And throughout some Catholic countries in Europe (e.g., the Bavarian countryside in southern Germany) wayside shrines still exist with crucifixes or religious art, giving the passerby a moment to stop and pay respects to Almighty God.

The following excerpt concerning the use of the Sign of the Cross is taken from an article published in 1950 by Didde Printing Company and written by Father Arthur Tonne which was re-published in *Sacred Music*, Volume 117, Number 4, Winter 1990:

> According to many, our Lord and the Apostles used it. Many affirm that our Lord blessed the Apostles with the Sign of the Cross on the day of His Ascension. Certainly, the early Christians used it constantly.
>
> It is used in all the public worship of our Church:
>
> The sign of the cross in some form or other is made about 54 times during Holy Mass.
>
> It is used frequently in the Divine Office or daily prayer of the priest.
>
> It is used in all blessings bestowed by bishop and priest.

---

[123] Ensure that a priest has properly blessed your crucifixes using the Rituale Romanum and not simply ad hoc prayers of blessing. There is a specifically beautiful prayer by which a crucifix is blessed.

> It is used in all the sacraments: 14 times in Baptism; 17 times in Extreme Unction. Yes, even in the semi-darkness of the confessional the priest makes the sign of the cross over you.
>
> It is used in everything blessed for the service of God: altars, linens, holy water, etc.
>
> It is used frequently in personal devotions: in the morning and evening to seek God's help; before and after prayer, against distractions; before and after meals, asking God's blessing; in dangers of soul, like temptation and occasions of sin; in dangers of body like storms, sickness, travel; before our chief actions and undertakings, to make them pleasing to God and to obtain God's help in performing them properly.

Father Tonne continues:

> An indulgence of 100 days is granted for making the sign of the cross and saying the words. An indulgence of 300 days for making the sign of the cross, with holy water. A love and devotion toward this sacred sign is the mark of a true follower of Christ... Use it frequently, use it thoughtfully, use it lovingly. It will bring you countless blessings.

The Holy Cross Weather Blessing

From May 3rd, the Feast of the Finding of the Cross, until September 14th, the Feast of the Exaltation of the Holy Cross, a special blessing beseeching God's protection against violent and damaging storms may be given with a relic of the True Cross of Our Lord Jesus Christ. As the month of September is often prone to hurricanes and violent storms, it would be most expedient for priests to take time on September 14th to bless the Faithful with the relic of the True Cross. Many parishes have such a relic and, for those who do, publicizing this practice in the weeks leading up to this day would be worthwhile. The following prayers are offered during the Holy Cross Weather blessing:

In Latin:

V. A fúlgure, grádine et tempestáte.
R. Líbera nos, Dómine Jesu Christe.

V. Osténde nobis, Dómine, misericórdiam tuam.
R. Et salutáre tuum da nobis.

V. Dómine exáudi oratiónem meam.
R. Et clamor meus ad te véniat.

V. Dóminus vobíscum.
R. Et cum spíritu tuo.

Orémus. Quaesumus, omnípotens Deus, ut, intercessióne Sanctae Dei Genetrícis Maríae, sanctórum Angelórum, Patriarchárum, Prophetárum, Apostolórum, Mártyrum, Confessórum, Vírginum, Viduárum, et ómnium Sanctórum tuórum, contínuum nobis praestes subsídium, tranquíllam auram permíttas, atque contra fúlgura et tempestátes désuper nobis indígnis tuam salútem effúndas de caelis, et géneri húmano semper aemulas, déxtera poténtiae tuae, aéreas cónteras potestátes. Per eúndem Christum Dóminum nostrum.
R. Amen.

V. Sit nomen Dómini benedíctum.
R. Ex hoc nunc et usque in saeculum.

V. Adjutórium nostrum in nómine Dómini.
R. Qui fecit caelum et terram.

Benedíctio Dei omnipoténtis, Patris + et Fílii, et Spíritus Sancti, descéndat super vos, locum istum et fructus terrae et máneat semper.
R. Amen.

English Translation:

V. From lightning strikes, hail, and violent storms.
R. Deliver us, O Lord Jesus Christ.

V. Show us, O Lord, Thy mercy.
R. And grant us Thy salvation.

V. O Lord, hear my prayer.
R. And let my cry come unto Thee.

V. The Lord be with you.
R. And with thy spirit.

Let us pray. We beseech Thee, O Almighty God, through the intercession of Holy Mary, the Mother of God, of the holy angels, patriarchs, prophets, apostles, martyrs, confessors, virgins, widows, and of all Thy saints, that Thou show us Thy continuing protection, permit tranquil winds, and also pour out to us, Thy unworthy servants, Thy safety from heaven above against lightning strikes and violent storms, and that Thou remain always protective of the human race and crush down the aerial powers by the right hand of Thy power. Through the same Christ our Lord.
R. Amen

V. Blessed be the Name of the Lord.
R. Now and forever.

V. Our help is in the Name of the Lord.

R. Who made heaven and earth.

May the blessing of Almighty God, the Father, + the Son, and the Holy Ghost, descend upon you, this place, and the fruits of the earth and remain forever.
R. Amen.

Chaplet of the Five Wounds

Another custom to begin observing on September 14th is the recitation of the Chaplet of the Five Wounds. Included in the *Raccolta* is this Chaplet. Praying these prayers in front of the family crucifix especially for this feast in honor of the Lord's triumph on the Cross would be a most praiseworthy endeavor.[124]

Autumnal Ember Days

As an additional reminder, the Feast of the Exaltation of the Cross "announces" the coming Ember Days. As stated in the 1962 Angelus Press Daily Missal:

> At the beginning of the four seasons of the Ecclesiastical Year, the Ember Days have been instituted by the Church to thank God for blessings obtained during the past year and to implore further graces for the new season. Their importance in the Church was formerly very great. They are fixed on the Wednesday, Friday, and Saturday: after the First Sunday of Lent for spring, after Pentecost Sunday for summer, after the Feast of the Exaltation of the Cross (14th September) for autumn, and after the Third Sunday of Advent for winter. They are intended, too, to consecrate to God the various seasons in nature, and to prepare by penance those who are about to be ordained. Ordinations generally take place on the Ember Days. The faithful ought to pray on these days for good priests. The Ember Days were until c. 1960 fast days of obligation.

May our fasting and abstinence on the Wednesday, Friday, and Saturday after September 14th be for the honor and glory of God and the good of souls.

Priests, encourage the faithful to keep holy the feast of the Exaltation of the Holy Cross. Encourage us to keep the Ember Days. Remind the faithful of the historical reasons for this

---

[124] Ibid., <https://acatholiclife.blogspot.com/2014/09/indulgences-for-feast-of-exaltation-of.html>.

feast, the power of the Sign of the Cross, and the opportunities when we should make the Sign of the Cross in our daily lives. Offer the Holy Cross Weather blessing and show us the power of the True Cross of Our Lord Jesus Christ, who truly lives and reigns now in Heaven *per omnia saecula saeculurm.*

XXVI

Michaelmas

Angels are pure, created spirits. The name angel means servant or messenger of God. They are celestial or heavenly beings, on a higher order than human beings. An angel has no body and does not depend on matter for his existence or activity. They are distinct from saints, which men can become. Angels have intellect and will and are immortal.

St. Michael – More Than An Archangel

Archangels are one of the nine choirs of angels listed in the Holy Bible. In ascending order, the choirs or classes are 1) Angels, 2) Archangels, 3) Principalities, 4) Powers, 5) Virtues, 6) Dominations, 7) Thrones, 8) Cherubim, and 9) Seraphim. For more general information on angels, see my article, "What are Angels? A Summary & Exposition on Angels for Catholics" which is taken from *A Tour of the Summa* compiled by Msgr. Paul J. Gleen for Aeterna Press.[125]

St. Michael is regarded as the special Guardian Angel of Saint Joseph and the Guardian Angel of each one of the Popes and one of the seven great angels who stand before the throne of God. As a result, it is taught that while we refer to St. Michael, St. Gabriel, and St. Raphael as "Archangels" we are not referring to their rank but rather denoting that they are a higher level than ordinary angels. It is believed that all three of them are actually seraphim – the higher-ranking angels.

---

[125] Ibid., <https://acatholiclife.blogspot.com/2016/09/what-are-angels-summary-exposition-on.html>.

The Liturgical Calendar
Enriched by Angels in Recent Centuries

While the Novus Ordo Calendar combined their feast on September 29, the Traditional Calendar in place for 1962 (and prior) kept St. Michael on September 29th, St. Gabriel on March 24th, and St. Raphael on October 24th. The feast day of St. Raphael was included by Pope Benedict XV for the first time in the General Roman Calendar in 1921, for celebration on October 24. By a decree of the Congregation of Sacred Rites dated October 26, 1921, issued by command of Pope Benedict XV, it was directed that the feast of St. Gabriel the Archangel should also be added and kept – this one on March 24th in connection with the Annunciation on March 25th. In addition to these three Archangels, the Eastern Catholic Churches also venerate the Angels Uriel, Selaphiel, Jegudiel, Barachiel and Jerahmeel. The Synaxis of the Holy Archangels is on November 8th in the Byzantine Rite.

Dr. Michael Foley in a piece published on the website of *New Liturgical Movement* in March 2022 provides a concise history of this gradual addition of angels to the Liturgical Life of the Church:

> Angels were added to the Church calendar gradually. In A.D. 530, Pope Boniface II consecrated a basilica in Michael's honor on the Salarian Way about seven miles from Rome, with the ceremonies beginning on the evening of September 29 and ending the following day. Subsequent celebrations of this dedication were held first on September 30 and later on September 29. In the traditional calendar, "Michaelmas," as it is also called, maintains the official title "The Dedication of Saint Michael the Archangel," even though the basilica it commemorates disappeared over a thousand years ago.

Michaelmas also commemorates all the heavenly hosts (including Gabriel and Raphael by name in the Divine Office), but the primary focus is on St. Michael. Over time, the Church began to see the wisdom of singling out particular angels for liturgical veneration. In 1670, Pope Clement X included the Feast of the Guardian Angels on October 2 of the universal calendar, the first available day after Michaelmas.[126]

The *Catholic Encyclopedia* provides an overview of St. Michael:

> St. Michael is one of the principal angels; his name was the war-cry of the good angels in the battle fought in heaven against the enemy and his followers. Four times his name is recorded in Scripture: Daniel 10:13… Daniel 12… In the Catholic Epistle of St. Jude: 'When Michael the Archangel, disputing with the devil, contended about the body of Moses', etc. St. Jude alludes to an ancient Jewish tradition of a dispute between Michael and Satan over the body of Moses, an account of which is also found in the apocryphal book on the assumption of Moses (Origen, *De Principiis* III.2.2).
>
> St. Michael concealed the tomb of Moses; Satan, however, by disclosing it, tried to seduce the Jewish people to the sin of hero-worship. St. Michael also guards the body of Eve, according to the 'Revelation of Moses'… Apocalypse 12:7, 'And there was a great battle in heaven, Michael and his angels fought with

---

[126] Michael Foley, "The Messenger Angel," *New Liturgical Movement* (Mar 23, 2022) <https://www.newliturgicalmovement.org/2022/03/the-messenger-angel.html>, accessed December 11, 2023.

the dragon.' St. John speaks of the great conflict at the end of time, which reflects also the battle in heaven at the beginning of time. According to the Fathers there is often a question of St. Michael in Scripture where his name is not mentioned. They say he was the cherub who stood at the gate of paradise, 'to keep the way of the tree of life' (Genesis 3:24), the angel through whom God published the Decalogue to his chosen people, the angel who stood in the way against Balaam (Numbers 22:22), the angel who routed the army of Sennacherib (2 Kings 19:35)...

Consequently, the Church attributes four offices to St. Michael as the *Catholic Encyclopedia* next summarizes:

1. To fight against Satan.
2. To rescue the souls of the faithful from the power of the enemy, especially at the hour of death.
3. To be the champion of God's people, the Jews in the Old Law, the Christians in the New Testament; therefore, he was the patron of the Church, and of the orders of knights during the Middle Ages.
4. To call away from earth and bring men's souls to judgment

Why Have A Devotion to St Michael?

The Benedictine Sisters of Perpetual Adoration in *Saint Michael the Archangel* (TAN, 2006) answered this question well:

> According to the great St. Alphonsus Liguori, veneration of the holy Angels, and particularly of St. Michael, is an outstanding sign of predestination. St. Lawrence Justinian says: 'Although we must honor all the Angels, we

ought to invoke in a very special manner the glorious St. Michael, as the Prince of all the heavenly spirits, because of his sublime dignity, his pre-eminent office and his invincible power, which he proved in his conflict with Satan, as well as against the combined forces of Hell.' Again, the same Saint says: 'Let all acknowledge St. Michael as their protector, and be devoted to him, for he cannot despise those who pray to him . . . But he guards them through life, directs them on their way and conducts them to their eternal home.'

The Two Feasts in Honor of St. Michael

Traditionally in the Liturgy of the Church prior to the year 1960, there were two feasts in honor of St. Michael. Those familiar with the Litany of Saints will also recall that his name is mentioned by name in the Litany. And those who attend the Traditional Latin Mass will be familiar with several references to St. Michael in the course of the Liturgy.

In the 6th century, the angelic St. Michael appeared in southern Italy on a mountain named Gargano. In this apparition, St. Michael asked that the cave in which he appeared would become a shrine to the True God in order to make amends for the pagan worship that once occurred there. The Sanctuary of Monte Sant'Angelo sul Gargano still remains to this day.

St. Michael later appeared with a flaming sword atop the mountain during a storm on the eve of battle for the Lombards. The Lombards attributed their victory in battle on that day, May 8, 663, to St. Michael. And the Church then established a Feast in honor of the Apparition of St. Michael on May 8th, the anniversary of the battle.

This feast is still kept by priests who offer the pre-1955 Liturgy. It's quite unfortunate that a decree was issued on July

26, 1960, that dropped this feast from the Universal Calendar. While the feast day is not kept even in the 1962 Missal, priests who offer the 1962 Missal may (and arguably should) say a Votive Mass on that day for St. Michael. Since in the 1962 Missal May 8th is a feria, a Votive Mass may be offered on that date (unless May 8th falls on a Sunday or another high-ranking day in the sanctoral cycle like Ascension Thursday).

On September 29th the Feast of the Dedication of St. Michael occurs, allowing us for the second time in the year to honor the Glorious St. Michael. The Feast of the Dedication of St. Michael the Archangel on September 29th is often just called: The Feast of St. Michael the Archangel.

St. Michael's Day as A Holy Day of Obligation

The first catalog of Holy Days of Obligation comes from the Decretals of Pope Gregory IX in 1234, which listed 45 Holy Days. In 1642, His Holiness Pope Urban VIII issued the papal bull *"Universa Per Orbem"* which altered the required Holy Days of Obligation for the Universal Church to consist of 35 such days as well as the principal patrons of one's locality. St. Michael's September 29th Feast day is present in both lists. While there was a divergence of holy days with no locality keeping all of them, his feast remained a day of obligation in Rome. His feast ceased being a universal day of obligation in the 18th century. It ceased being a Holy Day in Ireland in 1778.

Fasting in Preparation for Michaelmas

The Wednesday, Friday, and Saturday after the Feast of the Exaltation of the Holy Cross are the Autumnal Ember Days which are also known as the Michaelmas Embertide, since they come near the time of Michaelmas. Those Ember Days were covered in our chapter dedicated to the Customs of the Exaltation of the Holy Cross.

However, in addition to the Ember Days which were established as part of Church Law, there is an informal fasting period known as St. Michael's Lent which is a Franciscan Tradition. The Little Flowers of St. Francis, a collection of stories about St. Francis of Assisi that was compiled during the 13th century, relates these words of St. Francis to his brothers in reference to St. Michael's Lent:

> My sons, we are drawing nigh to our forty days' fast of St. Michael the Archangel; and I firmly believe that it is the will of God that we keep this fast in the mountain of Alvernia, the which by Divine dispensation hath been made ready for us, to the end that we may, through penance, merit from Christ the consolation of consecrating that blessed mountain to the honor and glory of God and of His glorious mother, the Virgin Mary, and of the holy angels.

This fasting period begins on the Assumption (August 15) and ends on the feast of St. Michael (September 29). It excludes Assumption Day itself and all Sundays, which are never days of fasting although they may be days of abstinence if one so chooses to keep them as such. For those interested in reviving this forgotten period of penance in preparation for Michaelmas, there are several resources available on *A Catholic Life*.

Michaelmas as an English Quarter Day

Also forgotten is how Michaelmas served as an important milestone in the English legal system. Michaelmas is one of the four English "Quarter Days," days which fall around the Equinoxes or Solstices and mark the beginnings of new natural seasons (i.e., Spring, Summer, Winter, Fall) and which were used in medieval times to mark "quarters" for legal purposes, such as settling debts. The other days like this are Lady Day (the Feast of the Annunciation) on March 25, the Feast of the Nativity of St. John the Baptist on June 24, and Christmas on

December 25. Debt collection was forbidden certain times of the year such as during the Octave of Christmas. We would do well to ensure all of our debts are paid to all rightful parties at this time.

The Foods of Michaelmas

Like at Martinmas, Michaelmas would often feature goose as one of the dinner's key meals (assuming Michaelmas did not fall on a day of abstinence). Roast goose with apples, St. Michael's Bannock, and Blackberry crumble were all eaten in various places for Michaelmas. In Mifflin County, Pennsylvania, Michaelmas has been observed since 1786 as Goose Day. Recipes for these may be found at *Fish Eaters*.

Dr. Foley describes these customs in more detail in the aforementioned piece:

> Michaelmas was also known as 'Devil's Spit Day.' When Lucifer was cast out of Heaven, he is said to have fallen on a blackberry bush and angrily spat on it. Consequently, one can eat blackberries on but not after either Michaelmas Day (September 29) or Old Michaelmas Day (October 4 or 11 in those parts of England that unofficially held on to the Julian calendar).
>
> Of course, Michaelmas revelers need something to wash down all that food. Michelsminne or 'Michael's Love' was the name given in parts of northern Europe to any wine consumed on Michaelmas. The custom was especially popular in Denmark.

Customs Celebrating the Victory of St. Michael over the Devil

Dorothy Gladys Spicer describes a Bavarian custom in *The Festivals of Western Europe* published in 1958:

On September 29, Saint Michael's Day, the city of Augsburg holds an annual autumn fair to which hundreds of peasants from far and near come for trade and pleasure. Chief among the day's attractions is the hourly appearance of figures representing the Archangel and the Devil. The figures are built in the foundation of Perlach Turm, or Tower, called Tura in local dialect. This slender structure, which rises to a height of two-hundred-and-twenty-five-feet and stands next to the Peter's Kirche, north of the Rathaus, originally was a watch tower. In 1615 the watch tower was heightened and converted into a belfry.

Almost a hundred years earlier the group depicting the saint and the devil had been installed in the tower's understructure. Annually on his feast day the archangel's armor-clad figure, holding a pointed spear, appeared whenever the tower bell struck, and stabbed at the devil writhing at his feet.

During World War II the historic figures—the delight of generations of fair-goers—were destroyed. Since then a new group has been made and installed. Today, as for over four centuries, spectators continue to gather about the Tura and to watch breathlessly the symbolic drama of Michael, head of the Church Triumphant, dealing death blows to the dragon which brings evil and destruction to the world of men.

The Blue Mass

St. Michael remains the heavenly patron of police officers in addition to knights, soldiers, paramedics, ambulance drivers, and anyone at danger at sea, amongst others. His connection with police officers is the basis for the Blue Mass custom that originated in the early 20th century.

The Blue Mass dates to September 29, 1934, when Father Thomas Dade started the service as part of his duties with the Catholic Police and Fireman's Society. The first Mass was held at St. Patrick's Catholic Church in Washington, D.C. and has grown to a nationwide celebration on September 29th.

Chaplet of St. Michael the Archangel

In 1751 AD, the Archangel Michael appeared to the Portuguese Carmelite nun, Servant of God Antónia d'Astónaco. In this apparition, St. Michael said that God wished to be glorified through a series of nine invocations in honor of the nine choirs of angels. Thus, the Chaplet of St. Michael was born. It was approved by Pope Pius IX in 1851 and was granted indulgences.[127]

The Leonine Prayers
& the Prayer of St. Michael the Archangel

Anyone who has assisted at a Tridentine Low Mass will be familiar with the Leonine prayers which are said immediately after the Last Gospel and the conclusion of Mass. The Leonine Prayers are so named as they were mandated by Pope Leo XIII in 1884.

Previously in 1859, Pope Pius IX ordered that all Masses offered in the Papal States were to be concluded with three *Hail Mary*s, the *Hail Holy Queen*, and a Collect for the temporal sovereignty of the Church. But it was not until January 6, 1884, that Pope Leo XIII ordered the prayers to be recited throughout the world after the anti-clerical Kingdom of Italy was created, which absorbed the sovereignty of the Papal States. Two years later, in 1886, he added to them the *St. Michael the Archangel* prayer, after the extraordinary vision

---

[127] Matthew Plese, *loc. cit.*, <https://acatholiclife.blogspot.com/2006/12/download-chaplet-of-st-michael.html>.

God permitted him to see. The Leonine Prayers were modified by Pope St. Pius X, who inserted at the end of these series of prayers the three-fold recitation of "Most Sacred Heart of Jesus, have mercy on us."[128]

The Forgotten Full Length St. Michael Prayer

The story of the vision is as follows. One day after Mass and in a Conference with the Cardinals in 1866, Pope Leo XIII fell down and received a vision of hell. Physicians ran to him to find no pulse; they feared that he had died. Yet, he opened his eyes only a few minutes later and screamed, "Oh what a horrible picture I was permitted to see!" In his visions, legions of devils flew from the depths of hell to cause destruction to the Church and damn souls. Suddenly St. Michael the Archangel appeared and fought the devils back into the abyss of hell. Following this, Pope Leo XIII created a prayer in honor of St. Michael. In addition to the short prayer which Catholics are most familiar, there is a full-length version which was

---

[128] In 1929, when Vatican City was officially established as a sovereign state in a treaty with the Kingdom of Italy, the purpose of the Leonine Prayers was seen by some as being fulfilled. However, others would hold that the real intent of Leo XIII was for the full temporal sovereignty of the Pope over the territory known as the Papal States to be restored. To date, this has yet to happen. The following year, Pope Pius XI ordered that the Leonine Prayers were to continue to be said but were to be offered for the intention "to permit tranquility and freedom to profess the faith to be restored to the afflicted people of Russia." And they continued to be prayed at the end of Low Mass until they were discontinued in March 1965, following the September 26, 1964, instruction *Inter Oecumenici*, which decreed: "The Leonine Prayers are suppressed." However, more than ever before, we see the need to restore these prayers and encourage the faithful to pray them every day – even from home. The Leonine Prayers are not strictly speaking part of the Mass. They occur immediately after Mass and may be said by anyone for the intention of the Consecration of Russia to the Immaculate Heart of Mary and for the restoration of the Catholic Faith in Russia and the end of the schism of the Orthodox. (Some priests we know even specifically pray for the consecration and/or the conversion of Russia at the conclusion of the Leonine prayers.)

listed in the *Raccolta*. That full length version is available online.[129]

Concerning who may say the full length prayer, the Angelus Press Daily Missal notes:

> The Holy Father (Pope Leo XIII) exhorts priests to say this prayer as often as possible, as a simple exorcism to curb the power of the devil and prevent him from doing harm. The faithful (laity) also may say it in their own name, for the same purpose, as any approved prayer. Its use is recommended whenever action of the devil is suspected, causing malice in men, violent temptations and even storms and various calamities. It could be used as a solemn exorcism (an official and public ceremony in Latin) to expel the devil. It would then be said by a priest, in the name of the Church and only with a Bishop's permission.

Conclusion

In heaven, St. Michael led the good angels against Lucifer and his rebel angels. The fallen angels pursue on earth that same war against the Man-God Christ which they began in heaven. Therefore, holy St. Michael continues to direct the battle against them here on earth.

The presence of St. Michael at the Holy Sacrifice of the Mass is particularly made clear to those at the Tridentine Mass, as St. Michael is at several times called out by name: As the standard-bearer of the Church, he introduces the departed souls of her children into God's holy light (Offertory Hymn of Requiem Mass). He also presents our prayers to God (Incensation of the Altar at High Mass), he conquers demons

---

[129] Ibid., <https://acatholiclife.blogspot.com/2006/07/st-michael-archangel-prayer.html>.

(Prayers after Low Mass), and he pleads for us sinners (Confiteor).

May we worthily invoke his patronage! St. Michael the Archangel, defend us in battle!

XXVII

Allhallowtide

Known in some places as Allhallowtide, the Vigil of All Saints, All Saints Day, and All Souls Day form a sort of triduum. While All Saints Day is still a Holy Day of Obligation, the Church's traditions and customs have enriched all of these three days with unique and time-honored customs that we need to restore to our world. Make a point to learn, share, and practice them this year.

The Vigil of All Saints (Halloween) Fasting

As we have mentioned previously, the year 1955 saw some of the most significant changes to the Church's liturgy since the Council of Trent. Pope Pius XII in *"Cum nostra hac aetate"* on March 23, 1955, abolished 15 Octaves in addition to the Octave for the Dedication of a Church, and particular octaves for patrons of various religious orders, countries, dioceses, etc. He also abolished roughly half of all vigils, leading to the removal of the liturgical vigils of the Immaculate Conception, Epiphany, All Saints, and All apostles except Ss. Peter and Paul. The total number of liturgical vigils was now reduced to 7.

Uncertainty existed on whether or not fasting was still required on October 31st, the Vigil of All Saints (commonly called Halloween). It had previously been for centuries a day of fasting and abstinence. The US Bishops requested an official determination from Rome on whether the custom of fasting and abstinence on the suspended Vigil of All Saints had also been terminated. They received a pre-printed notice in a response dated March 15, 1957, stating: "The Decree of the

Sacred Congregation of Rites… looks simply to the liturgical part of the day and does not touch the obligation of fast and abstinence that are a penitential preparation for the following feast day." The US Bishop thereafter dispensed both the fast and partial abstinence law for the Vigil of All Saints.

However, for those who strive to retain our traditions, the Vigil of All Saints is still a worthwhile day to maintain a fast and keep as a day of abstinence in preparation for All Saints Day.

Distributing Sacramentals on Halloween

The Vigil of All Saints is a day to be rescued from the pagan-inspired customs of our world today and restored to what it is. Part of our responsibility as Catholics is to spread the Faith to a world that has turned away from its Christian roots and embraced the idolatry of paganism, modernism, liberalism, communism, socialism, hedonism, and materialism.

What can we do? One thing we can do is distribute Sacramentals on Halloween in addition to candy! Think about passing out various items including:

- St. Benedict Medals
- Guardian Angel Medals
- St. Michael Medals
- Gospel Holy Cards
- St. Michael Holy Cards
- St. Benedict Holy Cards

But should children participate in Halloween? Especially when children are dressed as saints or as good role models, there is nothing inherently wrong with it. Father Weiser explains:

> Although the name of this tradition is taken from the great Christian feast (All Hallows' Eve), the observance of Halloween pranks,

masquerading, 'trick or treat' and similar features, are not based on any religious background nor connected with any Christian meaning. This practice has come down to us from the demon lore of the ancient Druids.

In a Catholic home, therefore, the participation of the children in such Halloween activities should not be explained as a part of the Christian feast, because such explanations would be erroneous. It is an ancient popular custom from pagan times which has never been associated with Christian meanings. Let the children enjoy their Halloween festival, if you wish, but apart from it direct their minds to the fact that this evening is primarily a time of preparation for the great feast of All Saints, and that after the Halloween frolics they should turn their minds to God in a devout evening prayer, and greet all the heroes of God on the eve of their feast.

Halloween is a day of preparation for All Saints Day.

All Saints

The term "saint" originated for Latin *sanctus* meaning "hallowed or consecrated." *The Essential Catholic Handbook: A Summary of Beliefs, Practices and Prayers*, by John O'Connor, defines a saint this way: "In the wide sense, any person known for Christian holiness; in the strict sense, a person who has manifested heroic devotion during his or her life and who is officially honored by the Church as one who has attained heavenly glory and as one through whom God freely chooses to exhibit exceptional generosity."

The first person honored individually as a saint was the first martyr, Stephen. For nearly 4 centuries, prayer to St. Stephen for his intercession and prayers was popular. Beginning at the end of the Second Century, special celebrations were created annually on the anniversaries of the martyrs' deaths. These martyrs (those that die because they refuse to renounce Jesus Christ) were witnesses of Christ and were certainly in Heaven.

The *Catholic Encyclopedia* provides a short account of the history of All Saints Day:

> In the early days the Christians were accustomed to solemnize the anniversary of a martyr's death for Christ at the place of martyrdom. In the fourth century, neighbouring dioceses began to interchange feasts, to transfer relics, to divide them, and to join in a common feast; as is shown by the invitation of St. Basil of Caesarea (379) to the bishops of the province of Pontus. Frequently groups of martyrs suffered on the same day, which naturally led to a joint commemoration. In the persecution of Diocletian the number of martyrs became so great that a separate day could not be assigned to each. But the Church, feeling that every martyr should be venerated, appointed a common day for all.
>
> The first trace of this we find in Antioch on the Sunday after Pentecost. We also find mention of a common day in a sermon of St. Ephrem the Syrian (373), and in the 74th homily of St. John Chrysostom (407).
>
> At first only martyrs and St. John the Baptist were honoured by a special day. Other saints were added gradually and increased in number when a regular process of canonization was established; still, as early as 411 there is in the Chaldean Calendar a "*Commemoratio Confessorum*" for the Friday after Easter.
>
> In the West Boniface IV, 13 May, 609, or 610, consecrated the Pantheon in Rome to the Blessed Virgin and all the martyrs, ordering an anniversary. Gregory III (731-741) consecrated a chapel in the Basilica of St. Peter to all the

saints and fixed the anniversary for 1 November. A basilica of the Apostles already existed in Rome, and its dedication was annually remembered on 1 May. Gregory IV (827-844) extended the celebration on 1 November to the entire Church. The vigil seems to have been held as early as the feast itself. The octave was added by Sixtus IV (1471-84).

We can pay no greater honor to the Saints than by offering up to God in their name the Blood of Jesus. The efficacy of their past merits and present prayers is greatly increased when offered to God in close association with the merits and prayers of Our Lord. Therefore, the Church commemorates on this day all the Saints in heaven without exception, and thus honors also those who are unknown and who have no public recognition in the liturgy. And it is our duty to honor them on this day. It is a Holy Day of Obligation and, as Father Weiser references, the Church commands us to honor the saints who intercede in Heaven for us:

> The feast of All Saints was established by the Church because a very large number of martyrs and other saints could not be accorded the honor of individual celebrations since the days of the year would not suffice. Therefore, as the prayer of the Mass states, "we venerate the merits of all the saints by this one celebration." There is another reason for the feast. Pope Urban IV mentioned it in the following words: "Any negligence, omission and irreverence committed in the celebration of the saints" feasts throughout the year is to be atoned for by the faithful, and thus due honor may still be offered these saints " (Pope Urban IV, *Decretale Si Dominum*).

The Evening of All Saints Day

In anticipation of All Souls' Day on November 2nd, when night comes on November 1st it was customarily in some places to darken the room, light a candle blessed at Candlemas (Feast of the Purification of our Lady which is on February 2nd), and pray the Rosary for the repose of the souls of the dead. Praying the 129th Psalm (the De Profundis) and/or the Litany of the Saints would also be a worthwhile custom to start as a family as All Saints Day turns into All Souls Day.

All Souls Day

This feast, dating back to the 11th Century, is a time to remember all of the faithful departed and pray that they are now in the grace of God. God certainly is love and He is mercy. The only thing we can do is trust in Him and pray for our loved ones.

In 998 AD, St. Odilo, the abbot of Cluny (France), said that all Cluniac monasteries were to offer special prayers and sing the Office for the Dead on November 2, the day after the Feast of All Saints. The custom spread from Cluny and was adopted throughout the entire Roman Catholic Church. Now the entire Church celebrates November 2nd as All Soul's Day.

During the First World War, Pope Benedict XV on August 10, 1915, allowed all priests everywhere to say three Masses on All Souls' Day. The two extra Masses were in no way to benefit the priest himself: one was to be offered for all the faithful departed, the other for the Pope's intentions, which at that time were presumed to be for all the victims of that war. The permission remains. So today, find a Latin Mass parish and attend all 3 Masses offered this day for the souls in Purgatory.

It has and always will be a pious and holy practice to pray for the repose of the souls who have passed on to the next life. However, in the past few decades, the occurrence of prayers said for the souls in purgatory and their blessed repose has fallen into such disuse that such a lack of charity for their souls is an atrocity. For generations, Catholics would pray for the souls of the faithful who have gone before them in the sleep of death and hope in the future resurrection.

It is a traditional and pious practice with references not only in the Magisterium of the Church but also through the Holy Scriptures. As stated in the holy book of Maccabees: "It is a holy and a wholesome thought to pray for the dead, that they may be loosed from sins" (2 Maccabees 12:46). In 230 A.D., Tertullian writes, "The widow who does not pray for her dead husband has as good as divorced him."

Many European Customs for All Souls Day

Few days in the Church's year have as many customs as All Souls Day, as it was a time for all families to come together and pray for the dead. The following short account from Poland, Hungary, and Austria is taken from *The Catholic World* published in November 1930:

> In Poland the farmers hold a solemn meal on the evening of All Souls' Day, with empty seats and plates ready for the "souls" of departed relatives. Onto the plates members of the family put parts of the dinner. These portions are not touched by anyone, but afterward are given to beggars or poor neighbors. In the Alpine provinces of Austria destitute children and beggars go from house to house, reciting a prayer or singing a hymn for the holy souls, receiving small loaves of the "soul bread" in reward. There, too, people put aside a part of everything that is cooked on All Souls' Day and give meals to the poor.
>
> In Hungary the "Day of the Dead" (*Halottak Napja*) is kept with the traditional customs common to all people in central Europe. In addition, they invite orphan children into the

family for All Saints' and All Souls' days, serving them generous meals and giving them gifts.

In the rural sections of Poland the charming story is told that at midnight on All Souls' Day a great light may be seen in the parish church; the holy souls of all departed parishioners who are still in Purgatory gather there to pray for their release before the very altar where they used to receive the Blessed Sacrament when still alive. Afterward the souls are said to visit the scenes of their earthly life and labors, especially their homes. To welcome them by an external sign the people leave doors and windows open on All Souls' Day.

In Austria the holy souls are said to wander through the forests on All Souls' Day, sighing and praying for their release, but unable to reach the living by external means that would indicate their presence. For this reason, the children are told to pray aloud while going through the open spaces to church and cemetery, so the poor souls will have the great consolation of seeing that their invisible presence is known and their pitiful cries for help are understood and answered.

Cemetery Visits on All Soul Day

Father Weiser writes:

> The main religious exercise we can perform on All Souls day is, of course, to attend the holy Sacrifice and offer it for the departed ones. That is why an ancient custom in many countries demands that at least one member of every family go to church and Mass. It is also a custom to say the rosary or other prayers at

home for the holy souls, and to do some acts of charity for their sake.

On the afternoon of All Saints day, and during the whole of All Souls, many Catholics go to the cemeteries to pray at the graves of their dear departed. They decorate the tombs with lights and lanterns, and all the graves are adorned with flowers.

Catholic parents might prudently explain to their children that we should not only pray for the holy souls to help them, but that we may also pray to them for their intercession and help. It is a fact often mentioned among sincere Catholics that the holy souls invariably show their great power of intercession by unusual and surprising answers to our petitions. Not only in big and serious matters but even in little things they seem anxious to help us if only we turn to them in great confidence.

Praying the Office of the Dead

The Office of the Dead is prayed by all on All Souls Day. You may also pray the Office of the Dead any other day of the year. The Office of the Dead on other days would be prayed in addition to the day's office. After Matins and Lauds for the day, you would pray the Office of the Dead's Matins and Lauds. After Vespers for the day, you would pray Vespers from the Office of the Dead. So, please feel free to pray this Office often for the Poor Souls.

Request Masses for Deceased Loved Ones

All Souls Day is a reminder to have Masses said for the repose of the soul for our departed friends and family. Ask a priest to offer a Mass for the intention of the repose of the soul of your friend or relative. We also highly encourage having Gregorian Masses said for the repose of the deceased. Gregorian Masses are highly involved but some religious orders, such as the Servants of the Holy Family, accept Gregorian Mass enrollments.

Also, see the Regina Caeli Purgatorial Society and enroll as many souls as you would like. There is no cost. There is also the perpetual enrollment available through the Purgatorian Archconfraternity. Remember that we have a duty and responsibility to pray for all departed souls.[130]

Indulgences for Allhallowtide

An indulgence is a removal of the temporal punishment due to sin. Although you are forgiven in Confession for sins, the punishment remains, which would have to be expiated through purification like that accomplished in Purgatory. If an indulgence is performed and earned, then part or all of this punishment is removed. Catechists often use the story of a boy hitting a baseball through his neighbor's window to explain indulgences. The neighbor forgives the boy for the offense – which corresponds to our forgiveness in the confessional – yet the boy must still make restitution and pay for a new window – which relates to our need for penance to remove the temporal effects of sin.

Indulgences are only possible because of God's infinite love, most perfectly displayed upon the Cross. Without Jesus Christ, Who won all the graces we can ever receive through indulgences or otherwise, we would have no chance to be forgiven and obtain salvation.

Taken from the *Raccolta*, the Church has enriched many different practices at this time with indulgences.

> The faithful who recite prayers or perform other devout exercises in supplication for the faithful departed during the month of

---

[130] Matthew Plese, *loc. cit.*,
<https://acatholiclife.blogspot.com/2022/09/may-catholic-pray-for-soul-of-hm-queen.html>.

November, may gain a plenary indulgence on the usual conditions, if they perform these devotions daily for the entire month.

Those, who during the aforesaid month, take part in public services held in a church or public oratory in intercession for the faithful departed may gain a plenary indulgence, if they attend these exercises on at least fifteen days and, in addition, go to confession, receive Holy Communion and pray for the intentions of the Sovereign Pontiff (Jan. 17, 1888).

The faithful, as often as they visit a church or public oratory, or even a semi-public oratory (if they may lawfully use the same), in order to pray for the dead on the day on which the Commemoration of All the Faithful Departed is celebrated (November 2nd) or on the Sunday immediately following, may gain a plenary indulgence applicable only to the souls detained in Purgatory, on condition of confession and Communion, and the recitation six times during each visit of Our Father, Hail Mary, and Glory Be for the intentions of the Sovereign Pontiff (June 25, 1914).

The faithful who during the period of eight days from the Commemoration of All Souls inclusive, visit a cemetery in a spirit of piety and devotion, and pray, even mentally, for the dead may gain a plenary indulgence on the usual conditions, on each day of the Octave, applicable only to the dead.

Additionally, there is the famous *Toties Quoties* Indulgence which states that from noon on All Saints Day through midnight of All Souls Day, the Catholic faithful, as often as they visit a church to pray for the dead, reciting six times during each visit the Our Father, Hail Mary and Glory Be for the intentions of Holy Mother Church may gain a plenary indulgence applicable only to the souls in Purgatory, under the usual conditions of making a good Confession within a week before or after, worthily receiving Holy Communion within the week and having the right intention of heart. While in times past this indulgence was connected explicitly with the Jubilee St. Benedict Medal, the toties quoties indulgence was extended in 1914 to anyone, even those who do not have or use the Jubilee Medal.[131]

The fourth edition of the *Enchiridion of Indulgences*, the post Vatican II successor to the *Raccolta*, published in 1999 (i.e., the indulgences currently in force) states the following indulgences:

- A plenary indulgence, applicable only to the souls in purgatory, is granted to the faithful who, on any and each day from November 1 to 8, devoutly visit a cemetery and pray, if only mentally, for the departed;

- A plenary indulgence, applicable only to the souls in purgatory, is granted to the faithful who on All Souls' Day (or, according to the judgment of the ordinary, on the Sunday preceding or following it, or on the solemnity of All Saints), devoutly visit a church or an oratory and recite an Our Father and the Creed.

- A partial indulgence, applicable only to the souls in purgatory, is granted to the faithful who, devoutly visit a cemetery and at least mentally pray for the dead;

- A partial indulgence, applicable only to the souls in purgatory, is granted to the faithful who devoutly recite Lauds or Vespers from the Office of the Dead or the prayer *Requiem aeternam* (Eternal rest).

---

[131] Ibid., <https://acatholiclife.blogspot.com/2020/03/the-jubilee-medal-of-st-benedict.html>.

Consequently, there are many opportunities throughout November, but especially until November 8th, when we should use our time to gain indulgences for the Poor Souls who rely on our prayers to expedite their time of suffering. November 8th is the forgotten Octave Day of All Saints.

Octave of All Saints

The Octave of All Saints, like the Vigil of All Saints, was another casualty in 1955 that few people spiritually celebrate anymore. This is a Common Octave meaning that the days within (i.e., Days 2-7 which are Semidouble) yield to all Double and Semidouble feasts but have precedence over Simple feasts. The Octave is commemorated daily at Lauds, Mass, and Vespers when a higher feast occurs except if the feast is a Double of the First or Second class in which case the Octave is not commemorated. In practice, as laypeople, we can add to our morning and evening prayers (in either the Divine Office or in personal prayer) the collect from All Saints Day which asks:

Almighty and eternal God, through Your grace we honor the merits of all Your saints in the one solemn feast of today. Grant us the abundant mercy we ask of You through this army of heavenly intercessors. Through Our Lord Jesus Christ your Son who liveth and reignth with You and the Holy Ghost, one God, world without end. Amen.

Feast of the Sacred Relics

Listed in the pre-1962 Missal is an often unknown feast for November 5th – The Sacred Relics. This Mass was a "Mass in Some Places" and was not universally celebrated. The great liturgical Dom Prosper Guéranger recounts the spirituality for this feast:

> Veneration ought to be shown by the faithful to the bodies of the martyrs and other saints, who live with Jesus Christ. For they were His living members and the temples of the Holy Ghost;

He will raise them up again to eternal life and glory; and through them God grants many blessings to mankind. Therefore, those say that the relics of the saints are not worthy of veneration, that it is useless for the faithful to honour them, that it is vain to visit the memorials or monuments of the saints in order to obtain their aid, are absolutely to be condemned; and as they have already been long ago condemned, the Church now condemns them once more.

Considering the unequal distribution of relics throughout the world, Rome has not fixed one universal feast for the essentially local cultus of these precious remains. She leaves the particular churches free to consult their own convenience, reserving it to herself to bless and sanction the choice of each.

Conclusion

While the secular world knows only Halloween, a Catholic grounded in the Faith and in the immemorial customs of his forefathers knows that the Vigil of All Saints, All Saints Day, and All Souls Day form a triduum when he has a responsibility to pray for the dead and honor the saints in Heaven. Let us not allow these days to pass without restoring and practicing in our own homes some of these customs.

XXVIII

All Saints Days for Religious Orders & Nations

> The saints don't need us to honor them. Our devotion adds nothing to what they already have. When we venerate their memory, it serves us, not them. But I tell you, whenever I think of them, I feel inflamed by a tremendous yearning. . . So let us long for those who long for us. Let us hurry to meet those who await us. And let us ask those who envision our coming to intervene for us.
>
> – Saint Bernard

While all Catholics should be aware of All Saints Day as a Holy Day of Obligation on November 1st, a much smaller subset are aware that All Saints Day used to have an Octave associated with it until 1955. And a much smaller subset is aware of various special All Saints Days throughout November. In fact, All Saints Day for various orders – and for many different countries – occur throughout the month of November. We do not need to belong to these orders to call to mind these days throughout the month, to invoke the saints of the orders or nations on these respective All Saints Days, and to encourage others to learn about and imitate saints they may have not known before.

All Saints of the Jesuit Order

November 5th is the Feast of All Saints and Blesseds of the Society of Jesus. This "All Saints Day" for the Jesuit Saints is kept to honor the many remarkable saints which grace their order. While the modern-day Jesuits have lamentably fallen far from their founder and often advance heresy and sin, we should still invoke the holy Jesuits that preceded them. May these holy and saintly Jesuits pray for restoration and cleansing of their Order.

Since the founder of the Jesuits, St Ignatius of Loyola, was canonized in 1622, there have been 52 other Jesuits canonized. Some of these holy Jesuits include:

St. José de Anchieta
St. Robert Bellarmine
St. Francis Borgia
St. John de Brébeuf
St. Edmund Campion
St. Peter Canisius
St. Peter Claver
St. Claude de la Colombiere
St. Peter Faber
St. Aloysius Gonzaga
St. Roque González
St. Alberto Hurtado
St. Isaac Jogues
St. Stanislaus Kostka
St. Ignatius Loyola
St. Paul Miki
St. Joseph Pignatelli
Blessed Miguel Pro
St. Alphonsus Rodriguez
St. Francis Xavier

The collect prayer for this feast day is as follows:

Grant us, we ask, O Lord, by the intercession of the blessed Father Ignatius and of all the Saints who have served under the banner of the Most Holy Name of Jesus, with him as their leader, so to serve Thee with a perfect heart; that after the course of this life, we may merit to share in their glorious end. Through Christ Our Lord. Amen

All Irish Saints

November 6th is kept in Ireland as the Feast of All Irish Saints. The blog *Pilgrim Progress* explains:

> Pope Benedict XV beatified Oliver Plunkett in 1920 and during his papacy also (1914-22) the Feast of All the Saints of Ireland was instituted. The same Pope also granted Ireland the honor of having a litany of its native saints approved for public recitation. Only four saints, St Malachy (1094-1148), St Lawrence O'Toole (1128-80) and St Oliver Plunkett (1625-81) and St Charles of Mount Argus (1821-93), have been officially canonized. All the other Irish saints, such as Saints Patrick, Brigid, and Colmcille, are saints, as it were, by acclamation of the local Church

One of the best ways we can honor this day is by praying for the intercession of the Irish saints using the Litany of Irish Saints. The website, *Daily Prayers* explains:

> The official Litany of Irish Saints commemorates sixty-five of the best known, among them St Patrick and St Bridget. Perhaps the less well known include greats like St Darerca and St Crea. However, there are many

hundreds of other Irish Saints, most having lived during the 4th – 6th Centuries which led to Ireland being named, "The Land of Saints and Scholars."

The Irish Ecclesiastical Record, Volume 18 (1921) provided the official litany in Latin. And the blog *Omnium Sanctorum Hiberniae* provided both that and the official English translation. Keep in mind when praying litanies for specific saints of nations or orders if the litany is a public or a private litany. The Church has an important distinction as private litanies should not be prayed in the context of the liturgy nor should they be prayed in common while priests, monks or religious are sitting in choir and would then normally be praying the Divine Office.

The collect prayer for All Irish Saints:

Grant, O Lord, an increase of Thy Grace to us who celebrate the memory of all the Saints of our Island; that as, on earth, we rejoice to be one with them in race, so, in Heaven, we may deserve to share with them an inheritance of bliss. Through Christ Our Lord. Amen.

All English Saints

November 8th is the Feast of All English Saints.

While many know that King Henry VIII broke away from the Church and that he is known for murdering and replacing a series of wives, few know the full history of Catholicism in England. After King Henry VIII's death, after a brief experiment with Protestantism under his son Edward VI who ruled at a young age mainly through regents, Catholicism returned to England under his elder daughter Mary I (1555-58). But after her reign ended, England officially adopted Anglicanism in 1559 under his younger daughter Elizabeth I

(1558-1603). Except during the reign of the Catholic James II (1685-88), Catholicism remained illegal for the next 232 years until the Catholic Mass could be legally celebrated again in 1791. Yet most Catholics could not hold any public office and had few civil rights. It took the Emancipation Act of 1829 to restore most civil rights to Catholics in England.

We can and should fervently pray for a restoration of the True Faith – that is the Catholic Faith – in England and Wales. England is blessed with thousands of canonized and beatified Saints and Martyrs – many known and many more unknown. For this reason, it used to be known as "Mary's Dowry." How sadly times have changed.

St Arsenios of Paros prophesized: "The Church in the British Isles will only begin to grow when she begins again to venerate her own saints." For this intention – the return of England and Wales back to the unity of the Catholic Faith – let us pray the Litany of the Saints and Martyrs of England, which is a private litany.

All Saints of the Dominican Order

November 12th is the Feast of All Dominican Saints. This Feast was moved to November 7th after Vatican II; however, those attached to Catholic Tradition, including Dominican communities that follow the Dominican Rite, still retain it on November 12th.

In *Short Lives of the Dominican Saints* published in 1901 by A Sister of the Congregation of St. Catherine of Siena, we read:

> It may not be without interest to record in this place the number of Saint Dominic's children who, up to the present date, A.D. 1900, have received the honors of canonization and

beatification. The canonized Saints of the Order are 14 in number; its Beati, 215. By far the majority of these belong, of course, to the First or Great Order; but the Second Order of cloistered women has 10 representatives, and the Third Order, 66. We may add to the figures given above, Blessed Jane of Aza, the mother of our Holy Father, Saint Dominic, 58 members of the Confraternity of the Most Holy Rosary, beatified with our Japanese Martyrs, and 7 Martyrs belonging to the Dominican Mission of Eastern Tonquin.

The General Chapter of Valencia caused a list to be drawn up of the martyrs of the Order between the years 1234 and 1335, and it was found to contain 13,370 names. In the sixteenth century alone, 26,000 of the children of Saint Dominic gave their lives for the faith; and an author writing in the year 1882 states as an ascertained fact, that, from the foundation of the Order down to our own day, there has never been a single decade of years without some addition to the blood-stained roll of its martyrs. The century now closing has furnished its quota in the far East, where the chronicle of the Dominican Mission in Tonquin may be said to be written in blood.

But there are other martyrdoms besides that of blood, and who shall reckon up the number of Saint Dominic's children whose lives have been consumed for the aim and object of his Order, the salvation of the souls for whom Christ died, in missionary labours, in the pulpit, the confessional, the professor's chair, the hospital, or the school, or in the humbler sphere of domestic labour in the service of their Community, or again in the cloistered seclusion of their Convents, by the secret crucifixion of the spirit and the holy apostleship of intercessory prayer and suffering?

And since that text was written, more Dominicans have been canonized. The collect prayer for this feast day, which we can joyfully pray on November 12th is as follows:

O God, who hast vouchsafed to make the order of Preachers fruitful in an abundant progeny of Saints, and hast sublimely crowned in them the merits of all heroic virtues, grant us to follow in their footsteps, that we may one day be united in perpetual festivity in heaven with those whom we today venerate in common upon earth. Through Christ our Lord. Amen.

All Saints of the Benedictine Order

November 13th is the Feast of "All Saints of the Benedictine Order." Published in 1944 by The Liturgical Press for the Benedictine Order, *A Short Breviary for Religious and the Laity* states: "Because this Office is also used by the Brothers and the Oblates of the Benedictine Order, the first and second class feasts of the Benedictine Calendar are added to those of the Roman Calendar."

The collect for this feast day is:

O God, who has promised that those who have left all things to follow Thee will receive a hundredfold and possess eternal life. Grant to us, through the intercession of our father Benedict and all monastic saints who have followed his Rule, that we may be detached from all earthly things and prefer nothing to the riches of Thy love. Through Christ Our Lord. Amen

All Saints of the Augustinian Order

November 13th is a day of multiple feasts. The Benedictines keep it as the Feast of All Benedictine Saints. In the Universal Church following the traditional calendar, November 13th is the Feast of Saint Didacus, the namesake for San Diego, California. And in some places, it is also the Feast of St. Frances Cabrini, the American saint.[132]

This day is also for the Augustinian Order their Feast of All Augustinian Saints. There are dozens of saints and blesseds of the Order. St. Fulgentius, St. Rita of Cascia, St. Clare of Montefalco, St. Nicholas of Tolentine, St. Thomas of Villanova, and others now see God face-to-face in Heaven along with St. Augustine and his mother, St. Monica.

May Our Mother of Good Counsel pray for all of us, especially for all who are members of the Augustinian Order on earth. And may we pray to all these Augustinian saints to keep the Order of St. Augustine faithful to Christ and Tradition.

On November 13th, we can add to our daily prayers an adapted collect:

Almighty, everlasting God, Who hast granted us to venerate in one solemnity the merits of all Thy Saints of [the Augustinian Order], we beseech Thee, that as our intercessors are multiplied, Thou wouldst bestow upon us the desired abundance of Thy mercy. Through Christ Our Lord. Amen

---

[132] Her feast day was assigned for the United States to November 22nd until the change to the calendar in 1960 when her feast was moved to November 13th, the day of her beatification, in order to avoid conflicting with the greater ferias of Advent. In both instances, her feast day is not kept on the Universal Calendar – it is kept only in the United States.

All Saints of the Premonstratensian Order

Joining an already crowded day, November 13th is kept by the Canons Regular of Prémontré (i.e., the Premonstratensians) the Feast of All Saints of the Premonstratensian Order. This Order is more commonly known as the Norbertines, after the name of their founder. Living a worldly life, St. Norbert decided to receive Holy Orders only as part of a career move. St. Nobert joined the Benedictines at Siegburg and after a narrow escape from death, took his vows seriously and experienced an interior conversion. Ordained a priest in 1115 AD, St. Norbert accepted the duty of preaching, particularly in France and Germany. St. Norbert founded a religious community of Augustinian canons at Premontre, France, who became known as the Norbertines or Premonstratensians.

As described in *The Life of Saint Norbert*:

Norbert established a clergy dedicated to the ideals of the Gospel and the apostolic Church. They were chaste and poor. They wore the clothing and the symbols of the new man; that is to say, they wore "the religious habit and exhibited the dignity proper to the priesthood." Norbert asked them "to live according to the norms of the Scriptures with Christ as their model."

The priests lived in community, where they continued the work of the apostles. When Norbert was appointed as archbishop, he urged his brothers to carry the faith to the lands of the Wends.

Faith was the outstanding virtue of Norbert's life, as charity had been the hallmark of Bernard of Clairvaux. Affable and charming, amiable to one and all, he was at ease in the company of the humble and the great alike. Finally, he was a most eloquent preacher; after long meditation he would preach the word of God and with his fiery eloquence purged vices, refined virtues and filled souls of good will with the warmth of wisdom.

Like other Orders which keep feast days in honor of their saints sometime during the month of November, today's Feast of the Norbertines should further inspire us to pray for the success of Traditional Norbertines active in our world today. May the intercession of all Norbertines in Heaven help them – and us – to spread the Catholic Faith, to do penance, and to one day save our souls. For a list of the many Norbertine saints, see the blog *Norbertine Vocations*.

All Saints of the Carmelite Order

November 14th is the Feast of All Saints of the Carmelite Order. Like other major religious orders, the Carmelite Order is blessed with many saints and blessed. It is thanks to the Carmelite Order that we have the Brown Scapular.

Who are the Carmelite Saints? The Order of Carmelites answers:

> They are hermits of Mount Carmel who "lived in small cells, similar to the cells of a beehive, they lived as God's bees, gathering the divine honey of spiritual consolation." They are

mendicants of the first medieval communities, who discovered the presence of God in the events of ordinary daily life and especially seeing God in his brothers and sisters. They are teachers and preachers, missionaries and martyrs who searched for the face of God among the people. They are nuns who have contributed to the growth of God's people by their mystical experience and especially through their fervent prayer and contemplative life. They are religious, who showed us the face of Christ through their apostolate in hospitals or schools, especially in the mission lands. They are laity, who were able to embody the spirit of Carmel and lived that spirit in the midst of the people. Simon Stock, Andrew Corsini, Albert of Trapani, John of Cross, Teresa of Ávila, Thérèse of the Child Jesus, Edith Stein, Titus Brandsma, Angelo Paoli and countless saints and blesseds of Carmel together with Mary, the Mother of Carmel, are now singing a song of praise to the Father in Heaven.

On November 14th, besides calling to mind all of these saints, we pray for the intercession of all Carmelites – known and unknown – that they especially intercede for all Carmelites on this earth. May everyone in the Carmelite Order – including the many Carmelite Third Order members – grow in sanctity, stay true to the authentic Catholic Faith, and persevere to the end. For this, let us add this prayer to our morning prayers on November 14th:

Almighty and merciful God, Who dost rejoice us by the memory of all the Saints of the Carmelite Order: grant that, inspired by their example and merits, we may live for Thee alone in the continual observance of Thy law and in the perfect abnegation of self, and that we may attain to perfect happiness with them in heaven. Through Christ Our Lord. Amen

All Saints of the Servite Order

November 16th is the Feast of All Saints of the Servite Order. While not as well-known as the Dominicans, Jesuits, or Carmelites, the Servite Order is illustrious in its own right. The Order of Servites is the fifth mendicant order, founded in 1223, and its primary ends are "sanctification of its members, preaching the Gospel, and the propagation of devotion to the Mother of God, with special reference to her sorrows."

St. Juliana Falconieri, St. Philip Benizi, St. Anthony Pucci, and others are canonized members of the Servite Order. The Seven Holy Founders of the Servite Order are remembered together with their Feast on the Universal Calendar on February 17th.

November 16th is also a good day to learn more about the Black Scapular, which comes from the Servite Order which began in 1255 and was sanctioned by Pope Alexander IV. This scapular honors the Seven Sorrows of Mary. It is one of 17 approved Scapulars in the Church.

All Saints of the Order of Malta

On November 19th, the Order of Malta keeps their Feast of All Saints of their Order, a feast day known as "All Saints of the Order of Saint John of Jerusalem of Rhodes and of Malta." This feast, like the various feasts of All Saints for other religious orders, commemorates both the known and the unknown saints of their Order who now possess the beatific vision in Heaven.

Let us pray to some of these holy intercessors ranging from Blessed Gerard, Founder and First Grand Master of the Order, St. Toscana, St. Nicasius, St. Nuno Alvarez Pereira, Blessed

Charles of Austria, Blessed Alfredo Schuster of Milan, and all others with connections to this venerable order.

We pray especially for an end to the controversies that engulf the Order now, including the illegal prohibition of the Tridentine Mass a few years ago by the Master of the Order at that time. May they also be unwavering in fidelity to the Teachings of the Church on the impossibility of artificial contraception, especially in light of the scandal from a few years ago.

To this end, we can add to our prayers the collect prayer from this feast day:

God, the source of all holiness and of varying forms of it that endow Thy Church and build up the Body of Christ, give us the grace to follow the saints of [this] Order in living for Thee alone by meditating on Thy law and by perfect self-denial so that we may come with them to the bliss of eternal life. Through Christ Our Lord. Amen

All Saints of the Franciscan Order

Rounding out the month of November, the Franciscan Order keeps a feast day in honor of all their saints on November 29th. November 29 was selected for this feast day because on that day in 1223 Pope Honorius III gave his approval to the final Rule which St. Francis gave to the Friars Minor. Known as the Feast of All Saints of the Seraphic Order, we can spend time honoring these saints with a private Litany in their honor and by similarly praying the collect prayer for this feast day:

Almighty everlasting God, we thank Thee for granting us the joy of honoring our holy Father Francis and his sainted followers and enjoying the protection of their unceasing prayers. Grant us also the grace to imitate their example and so attain their fellowship in eternal glory. We ask this through Christ our Lord. Amen.

All Souls Day for the Various Orders

Just as the Church celebrates All Saints Day and then immediately turns on November 2nd to commemorating and praying for the souls of all the faithful departed in Purgatory, so too the various orders keep various "All Souls" Days for their orders. We may also wish to add these to our calendars in November and pray in a special way for all departed members of these orders including Third Order members:

November 13th: All Dominican Souls
November 14th: All Benedictine Souls
November 15th: All Carmelite Souls
November 17th: All Servite Souls

Conclusion

There are over 10,000 known saints from all walks of life. While St. Ulrich of Augsburg was the first saint to be formerly canonized, thousands have followed him, and many others preceded him before formal canonizations began.[133] However, our goal is for the salvation of our own souls, those souls of our family and friends, the souls of our countrymen, and the souls of as many others as possible. We pray to be among them

---

[133] As summarized by Encyclopedia Britannica: "In the early church there was no formal canonization, but the cult of local martyrs was widespread and was regulated by the bishop of the diocese. The translation of the martyr's remains from the place of burial to a church was equivalent to canonization. Gradually, ecclesiastical authorities intervened more directly in the process of canonization. By the 10th century, appeals were made to the pope. The first saint canonized by a pope was Ulrich, bishop of Augsburg, who died in 973 and was canonized by Pope John XV at a synod held in the Lateran in 993. Pope Alexander III (1159–81) began to reserve the cases of canonization to the Holy See, and this became general law under Pope Gregory IX (1227–41)."

one day in Heaven and join the numberless myriad of unknown saints who we honor not only on November 1st but throughout the month of November. May our honoring of the saints of various orders and nations help us to learn more about different saints and truly pray for and work for the salvation of others.

XXIX

Martinmas and St. Martin's Lent

> That blessed man, Saint Martin, bishop of Tours, has entered into his rest. The Angels and Archangels, Thrones, Dominations and Powers have welcomed him. Alleluia!
>
> –Alleluia Verse for the Feast of St. Martin of Tours in the 1962 Roman Catholic Missal.

Armistice Day & Praying for the Dead

Armistice Day is kept in honor of the ending of World War I which concluded on the 11th hour of the 11th day of the 11th month. In 1954, the United States amended the holiday to include a remembrance of all the living and the dead of the nation's veterans. And the name was subsequently changed to Veteran's Day on June 1, 1954. We would do well to remember to pray for the souls of all who have died in battle on this day.

However, to the Catholic, November 11th is even more than a day to pray for the repose of the souls of all who have died in battle for the country's defense. November 11th is the Feast of St. Martin of Tours, the great worker of charity who is said to have raised three persons from the dead. Known as Martinmas, this day of celebration featured numerous festivities in honor of the life and charity of St. Martin of Tours, and it is still observed by some Catholics who keep the tradition alive of carrying lanterns and eating a traditional meal of goose on this day. *Note: No goose allowed on years when November 11 falls on a Friday.*

The Catholic Thanksgiving

Father Francis Weiser shows that Martinmas was the Thanksgiving Day of the Middle Ages. This is not a day we should forget:

> The most common, and almost universal, harvest and thanksgiving celebration in medieval times was held on the Feast of Saint Martin of Tours (Martinmas) on November 11. It was a holiday in Germany, France, Holland, England and in central Europe. People first went to Mass and observed the rest of the day with games, dances, parades, and a festive dinner, the main feature of the meal being the traditional roast goose (Martin's goose). With the goose dinner they drank "Saint Martin's wine," which was the first lot of wine made from the grapes of the recent harvest. Martinmas was the festival commemorating filled barns and stocked larders, the actual Thanksgiving Day of the Middle Ages. Even today it is still kept in rural sections of Europe, and dinner on Martin's Day would be unthinkable without the golden brown, luscious Martin's goose.

The Second Catholic "Mardi Gras" of the Year

But St. Martin's Day was more than just Thanksgiving, it also served as the "Mardi Gras" of Advent by ushering in the pre-Christmas fasting period known as St. Martin's Lent. St. Martin's Lent as a period of fasting leading up to Christmas originated as early as 480 AD. Dom Prosper Guéranger writes:

The oldest document in which we find the length and exercises of Advent mentioned with anything like clearness, is a passage in the second book of the History of the Franks by St. Gregory of Tours, where he says that St. Perpetuus, one of his predecessors, who held that see about the year 480, had decreed a fast three times a week, from the feast of St. Martin until Christmas.... Let us, however, note this interval of forty, or rather of forty-three days, so expressly mentioned, and consecrated to penance, as though it were a second Lent, though less strict and severe than that which precedes Easter.

Later on, we find the ninth canon of the first Council of Mâcon, held in 582, ordaining that during the same interval between St. Martin's day and Christmas, the Mondays, Wednesdays, and Fridays, should be fasting days, and that the Sacrifice should be celebrated according to the Lenten rite. Not many years before that, namely in 567, the second Council of Tours had enjoined the monks to fast from the beginning of December till Christmas. This practice of penance soon extended to the whole forty days, even for the laity; and it was commonly called St. Martin's Lent....There were even special rejoicings made on St. Martin's feast, just as we see them practiced now at the approach of Lent and Easter. The obligation of observing this Lent, which, though introduced so imperceptibly, had by degrees acquired the force of a sacred law, began to be relaxed, and the forty days from St. Martin's day to Christmas were reduced to four weeks.

The History of the Advent Fast

In historical records, Advent was originally called *Quadragesimal Sancti Martini* (Forty Days Fast of St. Martin). The Catechism of the Liturgy notes that this observance of fasting in some form likely lasted until the 12th century.

Turning to the *Catechism of Perseverance* by Monsignor Gaume from 1882, we read the following historical account of the Advent fast taking the form of a fast on the Mondays, Wednesdays, and Fridays from St. Martin's Day until Christmas:

> The institution of Advent would seem as old as that of the festival of Christmas, though the discipline of the Church on this point has not been always the same. For several centuries, Advent consisted of forty days, like Lent: it began on St. Martin's Day. Faithful to the old customs, the Church of Milan kept the six weeks of the primitive Advent, which had been adopted by the Church of Spain. At an early period the Church of Rome reduced the time to four weeks, that is, to four Sundays, with the part of the week remaining before Christmas. All the West followed this example.
>
> Formerly, a fast was observed throughout Advent. In some countries this fast was of precept for every one; in others, of simple devotion. The obligation of fasting is attributed to St. Gregory the Great, who had not,

> however, the intention of making it a general law…

> The abstinence [of Monday, Wednesday, and Friday until Christmas] was observed in other Catholic regions as a pious donation proves for us. In 753, Astolphus, King of the Lombards, having granted the waters of Nonantula to an abbey of the same name, reserved forty pike to furnish his own table during St. Martin's Lent. We may infer that, in the eighth century, the Lombards observed the fast during the forty days before Christmas, or at least abstained from flesh meat.

By the 1100s, the fast had begun to be replaced by simple abstinence. As stated in *A History of the Commandments of the Church* by Rev. Antoine Villien:

> Thus even before reaching full vogue, the Advent fast was on the decline. At the end of the twelfth century it was nearly abolished. The Council of Avranches AD 1172 made not only fasting but even abstinence in Advent a matter of simple counsel especially addressed to clerics and soldiers. In Rome, the observance still existed but in Portugal, it was not known whether it carried with it any obligation for the Archbishop of Braga questioned Pope Innocent III on this point and the Pope, instead of insisting that there is an obligation, simply states that in Rome the fast is observed. No very clear information is to be obtained from Durand de Mende if an Advent fast existed at his time. Durand does not speak of the way it was observed. In England, it was obligatory

> only for monks like the daily fast imposed by the Council of Tours for the month of December up to Christmas.

As indicated, in 1281, the Council of Salisbury held that only monks were expected to keep the fast; however, in a revival of the older practice, in 1362 Pope Urban V required abstinence for all members of the papal court during Advent. Yet this too did not last long. By the time of St. Charles Borromeo in the 16th century, the saint urged the faithful under his charge in Milan to observe fasting and abstinence on Mondays, Wednesdays, and Fridays of Advent. Dom Guéranger similarly testifies to this in *The Liturgical Year*:

> The discipline of the Churches of the west after having reduced the time of the Advent fast so far relented in a few years as to change the fast into a simple abstinence and we even find Councils of the twelfth century, for instance Selingstadt in 1122 and Avranches in 1172, which seem to require only the clergy to observe this abstinence. The Council of Salisbury held in 1281 would seem to expect none but monks to keep it. On the other hand for the whole subject is very confused owing no doubt to there never having been any uniformity of discipline regarding it in the western Church we find Pope Innocent III in his letter to the bishop of Braga mentioning the custom of fasting during the whole of Advent as being at that time observed in Rome, and Durandus in the same thirteenth century in his Rational on the Divine Offices tells us that in France fasting was uninterruptedly observed during the whole of that holy time.

This much is certain that by degrees the custom of fasting so far fell into disuse that when in 1362 Pope Urban V endeavored to prevent the total decay of the Advent penance all he insisted upon was that all the clerics of his court should keep abstinence during Advent without in any way including others either clergy or laity in this law.

St. Charles Borromeo also strove to bring back his people of Milan to the spirit if not to the letter of ancient times. In his fourth Council, he enjoins the parish priests to exhort the faithful to go to Communion on the Sundays at least of Lent and Advent and afterwards addressed to the faithful themselves a pastoral letter in which, after having reminded them of the dispositions wherewith they ought to spend this holy time, he strongly urges them to fast on the Mondays, Wednesdays, and Fridays at least of each week in Advent.

Even closer to our modern times, remnants of St. Martin's Lent remained in the Roman Rite through the 19th century when Wednesday and Friday fasting in Advent continued to be mandated in some countries. In the United States, fasting was kept on the Wednesdays and Fridays of Advent, as was the Universal practice of the Church, until 1840 when the fast on Wednesdays in Advent was abrogated for Americans. The fast on Fridays in Advent was abrogated in 1917 in America and abroad with the promulgation of the 1917 Code of Canon Law. The Code similarly removed the Wednesdays of Advent for any localities that continued to mandate them as well as the Saturdays of Advent which were kept elsewhere, such as in Italy.

But even the attempts to maintain elements of the Advent fast from the 17th through the 20th centuries were shadows of St. Martin's Lent. In fact, the Church still encouraged people to keep the venerable discipline of St. Martin's Lent, even if it was not obligatory under pain of sin. This fact is expressed with conviction in the *Catechism of Perseverance*:

> The Church neglects no means of revisiting in her children the fervor of their ancestors. Is it not just? Is the little Babe whom we expect less beautiful, less holy, less worthy of our love now than formerly? Has He ceased to be the Friend of pure hearts? Is His coming into our souls less needed? Alas! perhaps we have raised there all the idols that, eighteen centuries ago, He came to overturn. Let us therefore be more wise. Let us enter into the views of the Church: let us consider how this tender mother redoubles her solicitude to form in us those dispositions of penance and charity which are necessary for a proper reception of the Babe of Bethlehem.

Fasting from Martinmas Until Christmas

How far we have fallen from the times of St. Martin. Strive to keep at least Mondays, Wednesdays, and Fridays from St. Martin's Day as days of fast. Should you wish to do more, keep all forty days (excluding Sundays) as days of fast. Indeed, as St. Frances de Sales noted: "If you're able to fast, you will do well to observe some days beyond what are ordered by the Church." Tuesdays, Thursdays, and Saturdays would be appropriate to observe as days of abstinence without fast. The Immaculate Conception, where it is kept as a Holy Day of Obligation on December 8, can also be exempt from this practice of fasting.

While the world celebrates too early and ceases celebrating on the 2nd day of Christmas, let us not make that same grave mistake. And before any feast, there should be an appropriate fast. Martinmas ushers in to us that sacred time of preparation for Christmas.

Priests, encourage the faithful to celebrate as a true Catholic Thanksgiving the Feast of St. Martin of Tours. Encourage the faithful to celebrate a feast in his honor and carry lanterns with the family as venerably done for centuries by the faithful. And encourage the faithful to keep the whole of St. Martin's Lent or at the very least the discipline of fasting on Mondays, Wednesdays, and Fridays from St. Martin's Feast until we celebrate the birth of the Lord on Christmas.

XXX

Immaculate Conception

> The feast of the Blessed Virgin's Immaculate Conception is the most solemn of all those which the Church celebrates during the holy time of Advent; and if the first part of the cycle had to offer us the commemoration of some one of the mysteries of Mary, there was none whose object could better harmonize with the spirit of the Church in this mystic season of expectation.
>
> – Dom Guéranger

The Immaculate Conception is a dogma of the faith stating that Mary was conceived sinless in the womb of her mother, Saint Anne. While this truth has been believed since the early times of the Church, it was not until December 8, 1854, that Pope Pius IX dogmatically decreed this truth, thus ending any possibility of doubt.[134] All Catholics are required to believe in

---

[134] While they did not use the phrase "Immaculate Conception," the Early Church honored the Blessed Virgin Mary as sinless since her conception. For instance, St. Ephrem (306-373 AD) wrote alluding to Mary's sinlessness: "You and Your mother are the only ones who are totally beautiful in every way. For in You, O Lord, there is no stain, and in Your mother no stain." Hippolytus wrote in 235 AD: "He was the ark formed of incorruptible wood. For by this is signified that His tabernacle was exempt from putridity and corruption." And Origen wrote in 244 AD: "This Virgin Mother of the Only-begotten of God, is called Mary, worthy of God, immaculate of the immaculate, one of the one." And there are many other such instances. The dogmatic proclamation in 1854 by Pope

this dogma without exception. The decree of Pope Pius IX in *Ineffabilis Deus* reads in part:

> We declare, pronounce, and define that the doctrine which holds that the most Blessed Virgin Mary, in the first instance of her conception, by a singular grace and privilege granted by Almighty God, in view of the merits of Jesus Christ, the Savior of the human race, was preserved free from all stain of original sin, is a doctrine revealed by God and therefore to be believed firmly and constantly by all the faithful.[135]

The Immaculate Conception as a Holy Day of Obligation & Public Holiday

How wonderfully glorious that the Lord preserved Mary from all stains to make her a worthy dwelling place. Originally referred to as the "Conception of the Blessed Virgin Mary," December 8th became a Holy Day of Obligation in 1708 under

---

Pius IX merely ended a debate that had arisen in the past centuries – fueled often by the Protestants. For more on this, see the sources in the article by Nishant Xavier, "Eastern Orthodoxy and the Immaculate Conception," *OnePeterFive* (Dec 8, 2021) <https://onepeterfive.com/the-immaculate-conception-and-eastern-orthodoxy/>.

[135] We read thus in the Catechism of St. Pius X:
42 Q. How is it possible for original sin to be transmitted to all men? A. Original sin is transmitted to all men because God, having conferred sanctifying grace and other supernatural gifts on the human race in Adam, on the condition that Adam should not disobey Him; and Adam having disobeyed, as head and father of the human race, rendered human nature rebellious against God. And hence, human nature is transmitted to all the descendants of Adam in a state of rebellion against God, and deprived of divine grace and other gifts.
43 Q. Do all men contract original sin? A. Yes, all men contract original sin, with the exception of the Blessed Virgin, who was preserved from it by a singular privilege of God, in view of the merits of Jesus Christ our Saviour.

Pope Clement XI, nearly 150 years before Pope Pius IX dogmatically and infallibly defined the dogma of the Immaculate Conception. Pope Innocent XII in 1693 had already raised it to the rank of "Double of the second class" with an octave for the universal Church. According to Father Weiser in *Christian Feasts and Customs*, the Greek Rite has kept this feast day as a holyday since 1166 and Spain has kept it as a public holyday since 1644.

The Immaculate Conception is a Holy Day of Obligation in the United States and many other nations.[136] It is also a public holiday in Guam, Italy, Malta, Monaco, and Spain.

Fasting on the Vigil of the Immaculate Conception

On November 30, 1879, Pope Leo XIII added the Vigil of the Immaculate Conception to the Universal Church's calendar, increasing the number of liturgical vigils from 16 to 17, which not including Holy Saturday, consisted of "the eves of Christmas, the Epiphany, the Ascension, Pentecost, the Immaculate Conception, the Assumption, the eight feasts of the Apostles, St. John the Baptist, St. Laurence, and All Saints." At this time, the Vigil of the Immaculate Conception was not yet a fast day. These 17 vigils mentioned were still in place at the time of the writing of the *Catholic Encyclopedia* in 1909.

1955 saw some of the most significant changes to the Church's Liturgy since the Council of Trent. Pope Pius XII in "*Cum nostra hac aetate*" on March 23, 1955, abolished 15 Octaves – including that of the Immaculate Conception – in addition to the Octave for the Dedication of a Church, and particular

---

[136] In times past, Holy Days would often be referred to as days of single or double precept, with those of double precept requiring both hearing Mass and abstaining from servile works, whereas days of single precept would permit servile work. Nowadays, Holy Days of Obligation refer to days of double precept.

octaves for patrons of various religious orders, countries, dioceses, etc. He also abolished roughly half of all vigils, leading to the removal of the liturgical vigils of the Immaculate Conception, Epiphany, All Saints, and All apostles except Ss. Peter and Paul. The total number of liturgical vigils was now reduced to 7.

On July 25, 1957, Pope Pius XII transferred the fast in the Universal Church from the Vigil of the Assumption to the Vigil of the Immaculate Conception on December 7, even though he had previously abrogated the Mass for the Vigil of the Immaculate Conception. Thus, this day starting in 1957 was a day of mandatory fasting and abstinence. This is preserved in the laws in force in 1962 for instance.

By 1962, the laws of fasting and abstinence were as follows as described in *Moral Theology* by Rev. Heribert Jone and adapted by Rev. Urban Adelman for the "laws and customs of the United States of America" copyright 1961:

> Complete abstinence is to be observed on all Fridays of the year, Ash Wednesday, the Vigils of Immaculate Conception and Christmas. Partial abstinence is to be observed on Ember Wednesdays and Saturdays and on the Vigil of Pentecost. Days of fast are all the weekdays of Lent, Ember Days, and the Vigil of Pentecost. If a vigil falls on a Sunday, the law of abstinence and fasting is dispensed that year and is not transferred to the preceding day. Father Jone adds additional guidance for the Vigil of the Nativity fast: "General custom allows one who is fasting to take a double portion of food at the collation on Christmas Eve (jejunium gaudiosum)."

The Octave of the Immaculate Conception

By the 8th century, Rome had developed liturgical octaves not only for Easter, Pentecost, and Christmas but also for the Epiphany and the feast of the dedication of a church. After 1568, when Pope Pius V reduced the number of octaves (since by then they had grown considerably), the number of Octaves was still plentiful. Octaves were classified into several types. Easter and Pentecost had "specially privileged" octaves, during which no other feast whatsoever could be celebrated. Christmas, Epiphany, and Corpus Christi had "privileged" octaves, during which certain highly ranked feasts might be celebrated. The octaves of other feasts allowed even more feasts to be celebrated.

To reduce the repetition of the same liturgy for several days, Pope Leo XIII and Pope St. Pius X made further distinctions, classifying octaves into three primary types: privileged octaves, common octaves, and simple octaves. The Immaculate Conception was kept as a Common Octave.

Restore the 54 explains the particulars of this Octave in the Church's Traditional Liturgy of Advent:

> The Octave of the IC is a Common Octave. The days within (i.e. Days 2-7) are Semidouble and have precedence over Simple feasts/Advent Feriae, but yield way to any feast of nine lessons. When a higher feast or Sunday occurs, the day within the octave is commemorated at Lauds, Mass, and Vespers unless the feast is a Double First or Second Class; in this latter case, days within common octaves are omitted. The Preces at Prime and Compline are omitted entirely during the Octave. Except on the Advent Sunday occurring within the octave,

the proper doxology of the Incarnation sung in the BVM Tone holds for all hymns of iambic metre throughout the octave. At Mass, when there is no saint to commemorate, after the Commemoration of the Advent Feria, there is a third set of orations of the Holy Ghost. The Credo is sung daily by reason of the Octave.

The Sunday within the Octave: The Pledge Against Indecent Movies

The American bishops at a meeting in Washington in 1938 requested all Ordinaries to have the Pledge of the Legion of Decency taken by all the Faithful at all Masses, in all churches and chapels throughout the United States, on the Sunday within the Octave of the Feast of the Immaculate Conception. In a time when the number of indecent movies – and the perversity of culture intensify – we must rediscover this and, as parishes and families, make this pledge:

In the Name of the Father, and of the Son, and of the Holy Ghost. Amen

I condemn indecent and immoral motion pictures and television programs, and those which glorify crime or criminals. I promise to unite my efforts with all those who protest against them.

I acknowledge my obligation to form a right conscience about films and television programs that are dangerous to my moral life.

As a true Roman Catholic, I pledge myself to watch only good motion pictures and television programs. I promise, further, to stay away altogether from places of amusement and sources of entertainment which are offensive to God and occasions of sin for myself and others for whom I am responsible.

For more information, see *Vigilanti Cura*, the encyclical of Pope Pius XI on motion pictures, which was promulgated on June 29, 1936. This too has been forgotten and is never mentioned by priests nowadays.

Spanish Customs for the Immaculate Conception

The Spanish were some of the greatest proponents for our Lady's Immaculate Conception. This is the reason why in Spanish and its dominions, priests have the unique permission to wear cerulean (i.e., blue) vestments. It was a privilege originally given by Pope Pius VII to the Church in Spain in 1817 and later reaffirmed by Pope Pius IX in 1864, in recognition of the centuries-old Hispanic defense of Mary's Immaculate Conception. It spread to other places formerly under the Spanish Crown as well as seen in the indult granted by Pope St. Pius X to the First Provincial Council of Manila for their use in the Philippine Islands. No other nation is authorized to use it and doing so constitutes a liturgical abuse. The only exception is a rare dispensation that was given temporarily to Marian shrines on special occasions.

Father Weiser states the following regarding the Spanish customs:

> Because of its very recent establishment as a holyday of obligation, this feast has not developed any popular customs and traditions except in Spain and Spanish-speaking countries, where it has been a great public feast day for the past three hundred years.
>
> Since Mary, under the title of the Immaculate Conception, is the primary patron of Spain, her feast is celebrated everywhere with great public solemnity. People prepare themselves by novenas and nocturnal vigils for the feast,

solemn processions with the statue of the Immaculate are made after High Mass, and additional services are held in the afternoon of the holyday. In many places December 8 is also the day for the solemn first communion of children.

In the northern provinces of Spain it is the custom to decorate the balconies of the houses with flowers, carpets, and flags on the eve of the feast, and candles burn in the windows all through the night. In Seville, the famous "Dance of the Six" (Los Seises) is performed in the cathedral on the feast day and during the octave. Six boys, their heads covered according to special privilege, enact an ancient religious pageant before the Blessed Sacrament, dancing in the sanctuary and singing hymns in honor of the Immaculate Conception. This performance annually draws large crowds of devout natives and curious tourists.

All through Spain December 8 is the traditional day of great school celebrations. Alumni revisit their alma mater and spend the day in joyful reunion with their classmates and former teachers. In many countries of South America, it is the day of commencement celebrations, since the long summer vacations start around the middle of December.

Mary Immaculate is also the patroness of the Spanish infantry and civil guard (state police). On December 8 in all towns and cities, troops attend Mass in a body. It is a colorful pageant to watch. Detachments in splendid uniforms march with military precision, brass bands play ancient, stirring music, and the picture of the Immaculate Conception on each regimental flag is held aloft.

Finally, there is the interesting fact that our modern custom of an annual "Mothers' Day" has been associated in Spain with the Feast of the Immaculate Conception. All over Spain, December 8 is Mothers' Day, and thus the great feast of our Lady has also become an outstanding day of joyful family celebrations in honor of mothers everywhere in that country.

May Our Lady, the Immaculate Conception, pray for the people of Spain to return in earnest to the True Catholic Faith of their past.

Conclusion

While we may not think of liturgical customs associated with the Immaculate Conception, this Holy Day of Obligation is a light of brightness in the midst of Advent penance. Even for those seeking to keep St. Martin's Lent and the Fast of Advent, this holy day is a short reprieve as we press on to the joy of Christmas Day.

XXXI

Other Saints Days

In addition to the saints previously covered in this book, other saints provide opportunities for us to live a truly Catholic life. Likewise, the patronal feasts of our own areas should be restored as festive celebrations and occasions to publicly showcase our Catholic Faith.

Patronal Feast Days as Former Holy Days of Obligation

The *Catholic Encyclopedia* provides a concise, high-level overview of Holy Days of Obligation from 1150 to the changes in 1642:

> The Decree of Gratian (about 1150) mentions forty-one feasts besides the diocesan patronal celebrations; the Decretals of Gregory IX (about 1233) mention forty-five public feasts and Holy Days. It was subsequently reduced in 1642 to the days listed by Pope Urban VIII which took the older list and maintained it.
>
> In 1642, when Pope Urban VIII issued the papal bull *"Universa Per Orbem"* which altered the required Holy Days of Obligation for the Universal Church to consist of 35 such days, to these were added the principal patrons of one's locality. Such local patronal celebrations had previously been holy days of obligation. This is one of the reasons why

patronal feast days were celebrated with such fanfare and piety. For instance, the Feast Day of St. Roch painted by Canaletto (pictured above) beautifully illustrates the devotion of the Venetian people on St. Roch's Day (August 16th).

Diocesan Patronal Saints & Titular Feasts

Who are the patron saints for your Diocese? Do you know if your Diocese has secondary patrons in addition to your primary patron? Did you know that your Diocese's patron saint might not be the same as the Cathedral's titular patron? I was disappointed to find no list online of the various patron saints for each of the Roman Catholic Dioceses in the United States. Since the feast days of these patrons should be kept as first-class feasts in each diocese, they are important to honor in our prayers at Mass and in the Divine Office in the local churches. In fact, the primary patron saint for each diocese would have been a Holy Day of Obligation up until the time of St. Pius X's changes in 1911. As a result, I sought to create such a list.[137]

Care should also be taken to ensure that we understand the difference between a patronal feast day and a titular feast day. The Sacred Heart Review published on June 29, 1889, concisely teaches:

> At other times, in order to show special devotion to some mystery, or to some manifestation of God's love, the church receives a name that will keep that mystery or mark of love always before the people of the

---

[137] You can find this list here: <https://drive.google.com/file/d/1kK_NHWW7V7dVLTD4h6BGOl5K0vbTPZOO/view>.

parish. Thus churches are sometimes called after the Holy Trinity, the Precious Blood, the Assumption, or, as in our own case here, the church of the Sacred Heart.

The intention in so naming churches is, in the case of a saint, that the people should have special love for that saint, that they should place themselves under his protection, and, by the study and imitation of his life, make themselves worthy of his intercession before God. That saint, in whose honor the church is named, becomes the patron saint of the place, and his feast is called the patronal feast. But when a church is named in honor of some mystery or mark of divine love or divine object, the people are supposed to have great veneration and love for the mystery, mark or object commemorated by the church's name: and the name of the mystery, mark, or object is called the title of the church, and when the anniversary of the feast comes around, it is called the titular feast.

Practically speaking, we should honor the patrons and titulars of our parish and diocese by attending Mass on those days and celebrating, as far as possible, those days as holidays.

St. Luke's Day

In 1295, Pope Boniface VIII enacted the decretal *Gloriosus* which "commanded that each of the feasts of the twelve apostles, four evangelists, and four doctors of the Church be celebrated as an officium duplex."[138] As such, one

---

[138] *The Cambridge History of Medieval Canon Law* by Anders Winroth and John Wei.

of the former days preceding the changes in 1642 under Pope Urban VIII was the Feast of St. Luke the Evangelist on October 18th, which had been kept in the ecclesiastical province of Mexico previously.

St. Luke is the patron of butchers. For years when St. Luke's Day is not on a Friday, it would be an appropriate custom to honor him with a nice cut of steak. October 18th is also known as "Sour Cakes Day" in Scotland because baked cakes were eaten with sour cream in Rutherglen in his honor.

We can also honor St. Luke's Day by praying for doctors and artists, since he is the patron saint of both. And we can take time to read the Acts of the Apostles or the Gospel according to St. Luke on his feast day.

St. Clement's Day

While not commonly known, St. Clement's Day on November 23rd is also known for its' own unique customs as the Latin Mass Society related on its Facebook Page:

> [Today] is the Feast of St Clement (23rd November) and traditionally children would go clementing – knocking on doors begging for apples, pear, and nuts in exchange for reciting rhymes. Indeed, it is believed that is the origin of the nursery rhyme "Oranges & Lemons."

Also as Pope Clement I is the patron saint of metalworkers and blacksmiths and celebrations on Old Clem's Night began with a bang, quite literally. Blacksmiths filled a small hole in their anvil with gunpowder. This was then struck with a hammer, creating a shower of sparks and a loud boom. The village blacksmiths would dress up in a wig, mask and cloak to represent Saint Clement and gather in the streets, singing loudly and staggering from tavern to tavern.

St. Anthony's Day

The "Hammer of Heretics," St. Anthony, is one of the most beloved saints. Besides being the patron saint of lost things, he is honored in many nations as the patron of sailors and fisherman. He is also the patron saint of the poor, which is visible in some places were the title on poor boxes in churches is "Saint Anthony's Bread."

Father Weiser also relates the connection of St. Anthony to Tuesdays:

> Tuesday is devoted in a particular way to the veneration of St. Anthony because he was buried on Tuesday, June 17, 1231. In the 17th century, the practice began of holding weekly devotions to St. Anthony; even today, most 'perpetual novenas' to him are held on Tuesdays. Portugal and Italy, where the saint was born and where he died, honor his feast day with unusual festive splendor and great devotion. In Portugal, the epithet 'of Padua' is never used, for to the Portuguese he remains 'Anthony of Lisbon' or 'of Alfama,' the district of Lisbon where he was born. There, every house on June 13 displays, among other decorations, a shrine with a statue of the saint.

St. Christopher's Day

July 25th, besides the feast of St. James the Greater, is the Commemoration of St. Christopher (i.e., St. Christopherus). He is one of the 14 Holy Helpers and is the patron of travelers, especially motorists, and is invoked in storms and tempests.[139]

---

[139] Matthew Plese, *loc. cit.*,
<https://acatholiclife.blogspot.com/2017/06/fourteen-holy-helpers.html>.

This day is the ideal day to have a priest bless your vehicles using the traditional Roman Rituale blessing whose English translation beautifully asks:

Lord God, be well disposed to our prayers, and bless + this vehicle with your holy hand. Appoint your holy angels as an escort over it, who will always shield its passengers and keep them safe from accidents. And as once by your deacon, Philip, you bestowed faith and grace upon the Ethiopian seated in his carriage and reading Holy Writ, so also now show the way of salvation to your servants, in order that, strengthened by your grace and ever intent upon good works, they may attain, after all the successes and failures of this life, the certain happiness of everlasting life; through Christ our Lord. All: Amen.

Name Day Celebrations

Another way we can restore Catholic culture is by celebrating our names days. Turning again to the wisdom of Father Weiser we learn:

> It was a general custom before the Reformation, and still is in Catholic countries, to celebrate not so much the birthday, but, rather, the feast of the saint whose name was received in baptism. This 'baptismal saint' is considered a special and personal patron all through life. Children are made familiar with the history and legend of 'their own' saint, are inspired by his life and example, pray to him every day, and gratefully accept his loving help in all their needs. It is a beautiful custom, this close relationship of an individual to his personal patron saint in Heaven.

Do you celebrate your and your family members' name days? If not, when can you start?

Our Lady of Mount Carmel (July 16)

The Feast of Our Lady of Mount Carmel commemorates the appearance of Our Lady to St. Simon Stock, the superior general of the Carmelites, in Cambridge, England, on Sunday, July 16, 1251. The Carmelite Order was founded in the 1100s on Mount Carmel, the same place in the Holy Land mentioned in the Bible in 1 Kings 18:16-40. It was there that the prophet Elijah took his stand against the pagan prophets of Baal and Asherah by the power of God.

St. Simon Stock had appealed to Mary through prayer to help the new Carmelite order to overcome oppression. She appeared with the Brown Scapular and said to him:

> Take, beloved son, this scapular of the order as a badge of my confraternity and for you and all Carmelites a special sign of grace; whoever dies in this garment, will not suffer everlasting fire. It is the sign of salvation, a safeguard in dangers, a pledge of peace and of the covenant.

Later that day, St. Simon Stock was called promptly by Lord Peter of Linton: "Come quickly, Father, my brother is dying in despair!" St. Simon Stock placed his large Scapular over the dying man and prayed that Mary would keep her promise. The man instantly repented of his sins and died in a state of grace. Blessed Pope Gregory X was buried wearing the Scapular, only 25 years after the vision. When his tomb was opened over 600 years later, the wool scapular remained perfectly intact and had not degraded in the least. And to show just how important the Scapular is, the Church sanctions and encourages the promises of the Scapular.[140]

---

[140] See Ibid., <https://acatholiclife.blogspot.com/2006/07/our-lady-of-mt-carmel-brown-scapular.html>, accessed November 27, 2024.

On customs, *Fish Eaters* summarizes:

> The Feast of Our Lady of Carmel is grandly celebrated in various places in Italy. In Rome, a statue of Our Lady of Carmel – Madonna del Carmine – is dressed in beautiful clothes and precious jewels given by the faithful, and then processed from the Church of Sant'Agata in Trastevere to the Basilica of San Crisogono, where it will remain for eight days, when it is processed back again. Food, music, traditional markets, and fireworks are all part of the celebrations.
>
> In Avigliano, Potenza, Basilicata, in 1694, the people appealed to Our Lady of Mt. Carmel when they were suffering from both famine and earth tremors. They ran to the mountains and prayed there for 40 days, pleading with Our Lady that they would honor her if she would intercede for them. When no one died and no houses were destroyed by the great earthquake that came, they renamed their local mountain "Mt. Carmine" (Carmel), built a chapel in her honor, and bought a beautiful wooden statue of Our Lady of Mt. Carmel to adorn it. Every year on the eve of this feast, they crown the statue and lay a mantle fixed with treasures over its shoulders. Then, on the 16th, the statue is processed from Church of Santa Maria degli Angeli to the Sanctuary of Santa Maria del Carmine almost 6 1/2 miles away. The statue remains there for two months, being returned on the second Sunday in September.

Not far away from Avigliano is Viggianello, whose people honor Our Lady of Mt. Carmel on the third Sunday of August. Everyone wears their traditional clothing, but the women wear cirii on their heads – conical shaped structures decorated with wheat and ribbons. The men carry on their shoulders a great wooden structure – la meta – that is shaped and decorated in the same way, but with the addition of farm animals. All the while, bagpipers, accordionists, and tambourine players make music while people dance a tarantella called the "sickle dance."

In Palmi, Calabria, a miracle took place that was officially recognized by the Vatican: on October 31, 1894, a statue of Our Lady of Carmel began doing very strange things. Its eyes would move, and its face would blanche, like the flesh of a woman who's about to faint. This went on for seventeen days, and was written about not only in the local press, but nationally. On November 16th, the people spontaneously held a procession of the statue – and just when they made it to the end of the city, a violent earthquake struck, destroying most of the houses. But out of the 15,000 inhabitants of the town, fewer than ten were killed because most of them were taking part in the procession to honor the Blessed Virgin. Since then, every year on November 16, the people of Palmi have Mass followed by a procession of the statue of Our Lady of Mt. Carmel.

These customs did not only remain in Italy. Italian Immigrants to the United States brought devotion and customs to Our Lady of Mount Carmel to America and these customs are still publicly observed in some places such as in the greater New York City area as the article adds:

> Italian immigrants brought their love of Our Lady of Mt. Carmel to the United States, and in various places around America at this time, one can find festivals in her honor. Williamsburg, Brooklyn, New York City has a large one centered around the Shrine Church of Our Lady of Mount Carmel at 275 North 8th Street. It includes a procession of Our Lady and is famous for its "Dancing of the Giglio" – a tall, three-ton tower that is carried down the street on men's shoulders.

We can do our part to honor Our Lady of Mount Carmel by wearing the Scapular (after we have been properly invested in it) and by buying Scapulars for family or friends who are Catholic but who do not wear the Scapular.

St. Mary Magdalene (July 22)

According to the Latin tradition in the Roman Catholic Church, Mary Magdalene is mentioned in Lk 7:36-50, Lk 10:38-42, and Jn 20:11-18. The Catholic Church believes these references all refer to Mary Magdalene. Clement Harrold carefully and thoughtfully analyzes the Scriptures and historical evidence:

> Thus retrieved, Mary Magdalene shines forth once more as the one who loved much (Luke 7:47), the one from whom seven demons were cast out (Luke 8:2), the one who grasped the one thing necessary (Luke 10:42), the one who

moved the God-Man to tears (John 11:33–35), the one who did a beautiful thing for Him (Mark 14:6), the one whose deed would be proclaimed throughout the world (Mark 14:9), and the one who first saw the Risen Lord and believed (John 20:18).[141]

Gregory DiPippo writes:

> From the time of St Gregory, the Western Church accepted that Mary Magdalene was also the sinful woman who anoints Christ's feet in the house of Simon the Pharisee, as recounted in Luke 7, 36-50, the Gospel for her feast. This connection was probably made from the words that immediately follow this passage, or at least reinforced by them, Luke 8, 1-3. "And it came to pass afterwards, that he travelled through the cities and towns, preaching and evangelizing the kingdom of God; and the twelve with him: And certain women who had been healed of evil spirits and infirmities; Mary who is called Magdalen, out of whom seven devils were gone forth, And Joanna the wife of Chusa, Herod's steward, and Susanna, and many others who ministered unto him of their substance." (Mark 16, 9 also refers to the seven devils.)[142]

---

[141] Clement Harrold, "A Retrieval of the Traditional View of Mary Magdalene From the Fringes of Theology," *Church Life Journal* (July 21, 2023) <https://churchlifejournal.nd.edu/articles/a-retrieval-of-the-traditional-view-of-mary-magdalene/>, accessed November 27, 2024.

[142] Gregory DiPippo, "'Apostle of the Apostles' – Liturgical Notes on the Feast of St Mary Magdalene," *New Liturgical Movement* (July 22, 2021) <https://www.newliturgicalmovement.org/2021/07/apostle-of-apostles-liturgical-notes-on.html>, accessed November 27, 2024.

Because of her faith and repentance, she was privileged to be the first person (after the Blessed Virgin Mary according to tradition) that Jesus appeared to after His Resurrection (John 20:1-18). According to Roman tradition, in 45 AD, St. Mary Magdalene, along with Sts. Martha and Lazarus were seized by the Jews of Palestine. They were placed on a dilapidated boat without oars and cast into the stormy sea. They eventually reached France, where they settled and converted the people of Provence. St. Martha established a community of women, and St. Lazarus became a bishop. Mary Magdalene, however, is said to have retreated to a cave in the hills of La Sainte-Baume to live a life of penance for thirty years. Near her death, angels reportedly carried her to the Oratory of St. Maximinus in Aix, where she received Viaticum and passed away. Her body was initially interred at the St. Maximin Oratory in Villa Lata.

As the "Apostle to the Apostles," before the changes to the Missal in 1955, the Creed was also said on her feast day. In honor of that, it is fitting that we should all pray the Creed on her feast day.

As for regional customs, this day is an ideal one to make or buy French *madeleines*, which are a light, cake-like, shell-shaped cookie that require a special *madeleine* pan to make. There are also Spanish Magdalena tea cakes which can be baked for her feast day. And as you eat them, listen to the Italian hymn "*Magdalena degna da laudare*" which dates back to the 13th century.

Our Lady of Ransom (September 24)

The Order of Our Lady of Ransom was founded in the Thirteenth Century by St. Peter Nolasco (January 28) and St. Raymond of Peñafort (January 23), aided by King James of Aragon. The object of the Order was to redeem Christians held in slavery by the Mohammedans. Pope Gregory IX instituted the feast of Our Lady of Ransom on September 24th and afterward, it was extended by Pope Innocent XII in 1696 to the Universal Church.

There are various customs throughout the Catholic world in honor of Our Lady of Ransom's including the famous ones in Barcelona, Spain and in the Dominican Republic as *Fish Eaters* summarizes:

> In Barcelona, Catalonia, Spain, the Fiestas de la Mercé (Fiestas de la Merced in Spanish) lasts for a week. It is marked by the usual Masses and processions, and also includes marathons, dances, fireworks coordinated to music, and the presence of los gigantes y cabezudos – great papier-mâché giants with large heads, common in Southern European celebrations. During the fireworks, there is the Correfoc in which people dressed as demons run through the streets and frighten people. Finally, there is the building of Castells – great towers made of human beings. Participants dress in white pants, red shirts, and wide, black belts, and then, against a backdrop of medieval flute music, arrange themselves to form tall towers. Also in Barcelona is the Basílica de la Mercè, the mother church of the Mercedarian Order. At the top of its dome stands a statue of Our Lady of Ransom holding her Son.
>
> In the Dominican Republic, tradition holds that Our Lady of Mercy appeared in the middle of a battle between natives and Christopher Columbus and his men, her appearance frightening the natives and causing them to

scatter. But the natives came back for more and fought so aggressively that Columbus was about to leave when Fray Juan Infante told him to press on, promising him victory at the hand of Our Lady of Mercy. The Spanish won, and a church was built at the site of victory in Santo Serro. Great celebrations are had there on la Dia de las Mercedes, and also in Santo Domingo, the capital of the Dominican Republic, where September 24 is a national holiday.

September 24th is also the Feast of Our Lady of Walsingham and thus is an appropriate day for us to pray for the return of all lapsed Catholics and all heretics – especially those in the Church of England – to the True Catholic Faith.[143]

St. Gerard Majella (October 16)

Born on April 6, 1726, in Muro Lucano, Italy, St. Gerard grew up in a devout family but faced significant hardships early in life, including the death of his father when he was young. Despite these challenges, he remained deeply committed to the Catholic Faith.

Gerard initially sought to join the Capuchin order but was rejected due to his frail health. However, he eventually joined the Redemptorists, founded by St. Alphonsus Liguori, as a lay brother in 1749. In this capacity, he performed various humble tasks and became known for his deep piety, humility, and

---

[143] For prayers to say for this intention, see "Prayer for the Conversion of the Anglicans," *A Catholic Life* (Jan 21, 2013) <https://acatholiclife.blogspot.com/2013/01/prayer-for-conversion-of-anglicans.html>, accessed Novembr 27, 2024.

miracles. His profound spiritual insight and dedication to God earned him widespread admiration.

Throughout his life, Gerard was credited with numerous miracles, including healing the sick, multiplying food, and other extraordinary events. One of the most famous incidents involved a young woman who falsely accused him of fathering her child. Gerard chose to remain silent during the investigation, and the woman later recanted her accusation, vindicating him.

Gerard's reputation as a miracle worker grew, and he became particularly renowned for his intercession in matters related to childbirth. Many expectant mothers sought his prayers, and numerous reports of miraculous interventions during difficult pregnancies and births were attributed to him. This legacy continues today, with many people seeking his intercession for safe childbirth and the well-being of mothers and children.

Saint Gerard Majella died on October 16, 1755, at the age of 29. He was canonized by Pope Pius X in 1904. His feast day is celebrated on October 16th, and he remains a beloved figure, especially among those praying for a safe and healthy childbirth. October 16th is an ideal day to pray for pregnant mothers, for the pro-life cause, and for new mothers undergoing struggles.

St. Raphael (October 24)

The angels that we know by name (i.e., Raphael, Michael, and Gabriel) are called "Archangels" because of their high rank (arching above the other angels). They are not Archangels in terms of the second-lowest tier in the ninefold hierarchy of angels. Rather, these three are three of the seven *seraphim* angels, the highest-ranking, who continually stand before the presence of God in Heaven.

Archangel Raphael is known through the Book of Tobias in the Old Testament. He appeared in human form as a gracious young man called Azarias, to protect the younger Tobias on his journey from Ninive to a city of the Medes. In the process he found a wife for Tobias, and later delivered her from an evil spirit; he also healed the elder Tobias of blindness. Raphael is "one of the seven who stand before the Lord" (Tob. 12:15). The day's Collect speaks of him as a companion in journeys. The reading shows him as presenting our prayers to God. The Gospel is a reminder of Raphael's healing powers, for his name means "God has healed."[144]

The feast day of Raphael was included by Pope Benedict XV for the first time in the General Roman Calendar in 1921, for celebration on October 24. In honor of his feast day, pray the Litany to St. Raphael the Archangel and the Chaplet of St. Raphael.[145] It is also an ideal day to pray for the souls of the sick and for the souls in Purgatory. A prayer for the former through the intercession of St. Raphael is as follows:

O Glorious Archangel St. Raphael, great Prince of the Heavenly Court, illustrious for thy gifts of wisdom and grace, guide of those who journey by land or sea, consoler of the afflicted and refuge of sinners: assist me in all my needs and in all the suffering of this life, I beseech thee, as once thou didst help the young Tobias in his travels. And because thou art "the medicine of God," I humbly pray thee to heal me of the many infirmities of my soul and of the ills which afflict my body if this be for my greater good. I especially ask of thee for

---

[144] For more information on angels see Ibid., "An Exposition of Angels: All You Need To Know," *loc. cit.*
<https://acatholiclife.blogspot.com/2016/09/what-are-angels-summary-exposition-on.html>, accessed November 27, 2024.
[145] For the Litany, see <https://www.fisheaters.com/feastofstraphael-litany.html> and the Chaplet:
<https://www.fisheaters.com/chaplets.html#raphael>.

an angelic purity, which may fit me to be the temple of the Holy Ghost. Amen.

As for food, since fish is part of the story of St. Raphael in the Scriptures, it would be a fitting dish for the day.

Mother Cabrini (November 13 or 22)

From childhood, Frances Cabrini desired to become a missionary for Christ. After some unsuccessful starts, she founded the Missionary Sisters of the Sacred Heart of Jesus in Codogno, Italy; and in 1889 at the urging of Pope Leo XIII, she accepted the invitation of New York's Archbishop Corrigan to work among the numerous Italian immigrants of that era. Mother Cabrini founded orphanages, schools, and hospitals all over the United States, and extended her institute to Central and South America, France, Spain, and England. Everywhere her work succeeded only through her unbounded trust in God's providence. Though always in poor health, she traveled constantly, crossing the Atlantic twenty-five times in spite of a great fear of ocean voyages.

A naturalized citizen of the United States, Mother Cabrini died in 1917 in the convent of her great hospital in Chicago and was canonized in 1946, the first American citizen-saint. Her feast day was assigned for the United States to November 22nd until the change to the calendar in 1960 when her feast was moved to November 13th, the day of her beatification, in order to avoid conflicting with the greater ferias of Advent. In both instances, her feast day is not kept on the Universal Calendar – it is kept only in the United States.

For Italian Americans, this day is one that should be widely celebrated. Two dishes worth preparing on this day are pasta *fazool* or a simple *rigatoni* along with *Panna Cotta* for dessert. And at the meal, pray for more missionaries like St.

Cabrini who are willing to go to the limits of their physical abilities for the honor and glory of God.

For those in the area, the shrines in the United States in her honor can be found in New York, Chicago, and Golden (Colorado).

St. Cecilia (November 22)

Saint Cecilia lived in Rome during the 2nd or 3rd century. She is believed to have been a noblewoman who converted to Christianity and took a vow of virginity. Despite being forced into marriage with a pagan nobleman named Valerian, she persuaded him to respect her vow of chastity. Eventually, Valerian and his brother Tiburtius converted to Christianity and were martyred for their faith.

Cecilia was arrested and condemned to death for her faith. Multiple attempts to execute her failed; she survived being suffocated in a steam bath and decapitation. It is said she remained alive for three days after the latter attempt, during which she continued to preach and sing hymns to God.

Cecilia was buried in the Catacombs of St. Callixtus, later her remains were transferred to the Church of Santa Cecilia in Trastevere in Rome. She is often depicted in art with musical instruments, especially the organ or the violin, highlighting her association with music.

Her feast day is celebrated on November 22nd. It is a day particularly marked by musical celebrations in her honor and it is a great day to pray for Catholic musicians and to promote authentic, traditional Catholic music which is so needed for the restoration of Catholic culture.

There is also an inspiring Italian tradition associated with St. Cecilia as detailed by *Fish Eaters*:

In Taranto, Italy (in the region of Puglia, found at Italy's heel), St. Cecilia's day is seen as the beginning of the Advent and Christmas seasons. At 3:30am, the church bells are rung, and musicians are blessed. Then a great procession – with lots of music, of course – is held, with the statue of St. Cecilia being carried from the Cathedral of S. Cataldo to the Church of S. Giuseppe. In celebration, the people eat pettole, a fried, crisp-on-the-outside and chewy-on-the-inside snack that can be made up to be either savory or sweet (note that the accent is on the first syllable of the word "pettole"). According to a legend that has been handed down for generations, pettole were born thanks to a Taranto woman who let the bread rise too much on the feast of Santa Cecilia because she was so distracted by the music of the bagpipers parading through the streets of the city. When she realized that the dough was no longer good for making bread, she decided to make balls out of it and fry them in oil.

Any number of these traditions can be adapted for local use in all regions of the Church.

Catholic Culture: Our Birthright

Help Restore Catholic Culture through Customs

We do not even need to wait for liturgical years to change or saint days to occur. Each and every day is an opportunity for us to help restore Catholic culture through daily customs. Here are some ways we can all do so today:

1. Bow your head at the name of "Jesus" no matter where you are or what you are doing. And if you are wearing a hat, remove it for the head bow.

2. Say "Blessed be the name of God" in reparation any time you hear the name of God taken in vain.

3. When passing by a Catholic Church (whether on foot, bike, or car), make the sign of the Cross out of respect for our God who is present in the Church in the tabernacle.

4. Pray grace before and after meals (including making the Sign of the Cross) even in public.

5. Make the Sign of the Cross and offer a Hail Mary whenever an ambulance passes by.

6. When passing a cemetery, offer a prayer for the Poor Souls in Purgatory whose mortal remains rest in that cemetery.

7. Never eat meat on a Friday, even if it is a Holy Day of Obligation

8. Bless your children before bed with the sign of the Cross and holy water

9. Pray the Rosary as a family.

10. Pray the Angelus daily at least at noon (which is traditionally said kneeling except on Sundays when it is prayed standing and with a genuflection for the 3rd verse).

Through all our actions, including the small customs of day-to-day life, may Our Lord Jesus Christ shine in our conduct. And may the glory of His Church, the Catholic Church, shine ever brighter in our families, our parishes, our cities, and our nations. *Ad Majorem Dei Gloriam.*

Printed in Great Britain
by Amazon